M t **Prior** was born in South Africa in 1982 and educated at
B ton College. He made his first-class debut for Sussex while
   teenager and was awarded a benefit by the county in 2012,
   helped them to their first three County Championship titles
   history. Having made his England debut in a one-day
   ational in December 2004, he has gone on to play more than
   imes for his country, including 75 Tests by the start of the
   er of 2014. He lives with his family in Brighton.

  James, who worked with Matt Prior on the writing of this
     educated at Swansea and Cambridge universities. The
   England and Glamorgan cricketer now works as a
co   ist for Telegraph Media. His book, *The Plan*, about the rise
o   lish cricket under Duncan Fletcher and Andy Flower, was
th   icket Writers' Club Cricket Book of the Year in 2012.

THE GLOVES
ARE OFF
My Life In Cricket
MATT PRIOR

**SIMON &
SCHUSTER**

London · New York · Sydney · Toronto · New Delhi

A CBS COMPANY

First published in Great Britain by Simon & Schuster UK Ltd, 2013
This paperback edition published by Simon & Schuster UK Ltd, 2014
A CBS COMPANY

1 3 5 7 9 10 8 6 4 2

Simon & Schuster UK Ltd
1st Floor
222 Gray's Inn Road
London WC1X 8HB

www.simonandschuster.co.uk

Simon & Schuster Australia, Sydney
Simon & Schuster India, New Delhi

A CIP catalogue record for this book is available
from the British Library

ISBN: 978-1-47112-792-2
Ebook ISBN: 978-47112-793-9

Typeset in the UK by M Rules
Printed and bound by CPI Group (UK) Ltd, Croydon, CR0 4YY

To my mum and dad
whose love and support
made all of this possible

Acknowledgements

There are a number of people I would like to thank: Steve James for telling my story for me; Ian Marshall and all at Simon & Schuster for helping me to put the book together, and Luke and Gaia at Activate Management. Thanks to Sussex CCC and England and to all my team-mates who have brought me so many fond memories that I will treasure for the rest of my life. To Bruce French, my fantastic cricketing mentor, and also to Jono Alexander for all his continuous support. And, finally, my amazing wife Emily and our three boys: JJ, Zac and Finn. I love you.

Contents

1

An England Cap

Every young cricketer growing up in England wants to play Test cricket for their country. I was no different. That was always my ultimate dream. And I know how lucky I am to have realised that dream.

But there is a flip side to that. For those lucky enough to play for England, there is also the ultimate nightmare. It is the ignominy of being dropped. It happened to me in the early days of 2008 when I was dropped from the England Test team. I was actually in New York at the time, having taken my then fiancée Emily there as a present after Christmas.

We had arrived only the day before. I rose the next morning rather tired, and checked my mobile phone. There were about 20 missed calls showing on it. Most of them were from my mentor and then manager, Alec Stewart. Some were from David Graveney, the chairman of selectors.

There was also a text from Alec: 'Give me a call as soon as possible, mate,' it read. 'You're not in the squads.'

What? Surely I was going to New Zealand with the England

team. Just before I had left for New York, I had received another text, from the late Christopher Martin-Jenkins, father of Robin, with whom I played at Sussex, and then still the chief cricket correspondent of *The Times*. We had not seen much of each other on the tour of Sri Lanka that had just ended before Christmas, and he wrote something along the lines of: 'Sorry that we didn't catch up in Sri Lanka, but I look forward to seeing you in New Zealand.'

I took that to mean that I was fine, and that my place was safe. I felt sure that CMJ would have known what was going on, as I was convinced that he would have had the inside track. He almost always did, being probably the most respected journalist or broadcaster on the circuit.

Therefore it was with great sadness and shock that I learnt on New Year's Day 2013 that he had passed away. I was in Australia at the time, playing in the Big Bash League Twenty20 competition for Sydney Thunder, and when I returned home in early January I found that, before his death, CMJ had sent me, with a personal note inside, a copy of his book, *CMJ: A Cricketing Life*, which had been published in April the previous year. It was incredibly poignant reading the book afterwards. He loved cricket and he loved Sussex, and he will be much missed.

Talking of the death of such a wonderful man puts things into perspective, and looking back at my reaction to the news that I had been dropped by England might seem a little over the top. But it was still a huge blow at the time. I was in New York and suddenly having to come to terms with the fact that I was out of the England team. It was awful. I phoned Stewie and he told me that the squad had just been announced. Tim Ambrose and Phil Mustard were going to be the wicketkeepers in New Zealand. It was public knowledge: I had been axed.

At that moment my cricketing world fell apart. I can honestly say that I thought I would never play for England again. It was over.

No one should ever underestimate the effect being dropped can have on you. Mentally it can leave the deepest scars. I've seen it happen to other players so many times. They come into the England side and do reasonably well, but then the axe suddenly falls, and it is as if they have been chewed up and spat out again. Some just never come to terms with being left out by England.

Out in New York, I was struggling to come to terms with it. I was questioning everything about myself and my cricket. Was it all worth it? Wouldn't I be better off having a go at baseball? 'I wonder if the New York Yankees fancy giving me a trial?' I thought.

I was that down, I tell you. OK, it wasn't that long before I realised that I probably wasn't going to be a Major League baseball star, and that cricket was probably a better way forward, but it took an awful lot longer for me to convince myself that I wanted to be a wicketkeeper any more.

Yes, I was very close to knocking keeping on the head for good. At one stage, I had decided that I was going to be just a batsman. I had decided that I was going to force the selectors to pick me solely as a batsman, and in order to do that I had to a Ramps.

Mark Ramprakash had finished the 2007 season with 2,026 first-class runs, including ten centuries, at an average of 101.30. That was the second season in a row that he had averaged over 100, and despite his age – he was 38 then – there was still talk about him being recalled for England. I decided that my goal was to be the best batsman in county cricket. I had to be as good as, if not better than, Ramps.

But then I spoke to Alec Stewart again and he persuaded me not to give up keeping just yet. He said: 'Do yourself and do me a favour and have one more year at it. And, if you do that, make sure you give it absolutely everything. If, after that, you can look me in the eye and say that you have given it everything, but it hasn't worked out, then fine.'

It was obvious that I had been dropped because of my wicket-keeping. After all, I had played ten Tests and was averaging 40.14 with the bat. I had done well on the tour to Sri Lanka too, being third in the averages behind Alastair Cook and Ian Bell, having scored two fifties for an average of 41.25.

I had missed the one-day series that preceded the Tests (which had been won 3-2) because I had broken my thumb in practice at the ICC World Twenty20 in South Africa, leaving Vikram Solanki to keep wicket in our last two Super Eight matches against New Zealand and India. The Colonel (Mustard) had then kept wicket in those one-dayers in Sri Lanka.

But when I returned from that injury I really felt that I had made strides with my batting in the Tests. I had changed my method considerably. I had had to rein myself in against the spinners, and I thought I had dealt with Muttiah Muralitharan pretty well.

His 19 wickets in the series were obviously crucial in Sri Lanka's 1-0 victory, but I had been especially proud of my efforts in the first Test at Kandy, where I'd batted with Ian Bell for more than two and a half hours on the last afternoon and into the evening session, as we attempted to save the Test.

I worked so hard in that innings. Our captain Michael Vaughan had told us at the start of the day that we had to fight, and that's what we did. I'd been hit on the head by a bouncer from Dilhara Fernando, and against Muralitharan it was a real war of attrition, but, in such tricky conditions, I took a huge amount from my innings of 63. Sadly, I was eventually bowled by a Muralitharan 'doosra' that I didn't pick, and Belly went just eight balls later for 74, and Sri Lanka ended up winning by 88 runs.

It was the third Test in Galle that proved my downfall. I

dropped three catches there: Mahela Jayawardena twice and Tillekeratne Dilshan once. The problem was that when Sri Lanka declared on 499 for eight, Jayawardene was still there with 213 not out, and Dilshan made 84.

Whenever you drop a batsman, you are praying for the next 15 minutes or so that he gets out so that no one will remember the drop. Unfortunately, I spent rather more than quarter of an hour in that Test praying for those two to get out.

What made it worse was that I took a stunning catch down the leg side off Matthew Hoggard in that innings, but it wasn't given out. I thought it was a clear glove from Dilshan, and to this day, as I dived a long way to reach it one-handed, it remains one of the best catches I have ever taken, but for some reason the umpire, in the days before the Decision Review System, did not give it out. All I remember thinking was: 'Somebody give me a break here, please!'

It is hard enough keeping in Asia as it is. There is the obvious heat and humidity but also, because the ball generally keeps so low, it means that you have to stand closer to the stumps than you normally would. And you have to stay lower for longer, which works the legs harder. Not that fielding in general in these conditions is easy. I think we missed 12 chances in total in that series. It was not just me who made mistakes!

I had kept well in that first Test in Kandy and decently in the second Test in Colombo, where the heat was stifling and we were in the field for nearly 187 overs, after I'd batted from the previous afternoon and was last man out for 79. I still conceded only seven byes.

Everyone said I had kept terribly after my mistakes in Galle, where, if I'm honest, I was shattered, but I actually conceded only one bye in nearly 149 overs there. And at the end of the tour my opposite number, Kumar Sangakkara, had said to me: 'You've done brilliantly, because Sri Lanka is the hardest place in the world to keep wicket.' That was a massive compliment from someone who had plenty of experience.

That is not to say that I wasn't aware that there were flaws in my wicketkeeping technique. Of course there were. And when you are placed under extreme pressure, it is then that your flaws will show up most. I had been placed under pressure in Galle and my flaws had been revealed.

My biggest flaw then? To be honest, it was the fact that I still considered myself a batsman who also did a bit of wicketkeeping. I simply didn't do enough work on my keeping in those days. I can see that looking back now. Wicketkeeping is just so much about volume of work.

In fact, I have to say that I reckon I actually did pretty well to play ten Tests with my keeping in the state that it was and the amount of work I used to do. I can't believe I got as far as I did.

As a youngster I was always a fielder. I loved fielding and I fell into wicketkeeping only by accident. I was playing an Under-13s match for Sussex one day and our wicketkeeper, a lad by the name of Tom Dowdall, was delayed in traffic and our coach, David Randall, asked who fancied having a go behind the stumps. I volunteered. 'I'll have a go,' I said. It sounded like fun.

And it was. I really enjoyed keeping that day. David was impressed. He saw something in me. He said to me: 'I reckon you should give it a go.'

Before I knew it I was at the County Ground at Hove having my first coaching session with none other than Peter Moores, who was then still on the Sussex playing staff. It was the first time I had ever met him. Who would have thought then that one day he would be coach of the England team in which I was keeping wicket? He became my mentor.

Our first session was supposed to last only an hour. Long after that, I was still there diving around on the mats. I was absolutely loving it. I walked away thinking: 'I really like this keeping lark.' But, first and foremost, I was still a batsman. And in truth I never kept up the enthusiasm I showed in that first session with Pete. I didn't put in the work I needed to. I have always had decent hands and for most of the time I relied on natural ability to get me through.

And it was natural ability that got me through to an England Test cap. That came in the summer of 2007 in the first Test against West Indies at Lord's. I'd already played 12 one-day internationals by then, but I had kept wicket in only one of them – at Jamshedpur in India in 2006.

I'd made my one-day debut in Zimbabwe in the fourth and last limited-overs international of the very nearly cancelled tour of late 2004. But, if I'm honest, it didn't really feel like an international debut. Because of the political problems there, which meant that we were delayed in Johannesburg en route after the Zimbabwean authorities said they were not going to allow some journalists in to cover the tour, the five-match series was reduced to four.

And some key players, such as Andrew Flintoff, Marcus Trescothick and Steve Harmison, missed the tour, either because they were rested or because they objected on moral grounds. That was the only reason I got my chance, I suppose, although it is worth pointing out that Kevin Pietersen also made his international debut on that trip. It was a strange tour in other ways, too, because we were basically told that we couldn't be seen to be enjoying ourselves. There was to be no golf or anything like that. It was just hotels, coaches and cricket grounds. And serious faces.

Because of those factors, when I played in Bulawayo it felt like a lesser deal than a county match. There were probably fewer people watching for a start. It was certainly not as I imagined playing for England would be, with packed grounds and a great atmosphere.

That feeling came in Lahore the following year when I played against Pakistan. The crowd and its noise, along with Shoaib Akhtar steaming in to open the bowling as I opened the batting with Marcus Trescothick, made it feel as if I was playing international cricket for sure. I made 45 that day, and I'd made 35 on debut. Sadly, that has been the story of my England limited-overs career. I have always been able to 'get in', but the big scores have proved so elusive. As I write I have played 68 one-day internationals, and yet I have made only three fifties in that time, with a best of 87. It is baffling.

Well, I know what the problem was early on in my career. Then I was mainly opening – in fact in all but two of those 12 matches before my Test debut I had opened – and I was given the role of 'pinch-hitter'. I would go in and play a lot of big shots that would come off, but then, once the fielding restrictions were lifted and field was set back, I did not change back down the gears and knock the ball around. You just cannot keep playing big shots. Your luck will run out sooner or later.

That was the problem early on. In latter times I'm not so sure what it has been. It has been a huge frustration, I know that. I've done really well for Sussex in one-day cricket and Twenty20, but just haven't been able to translate that into international cricket.

At least getting those solid scores early on gave me the confidence that I could play international cricket. I was facing some serious bowlers such as Akhtar, Rana Naved-ul-Hasan (with whom I played at Sussex), Mohammad Sami and Abdul Razzaq in Pakistan, and then in India Irfan Pathan and Sri Sreesanth. I was doing OK against them. I just needed that substantial score.

Fortunately that was not a problem in Test cricket. I began this chapter talking about the dream of playing Test cricket. Well, that dream becomes even wilder when you think of scoring a century on Test debut, and at Lord's, too. It is a cricketer's wildest dream probably. And, remarkably, it came true for me.

I thought I deserved to play in that first Test of the 2007 summer against West Indies. I reckon I had been knocking on the door for a while. There had been some talk before the Ashes tour of the previous winter that I might have been on that trip (I had been the reserve wicketkeeper on the Test tours to Pakistan and India in the winter of 2005-06). But the selectors went with Geraint Jones (who had played in the 2005 Ashes) and Chris Read instead.

I had set myself the goal of playing in the first Test of the 2007 summer at the end of the 2006 season, so it was not a huge set-back. I still went to Australia, but with the 14-man National Academy squad that was based in Perth for five weeks during the Ashes under Academy director Peter Moores and batting coach Andy Flower. I thought I might have had a chance for the Commonwealth Bank one-day series (also featuring New Zealand) that followed the Ashes, and indeed the World Cup in the Caribbean that followed that, but Paul Nixon was picked instead.

Of course, as we all know now, the winter as a whole went as badly as it possibly could. By the end of it, Duncan Fletcher had gone as coach and it was obvious to me that the Test team would be looking for a new wicketkeeper. That winter was a busy one for me, as I had also gone to Bangladesh in February and March with the A team, as it was still called then, and had done well, being the leading run-scorer on the tour overall.

With Fletcher gone, Mooresy stepped up to take charge of the England side, and I know it was widely perceived that I was selected only because of my obvious closeness to him. I was certainly well aware of that when I was being interviewed beforehand.

'I'd like to think that it is hard work and performance that has got me into the side rather than my link to Peter Moores,' I said. 'I am averaging nearly forty in first-class cricket and I had a great winter tour in Bangladesh, and everyone has stated that runs are important for a wicketkeeper. Mooresy was my first keeping coach. He is a fantastic coach and will have a good effect on anyone. He is a very important role model in my keeping. It is going to be nice to have him there in the changing room, but the main thing is to feel confident in myself. The catches and the runs are in the middle.'

There also seemed to be a lot of questions about how noisy I was on the field. There were comparisons with Nixon, or the Badger, as everyone was calling him then.

'I'm naturally outspoken, especially on the pitch, and I like to give out as much energy as possible,' I said. 'There are different ways you can do it and I'm not necessarily talking about sledging, but trying to have a presence on the field is part of my game and something I feel I'm good at. The role of the keeper now includes trying to get the other guys buzzing around. Without having to say too much, you can create an intense atmosphere and get in the opposition's faces. Am I noisier than Nixon? Watch the game and then you tell me.'

Looking back now, and knowing what was to happen later that summer against India, I wish I hadn't said some of those things. But I was young and excitable. I'd been picked to play Test cricket for England. I was buzzing. And, yes, I could be a little noisy in those days.

As Robin Martin-Jenkins said of my selection: 'If you want your keeper to make noise on the pitch, Prior's your man. He may not be in the same league as the certifiably insane Jack Russell or Paul Nixon, but his vocal chords get plenty of exercise.'

Ha! Cheers, Tucker.

I also said to the press: 'I think consistency is the difference between an international and a county cricketer – both the performances and how you behave as a person day in and day out. This is an area I have targeted. I have wanted to make sure that when I step out on to the pitch that I am ready to do this, not just to try and survive but to compete.'

The first part of that quote is interesting, because I hadn't actually had a great start to the season with the bat. I'd got a hundred for Sussex in a pre-season warm-up match against Surrey, but in ten competitive innings before the Test against West Indies I hadn't made a fifty.

The last part of that quote was very important to me, though. I'd received the call from David Graveney saying that I had been selected. And naturally I was extremely excited. I rang my mum and dad, and the third person I phoned was Alec Stewart. But then later that day it sunk in. I thought: 'Right, I've got to go and play now.' It's all right being selected, but then you've got to go and perform. I think that it is one of my strengths that I never want just to be a number in a team. I have always wanted to be a person that is a big part of that team, someone that can make a significant contribution and make a difference. So, for me, getting selected wasn't even half the journey.

That said, it was a special moment when Andrew Strauss (captaining in place of the injured Michael Vaughan) and Grav presented me, a rather happy 25-year-old dressed in my England blazer over my cricket whites, with my England Test cap on the outfield at Lord's on Thursday 17 May 2007. I still wear that cap on the field now.

I was the 635th player to be capped by England in Tests. That number – 635 – was there on my shirts below the badge of the crown and three Lions. And below that on my short-sleeved batting shirt, as did all of our team in that match as a show of support, I attached a yellow ribbon for Madeleine McCann, the four-year-old English girl who had gone missing. It was the least we could do at such a terrible time, which, tragically, continues even now for her family.

I then just sat back and watched. Ramnaresh Sarwan, captaining West Indies, had asked us to bat and by the end of a rain-shortened first day we were 200 for three, with Alastair Cook 102 not out. I did not even make it onto the field on my first day of Test cricket.

Was that a good thing or a bad thing? No bad thing, I would say. I usually give a sigh of relief when we're batting anyway. And it gave me time to acclimatise, to get used to the surroundings. I'd played at Lord's for Sussex before, but this was rather different.

The ten minutes before the toss are always the most nerve-wracking, whether it is your debut or not. Any cricketer will tell you that. It is that uncertainty that is so hard to deal with. What are we doing? Are we batting or bowling? If we lose the toss in any match and are asked to field, I will admit that my default reaction as a wicketkeeper is to swear a bit. But then it is straight into a routine that never alters, ending with the slamming of my own cricket ball that I always carry in my bag into my gloves just before I go out onto the field. Sometimes I might do that only three times, on other occasions as many as a hundred. It's all about the feel, about the way it is hitting the gloves. I've just got to keep doing it until it feels right. Then I can go out on to the field.

I have always had totally different gear for wicketkeeping and for batting – from shirts, trousers down to my boots. There is no difference in the type of boots – I wear half-spiked and half-rubber boots for both – except that I use newer pairs for batting, then, when they are more worn in, I use them for keeping. I just feel more comfortable that way. That complete change of clothing and gear was something I picked up from Peter Moores. He always felt it helped the change to the required mindset, so that there was no blurring of roles. You bat and you keep, and you wear different clothes for each.

When I'd been selected, Alec Stewart had said something to me that I didn't really understand at the time, but nonetheless it lodged in my mind. He said: 'You will know the moment you step onto the field if you are made for Test cricket or not. If you go out there and it's the last place on earth you want to be, then clearly you will struggle. But if you walk out there and you feel like you never want to leave, then it's definitely for you.' I think I said to him in response something like: 'What are you on about?'

I soon discovered. It was just before tea on the second day that Paul Collingwood was bowled by a good in-swinger from Dwayne Bravo for an excellent 111. We'd lost our fifth wicket. I was in.

I'm not a great watcher, so I wasn't out on the balcony observing every ball as I waited to bat. I was inside. I quite like to be involved in any conversations going on there to take my mind off batting. As we had been three wickets down, I'd been ready since the start of the day. Then, in terms of protective equipment, I'd just had my box, thigh pad and inner thigh pad on. I'd put my pads on later when Alastair Cook was fourth out for 105 in the day's eighth over.

I was wearing a short-sleeved shirt. I always do when I bat. But when I keep wicket, it is always a long-sleeved shirt that I wear, however hot the conditions. Sorry, but I just think it looks 'village' to wear a short-sleeved shirt when keeping. You just can't do that. Please don't do that, if there are any young wicketkeepers reading.

Quite often, especially in the heat of the sub-continent, Jonathan Trott will rib me, saying: 'Come on, mate! Wear a short-sleever and a wide-brimmed sun hat.'

And I'll reply: 'OK, Trotty, I will do that if you go out to bat wearing left-handed batting pads!' That's how much my preparation and kit means to me. A long-sleever and cap it always has to be when I'm keeping.

Oh, and as I waited to bat at Lord's I had my sweatband on my left arm, of course. That goes on first. That's very important. I never wear an armguard, although I did try one once in a National League match for Sussex in 2003 when Shoaib Akhtar was playing for Durham. I scored only two – caught behind off Akhtar – and cursed myself for being weak. So I've never worn one since.

And I've never been hit there – touch wood! – although I have taken the odd blow on my back (right) elbow. Jack Russell used to wear an armguard on that back arm (left for him, obviously, because he was a left-hander) as well as his front arm, but I don't think I'll be going down that route.

As I made my way out of the door at the rear of the England changing room at Lord's, I was more worried about getting lost as so many players have – most famously, David Steele on his debut against Australia in 1975. I was OK, though. I made sure I walked down only one flight of stairs, through the noise of the Long Room, down the steps and out on to the Lord's turf.

The moment I stepped on to the outfield I felt as if I was at home.

Stewie had been right. I remember thinking: 'I absolutely love this.' And I'd only taken three steps. It was just amazing. The crowd, the noise, everything was incredible.

I took guard. I usually take a middle-stump guard, although I do move it against spinners quite often, say going over to off stump for an off spinner on a pitch that is turning a lot. Or against a seamer such as South Africa's Makhaya Ntini, who used to bowl from very wide of the crease and angle the ball in, I would take an off-stump guard then too, just to straighten everything up. I try not to be too set in my thoughts on this and try to adapt to how the game is going and how different bowlers are bowling at me.

But middle stump it was now. The first ball from Bravo was wide of the off stump and I just let it go through harmlessly to wicketkeeper Denesh Ramdin.

My partner was Ian Bell, who had already passed his half-century. He was facing Daren Powell at the other end. Off the third ball of the over, he took a single. It was time to get off the mark now, surely. But no, I couldn't. I'd have to wait.

Belly faced Bravo and we took a single off the first ball of the next over from a bye down the leg side. I was facing again. Bravo ran in and bowled me a bouncer. Now, he may not be the quickest bowler in the world or possess the fieriest bumper, but, still, it wasn't a bad bouncer. That was what I had been expecting all along. They always say that when you walk into Test cricket you should expect a few short ones. They also say that you had better make sure you play them well, otherwise you can expect a whole lot more of them!

I thought I played it pretty well, avoiding it reasonably comfortably. Bravo clearly didn't see it that way. He ran in and bowled me another one, and, after I had again swayed out of the way, this time he accompanied it with a stare. I stared back. That was what I have always done. The crowd roared. The noise was just unbelievable. As I said, I was just loving this.

'I could do with getting off the mark,' I thought to myself, though. Thankfully, the next ball came gift-wrapped. It was a nice, juicy in-swinger on my legs. I clipped it away. I was up and running.

There might have been a small problem, however. There was the hint of a leading edge, as I was a little early on the stroke. The ball went in the air. It went about chest-high, in fact. And there was a fielder in front of square on the leg side. I've never told anyone this before, but I thought that I was gone. I thought I had chipped it straight to the man there. 'I haven't done that, have I?' I said to myself. A duck on Test debut!

Thankfully I hadn't chipped the ball to the man there. I hadn't got a duck on debut. The ball raced to the mid-wicket boundary, and I was away. I had my first runs in Test cricket. Umpire Rudi

Koertzen signalled the boundary, and, out of habit, I tucked my bat under my left arm to adjust the Velcro on my left glove.

The noise was amazing. I look back now and realise that is as good an example as I have seen in my time in the game of the fine margins on which we operate in this great game of ours. Sometimes it is as if you are in the hands of someone or something else. I could so easily have been caught for nought. As it was, I ended up making a century on debut, the first England wicketkeeper to do so, and only the third ever, so I'm told, after two Sri Lankans: Brendon Kuruppu (201 not out against New Zealand in 1986-87) and Romesh Kaluwitharana (132 not out against Australia in 1992).

I also learned that I became the fifth batsman to score a hundred on Test debut at Lord's. Harry Graham (for Australia in 1893), John Hampshire (for England against West Indies in 1969), Sourav Ganguly (for India in 1996) and Andrew Strauss (against New Zealand in 2004) were the others.

While we are doing the statistics, I should also mention that Belly went to make a century too, making four of us in the innings. That was only the second time in history that had been done by England.

Lord's is just such a wonderful place to bat. The pitch is good and you get real value for your shots. And on that day I just decided to play my shots. I just 'went with it', as they say. It was classic 'see ball, hit ball' batting.

There were three fours in an over from Bravo, the first a drive down the ground. It may have been in the air for a while but I hit it nicely. My balance felt good. It really gave me confidence. Two balls later I found the third-man boundary, before following that with a pulled four. There were a lot of pull shots in that innings. Indeed, I reached my fifty with one off Powell. 'This is incredible,' I thought. 'I've just got a Test fifty.' It had taken just 55 balls and I'd hit nine fours.

It was time to cash in. You have to pay due respects to your team-mates in such situations, because Cook, Collingwood and Bell had all laid the foundations for me. They had all had to bat when the ball had been moving around much more than it was now. I could just play my natural game, and that was because of the platform they had laid.

Sarwan tried to slow things down a little by using his own leg-spin and the off-spin of Chris Gayle. There was no way I wanted to slow down, but there were occasions when Belly would have a quiet word: 'C'mon mate, keep pushing the ones, try to milk the spinners,' he'd say. He was fantastic, actually. He's younger than me – if only by 45 days – but this was his 24th Test and it was brilliant to have someone like him out there guiding me through.

Before I knew it, I was on 97. Ninety-seven in a Test match! I was facing Gayle. And I had a dilemma. One of my very closest friends – he was best man at my wedding, in fact – is Carl Hopkinson, with whom I played at Sussex, where he is now on the coaching staff. I've known him since we were 12 and at Brighton College together. We obviously played loads of cricket together, so we also talked a lot of cricket together. And we had this agreement, a pact even. If a spinner is bowling and you are 49 or 99, the easiest way to get to the milestone is to lap-sweep; to get down on one knee and just paddle the ball around the corner. But I was on 97. What did I do? There was no fielder 45 degrees behind square on the leg side.

I went for it. I thought I had four, too, and my hundred, but it was stopped on the boundary (and I may just have cursed the fielder under my breath!), and I settled for two. Ninety-nine not out now. What to do now? Did I go for it again? The field certainly wasn't altered, but Gayle was taking ages over this ball. He was making me wait. He was making me think.

'That's the rule,' I thought. 'I'm going to do it. I'm going to lap-sweep. Hoppo would be proud.'

So as Gayle walked to the wicket (he doesn't run, of course), I got down to lap-sweep. And what did he do? He only stopped, and didn't deliver the ball. There were plenty of smiles, and the crowd loved it. But there was also a real battle going on inside my head. 'Do I still do it? I'll have to be very careful in case it is full, straight and fast,' I thought.

I was still deliberating as Gayle walked in. 'To do it, or not to do it? Lap-sweep or not? Lap-sweep or not?

'Oh, hang on. It's short. It's really short. In fact it's a long hop. It's a long hop outside off stump.'

I wasn't missing out on that. I whacked it through the covers for four. That was it. I'd made a Test century. And at Lord's, too. I was going to have my name on the famous honours board. Every aspiring cricketer must have thought or dreamed about this moment. I certainly had. I'd imagined that I would milk the applause quite coolly; nothing too outrageous or out of control.

Well, it didn't quite happen like that. I just hit the ball and screamed. It was the sort of roar I didn't think I had in me. Then I was jumping around like a schoolkid. I took off my helmet and punched the air with my bat. I raised my arms aloft, helmet in one hand, bat in the other. Then I kissed my bat, and embraced Belly before acknowledging my team-mates and the rest of the crowd. What a moment!

The hundred had taken me only 105 balls. We were 515 for five. It was time to declare really, but the light was poor. So there was time for some more fun. I even brought out the reverse sweep. Belly's own hundred soon followed and he finished the day 109 not out. I was 126 not out, and we walked off to a standing ovation.

It was nice that Belly was there with me. We played a lot of schoolboy cricket against and with each other. He was always in the Midlands side and I was in the South. I remember the

Bunbury Under-15 festival in 1997, played up in Lancashire, where I was in the South team alongside Hoppo and James Tredwell (now of Kent and England) and we were hammered by seven wickets by the Midlands, with Belly making 88. He was always the golden boy who everyone knew was destined to play for England. Me? They may not have been so sure about me. But here I was now, having made a Test hundred for England at Lord's.

'If I rewrote it all again, I don't think I'd change a thing,' I said afterwards to the press. And I wouldn't.

I was also asked about the influence of Alec Stewart upon my career. I was more than happy to talk about 'Stewie'. I owed him so much. 'He's been fantastic,' I said. 'There are times when you feel a bit anxious, times where you need to ask a few questions – even little things about my keeping gloves. To have someone like Alec, with all that experience, at the end of the phone, to calm you down and say: "Look mate, it'll be all right . . ." He's a legend.'

And soon the plaudits were ringing out for me, too. I read them all. I thought that's what everyone did. I had no real plan in place on how to deal with the media. So I lapped up all the compliments. Who wouldn't?

People were saying: 'We're all done now for the next ten years; you'll be England's keeper-batter.' I was the man. Life couldn't get any better. And the next three Tests went well. I scored 75 at Headingley, 40 (and a duck) at Old Trafford and 62 at Durham as we won the four-match series 3-0.

A month after the end of that rubber, we began a three-Test series against India. The first Test was drawn at Lord's. We should have won that actually, but rain hampered us on the last day, as did an LBW decision – Monty Panesar on Sri Sreesanth – which looked plumb to me but was not given.

The second Test took place at Trent Bridge. It was a match we lost by seven wickets, but it was much more than that. It was a game for which I was long remembered, for all the wrong reasons. It was a Test in which my reputation plumbed depths I never thought possible. In fact, I don't think I am exaggerating if I say it was a match that began my rapid rise to public enemy number one.

To describe the initial source of my character assassination – which is what it most certainly was – I need only mention two words: Jelly Beans.

The first thing to say is that this was an ill-tempered Test all round. Sreesanth was involved in a lot of it: there was a collision with Michael Vaughan, he bowled a no-ball bouncer to Paul Collingwood and also accidentally beamed Kevin Pietersen. But I bet most people have already forgotten those incidents, and all they can remember is 'Jellygate', as it became known. And I also bet that most people will recall that I was involved, maybe that I was the instigator of this little prank that turned into such a huge story.

Well, I wasn't involved, and I wasn't the instigator. This is what happened. It was after tea on the third day as India compiled a huge score in response to our 198 after we had been put in in damp, swing-friendly conditions. I had just caught V.V.S.Laxman off Chris Tremlett for 54 to make the score 464 for seven. As Zaheer Khan walked to the wicket, we took a drinks break.

As well as drinks, some Jelly Beans were also brought out to boost our energy levels. Some of them dropped onto the floor and someone decided to kick them towards the pitch as a joke, pre-sumably to wind up Zaheer. It certainly did wind him up because they had ended up right by his crease. After he'd edged his first ball down to third man for four past a diving KP in the gully, he went after KP, pointing his bat at him and having a real go. KP was innocent and he was saying things like: 'You sure you've got the right man?'

But Zaheer was not happy, because he thought we were being disrespectful by leaving the Jelly Beans around the crease. Something similar had actually happened in the series against West Indies, and Marlon Samuels had picked one up, said thank you and ate it!

Zaheer did not find it quite so funny, and he was quick to show umpire Ian Howell the Jelly Beans, indicating them with his bat. Vaughany happened to be off the field at the time, so Howell spoke to Andrew Strauss who was in temporary charge. When Vaughany returned, the other umpire, Simon Taufel, also had a word with him. But we thought that was that. End of story. Get on with the game.

Certainly what nobody remembers about that day is that I took five catches. That was the reason I was asked to do the post-match press conference. When our press liaison officer, Andrew Walpole, came in to tell me I was doing it, I was delighted. I thought: 'Fantastic. They'll want to talk about my catches and another good day for me. This Test cricket lark is great.'

How wrong I was. All they wanted to talk about was the aggro on the field. I was asked about the incident involving Zaheer and KP. I just played dumb and said that I didn't know what had started it all. I said: 'We play the game hard, it is competitive and there's a lot at stake. Sometimes things boil over. It's a tough game. There are a lot of people under a lot of pressure. If you can do anything to get one up on your opponent, you're going to do that, as long as it's kept in the spirit of the game. When you are fighting that hard, no one wants to take a step back, but from what I saw out there, nothing went over the line.'

On and on went this line of questioning: 'It's a tough game at the top end and if you don't enjoy it, you're going to struggle,' I said. 'It's never nice when it's you batting, and eleven blokes are giving you a barrage, but it comes with the territory. It's Test cricket, it's a hard game. We all want to win; we're all playing to win. You're going to try anything to get one up on your opponent, as long as it's within the spirit of the game.'

There was more: 'It's important to have eleven people hunting together on the pitch, creating an intensity and an environment that's uncomfortable for people to bat in,' I continued. 'It's even more important on a flat wicket – you might still lose the session, but by holding on to that intensity, you might not lose it as heavily.'

There was no mention of Jelly Beans at this stage. That came later in the game. And, of course, Zaheer was then wheeled out for an interview, primarily because he had taken five second-innings wickets to add to his four in the first innings, but also because he had something else to say about his own innings.

'When I got out to the crease there were some Jelly Beans there,' he said. 'I just swept one off the wicket, and when I played the next ball there were some more, so obviously someone was chucking them from behind. I was upset about it. I went to speak to them and asked what was going on. I didn't know exactly where they were coming from, and maybe I picked the wrong one, but they definitely came from a fielder and I just felt it was insulting. When I go out on to the cricket field I am serious. This is a Test match we are playing. It definitely inspired me to do well.'

He was asked why he went after KP. 'I didn't know where exactly it was coming from,' he said. 'Maybe I picked the wrong one, but I was just not bothered at that time. I just felt it was insulting. It was definitely from a fielder, because if it was placed unknowingly, it shouldn't have come there again when I removed it.'

That was it. 'Jellygate' exploded. It was Jelly Bean Central. Because it was me who went to that press conference and because I was closest to the stumps, I was somehow implicated. I was the main suspect. Maybe I should have said more in that press conference. But that is not the way I go about things. I will always stand by the saying that 'what happens on the pitch stays on the pitch'. You play the game hard, but I can't stand it when people bring up things that happen on the field off it. If you maybe cross the line and that individual comes to corner you one on one in the dressing room, then that's a different story. But you should never go into the media and start blurting off.

It is reasonably common knowledge now who the culprit was in this incident, but I'm not going to name him. That is not my way. But the problem was that because I was so conscious of acting that way in the press conference, I didn't actually clear my own name. And nobody else did either.

Afterwards, we were all getting phone calls urging us to make sure that the name of the culprit didn't come out, which was fair enough, but it still meant that everyone thought it was me. Nobody stuck up for me. If I had been a senior player, it might not have been so bad, but I was a junior player making my way in Test cricket. Couldn't somebody have just said: 'We just want to say it was not Matt Prior'? It's one of the reasons why I am so precious about looking after the team ethic these days. In this instance, I felt isolated, and that shouldn't happen to any player.

Worse was to come. There then emerged a story about my sledging Sachin Tendulkar in the same game. It was alleged that I said something like 'I drive a Porsche. What car do you drive?' to Tendulkar. It was absolute garbage, of course. Again, I will tell you exactly what happened. The sponsors of England's Test cricket were nPower at the time, and at some stage during our long stint in the field I said something like: 'Come on lads, let's look to nPower for some energy.'

It's the sort of thing you say in the field. Some of the chat on the field is directed at the batsman, but a lot of it is just an attempt to keep spirits up among the fielders. As wicketkeeper you are expected to encourage your team constantly, to be the heartbeat of the side, or, as Peter Moores always says, 'the drummer of the band'. I was just doing that.

But obviously this comment about nPower was picked up on the stump microphone, because the next morning there was a bottle of champagne waiting for me in my cricket bag. One of the main men from nPower had heard my comment and sent it, with a note of thanks. 'Thanks for the plug,' it said.

The boys loved this. So the next day in the field, all the fielders around the bat were trying to make comments about things they might have wanted. Alastair Cook was at short leg and he quite fancied a Bang and Olufsen television, so he said: 'I like Bang and Olufsen televisions,' hoping one would magically appear underneath his peg in the dressing room the next morning. And then I said to him in reply that my favourite car was a Porsche Carrera.

That was all it was, I swear. It was that innocent; just a joke between two cricketers. Why would I try to boast to Tendulkar anyway? I mean the bloke owns aeroplanes and fleets of cars. And I wasn't driving a Porsche. As a team we had a deal with Volkswagen then. Now it is Jaguar.

But, no, the story was believed and my character was duly assassinated. The criticism I got was unbelievable. I was called an 'uneducated skinhead' by one writer. In another paper, the headline to one piece read: 'Matt Prior the buffoon should grow up.' That was a piece by Michael Henderson in the *Daily Telegraph*, I think. To this day I've never met him, but I have been hoping that he would come up to me and shake my hand because he owes me an apology. It was a very, very poor piece from a man who did not know me at all.

I suddenly realised that international cricket was a whole different ball-game from that which I had known before. My honeymoon period with the media had ended. I had been praised; now I was being pummelled. I was reading these pieces and I was phoning my family to ask: 'Is this really me?' I certainly didn't like the person I was being portrayed as.

What took me by surprise was that the people who were writing these things didn't know me. My character was coming across as all wrong. I am not and have never been a confrontational bloke. I am just competitive. I don't go out to sledge the opposition, but I'll stand my ground if, say, a fast bowler gives me the stare. But, as I have said, I will make a noise behind the stumps, and increasing a batsman's anxiety with some mild banter has been part of the game for years.

I was just an excitable young guy playing cricket for England, and I was loving it. I was playing the role behind the stumps that the team wanted, but it was all construed wrongly. I was construed as lippy and arrogant. I'm not. Even my mother was taking flak for things I was supposed to have done and said. There was one letter in particular which hurt me. It was from a woman who wrote: 'I can't let my kids watch cricket any more because of the way you behave.'

It all hit me hard. How could it not have done? I defy anyone to receive all that criticism without being affected. I was booed at grounds – so much so that I told my parents not to come to games – and I was being sworn at left, right and centre by the Indian players when I went out to bat. They knew that I couldn't answer back, because I would be crucified again in the press if I did. And it all began to affect my form. It had to; I felt that everyone wanted me to fail.

So it was little surprise that I had a poor game in that Test at The Oval. I dropped a couple of catches, one of them off V.V.S.Laxman and the other off Tendulkar, as India reached a huge total of 664. And, of course, much was made of the

Tendulkar drop. He had made only 20 at the time, and went on to score 82. The edge was off Ryan Sidebottom (I dropped a few off him that year!) and I dived to my right but couldn't hang on. I also let through quite a few byes in that total and made a first-innings duck with the bat. What a game! The only consolation was that we didn't lose the game, it ended in a draw.

Naturally I got slaughtered by the press, though. Most of them seemed happy that the gobby keeper had got his comeuppance. When asked about it, I responded by saying: 'This week has been the hardest in my cricketing life, without a shadow of a doubt. My performance has been criticised, but I am still learning. Mistakes do happen – we're all human. I'm still new to Test cricket, but there are always things you can work on. I want to have that feeling of getting a hundred again, to take five catches again, but then I get a nought and drop a high-profile player like Tendulkar.

'You're not going to every day walk out and feel a million dollars. But I am my own biggest critic and I'll work very hard with Peter Moores and Andy Flower [then still the batting coach] to make sure I do make improvements. I don't feel I have to suddenly criticise or scrutinise myself massively.'

Not unexpectedly England did not give me a central contract (or any other keeper for that matter) at the end of that 2007 summer. Looking back now, I wonder how I even made it through to the Sri Lanka tour in the first part of that winter. I had to be dropped really. I couldn't carry on for much longer in the state I had been in at the end of that summer. I was kidding myself.

I kidded myself so well that, at the end of the Sri Lanka tour, by which time I had played ten Tests, I asked Mark Garaway, our team analyst, to look up the statistics of the great Test match batsmen/wicketkeepers such as Australia's Adam Gilchrist, Sri Lanka's Kumar Sangakkara and India's Mahendra Singh Dhoni at the same stage of their careers so that we could compare my stats with theirs.

And I didn't fare too badly. I was averaging 40.14 with the bat compared to Sangakkara's 39.87 and Dhoni's 37.28, while Gilchrist was on 56.41. I then got Garrers to look at their figures after 20 Tests (Gilchrist 53.75, Sangakkara 53.00 and Dhoni 36.39) so that I could plot my route ahead. I even sat down with Peter Moores to talk about what I had to do in those next ten Tests.

There was a problem, though. As we talked, Mooresy probably knew that I was going to be dropped. I did not play in England's next ten Tests. I did not play my 20th Test until July 2009 against Australia (by which time I was averaging 46.30). I was looking too far ahead. But it taught me a valuable lesson. It taught me the value of an England cap. You should never take it for granted.

Even now the question I hate most in any interview is if I am asked something with the assumption that my place is secure. I never let myself believe that. Obviously I have long-term goals if everything comes off, but, as clichéd as it is, it is the God's honest truth that I feel that I cannot look further ahead than one Test.

I just have to do it that way now.

2

French Lessons

Alec Stewart had some good advice for me: 'Mate, do me a favour and do two things please: have a shave and get rid of that bloody ear-ring!'

After being dropped I had to change in lots of ways. 'Why didn't you tell me that a year ago?' I said to him with a laugh. 'You could have saved me a lot of hassle!'

So, yes, I did ditch the diamond stud in my ear, and I did start shaving more regularly, even if I now sport a beard. I first grew that before the 2010-11 Ashes and haven't shaved it off since. I was just being a little bit lazy with my shaving at the end of the summer and then I had to go to a Professional Cricketers' Association golf day at Stoke Park in Buckinghamshire. I was late and suddenly realised how scruffy I looked, so I just trimmed up and groomed a little bit of a beard and off I went. To my surprise, it seemed to be a bit of a hit among the boys. They all said: 'We think you should keep it!'

So I did keep it. However, I forgot one other rather important opinion in the matter: my wife Emily's. She wasn't happy with it and kept asking: 'When are you going to shave it off?' So I did as she asked, but when I looked in the mirror I just didn't like it at all. I wanted my beard back, so I grew it back straight away.

But then, in my first innings in Test cricket with a beard, I got a first-ball duck in the first Ashes Test in Brisbane. I did think about ditching it again immediately, but I decided to stick with it and I still have it today (or at least I did when I was writing this).

Strangely enough, I wasn't the only one considering any role my beard might play in my form. In 2011, somebody sent me a message saying something along the lines of 'Do you know that before you had a beard you averaged 42 in Test cricket, but since you've grown a beard your average is 57!' Actually, the figures as I write before the New Zealand tour of 2012-13 are that pre-beard I averaged 42.13 and with-beard I average 44.68. I've got three centuries without and three with. But that's good enough for me. I'm keeping it for the foreseeable future.

Perhaps surprisingly, my beard seems to have helped the way I am seen by some. The stubble I sported on my arrival in Test cricket, along with the ear-ring and my shaven head, had contributed to an unfavourable image. The beard seemed to create a better impression.

It's amazing that when you go through a difficult experience you lose a lot of friends very quickly. When I'd made my debut at Lord's and scored a century, everybody seemed to want to be my friend. Now I'd dropped a few catches, had my character questioned and been dropped from the England team, and those friends seemed to be disappearing by the minute. Funny that.

The change in the way people were responding to me meant I had a serious issue with trust at this point. Who should I listen to? Who was advising me in the right way? Who actually had my best interests at heart? It came down to Alec. He was the one I knew I could trust implicitly. He was the one I listened to. He was the one who persuaded me to give wicketkeeping one final go. He was the one I knew I could pick up the phone to at any time. He was the one who had been through similar experiences himself.

I did not even speak to Peter Moores at this stage. He didn't phone me and I didn't phone him. I know that some players would have wanted to speak to him. He had dropped me and that was that. I didn't want to know the finer details of why I had been dropped. That is not how I work. I knew there was a reason. I knew it was my wicketkeeping. It was up to me to sort that out and to make sure that I got back into the England team, and that when I did that, there would be no reason for being dropped again.

But this was never going to be a swift process. Players who are dropped from international cricket rarely return quickly. That does not mean they cannot have hugely successful international careers in the end, though. Think of Matthew Hayden and Justin Langer in that respect. They were dropped and then spent long periods in first-class cricket before returning to the international arena. Steve Waugh was dropped, too. It takes time to get back on the horse. And before that, it takes time to realise what it takes to get back on there.

Of course, some never return at all. As I mentioned earlier, some struggle to cope with the effects of rejection by their country. I've seen that happen a lot. I saw it happen to my mate Tim Ambrose, who was a wicketkeeping rival at Sussex and then with England.

But, after my initial period of sulking in New York and beyond (it may have lasted a couple of months in total), I decided I was going to come back. I was going to continue with keeping and I was going to do everything within my power to make sure I got back into the England team and became a match-winner for them. And in doing all that, I was going to make sure that I was liked as a person again; that my true character was portrayed. I had never been so determined. I actually hate that phrase 'what doesn't kill you makes you stronger', which always seems very harsh, but that was exactly what this was.

And there are always silver linings to any disappointment. Being dropped meant that I could get married to Emily much earlier than planned. As any cricketer knows, it is very hard to fit in weddings in such a crammed schedule. So we had originally thought we might get married at the end of the 2008 season. I had thought that in March of that year I would have been in New Zealand with England. I'd been looking too far ahead. But, as it was, I was free in March 2008. And as both Emily and I had fallen in love with New York during our time there, it seemed only natural that we should get married there.

So I was feeling pretty good about life when I began the 2008 county season, and it was reflected in my batting. I scored county championship hundreds against Kent (twice) and Nottinghamshire where some bloke called Graeme Swann, then uncapped in Tests, eventually bowled me for 131. He bowled me again in the second innings, but I had made 64 by then, too. In fairness, it was a pitch more suited to the seamers, as it usually is at Trent Bridge. And, in fairness too, the ball that bowled me in the first innings was an absolute jaffa – the classic off-spinner's dismissal – with it pitching outside off stump and turning back sharply through the gate.

However, the second one was just downright unlucky for me, lucky for him. Swanny was bowling around the wicket to me and I went to sweep him. I bottom-edged the ball onto my pad and then, as my hands came around in trying to complete the sweep shot, I gloved the ball back onto my stumps. Swanny and I still laugh about it today.

And we still talk about the first-innings ball, too. In fact, it's got a name of its own: it's called 'the Cheese ball'.

I'd better explain. My nickname is 'the Cheese', or just 'Cheese'. It's a terrible nickname, but complaining about nicknames is never a wise policy. You just hope they go away. Unfortunately this one hasn't, and most of the England team still call me by it, especially Stuart Broad, who absolutely delights in calling me by it.

Swanny and Jimmy Anderson quite like it too, as you can imagine. Andy Flower? He just calls me Matt. I like that, not just because it's actually my name, of course, but because I think he really makes an effort to get the relationship between coach and player right. It's always a very fine line, because deep down the coach probably wants to be good mates with you, but he must also realise that ultimately there are big decisions that have to be made. If he gets too close to the players, that will make those big decisions even more tricky than they might have been anyway. I think he gets it just right.

'The Cheese' stems from my early days at Sussex. I can't even remember who first called me by it, but, as I say, it has certainly stuck. Basically, with the blonde tips and highlights in my hair (believe it or not, I did have hair once) and my stud ear-ring, I used to strut around a bit in those days. I didn't think I was 'the Big Cheese', but others obviously did believe that was how I saw myself.

There are many players in the game who have a bit of a strut, but often they put it on. For others it is just the way they are. Take Kevin Pietersen. He walks around any cricket field on which he is playing as if he owns the place. But that is what makes him the player that he is. It is not at all forced. That's the way he is. It's the aura that he holds.

So when I first toured with the England Test squad in the winter of 2005-06, to Pakistan and India, I was just being myself. But that did not go down too well with many of the senior players on that trip. A couple of them came up to me and said: 'There are no show ponies in this side. There is no space for them.'

I thought that was very harsh and told myself: 'There is a lot more to me than that!' Yes, I had (and still have) certain mannerisms, such as having my collar up and regularly making sure it is turned up, which some might find cocky. Although I'm not as bad as I used to be (I'm bald now, so I can't be too vain), it's amazing how, when you are a young player doing such things, it is regarded merely as being a show dog, yet when you've played quite a bit it is construed as you just being particular with your kit.

Anyway, Swanny was also pretty pleased with himself when he bowled Ricky Ponting during the 2009 Ashes at Edgbaston. It was that perfect delivery again, and he immediately acclaimed it as being 'the ball of the century' – to us out on the field, and then afterwards, even if it was in jest, to the press. But he did also mention that he'd only ever bowled one ball before that was close to being as good as that, and that was to me, back at Trent Bridge in 2008. As I'd been the first recipient I thought it should be named after me. 'Ponting ball'? Nah, 'Cheese ball' sounds better. So now, whenever we really need a wicket and Swanny is bowling, you might hear me chirp up from behind the stumps: 'C'mon Swanny, give us the Cheese!'

Apart from scoring runs during that summer of 2008, I was also keeping reasonably well, if maybe still not quite well enough. That was about to change. It had been mentioned to me that Bruce French was available to do some work with me if I wanted, but for some reason I had never taken up the offer. But now when I was picked to play for the England Lions against South Africa in two one-day matches at Leicester and Derby, I asked our manager David Parsons, the England & Wales Cricket Board's performance director, if I could get Bruce along.

I didn't know him at all then, and at that time he was just doing some part-time wicketkeeping coaching with the ECB. I knew he'd played for England (16 Tests and 13 one-day internationals in the 1980s, apparently) and was renowned as an expert gloveman because he'd kept Jack Russell out of the side for a while. And I knew that he had long, dark curly hair that made him look a lot younger than he was. But that was it.

Before I knew it, I was doing a session with him at the national cricket performance centre at Loughborough. 'Crazy' is the first word that springs to mind. 'Mad as a badger' were others that soon followed. Those were my impressions of him anyway. As for his first impression of me? Well, I'm not sure he was too impressed. He was a bit stand-offish. I'm pretty sure he was shocked that I had played so much top-level cricket while being so rubbish as a wicketkeeper.

The session he had planned for me was just too hard. I couldn't cope with it. He was asking me to do stuff that I considered impossible. We were using some reaction boards (called 'Katchet' boards, which are orange and are sloped and ridged) and he was flinging balls at them and they were flying off in all directions. Basically, I wasn't getting near any of them. It was so frustrating. It drives me crazy when I am hopeless at something. I was standing there thinking: 'I cannot do any of this. I'm wasting my time here with this bloke.'

But, despite my frustration and his disappointment, we were still just about talking to each other by the end of the session. And so we had an honest discussion. It was pretty obvious that we had to start from scratch. There was some very basic work to be done.

And one of the things that had attracted me to working with Frenchy in the first place was the knowledge that he had previously done a lot of work with Chris Read, the Nottinghamshire wicketkeeper who played 15 Tests for England and whose place it was I actually took (he had played in the last two Ashes Tests in Australia in 2006-07) when I made my Test debut in 2007. For years I had played against and watched Readie. I loved watching him. I thought he was the best gloveman ever. He made the job look so easy, and still does so today.

So I said to Frenchy: 'I want you to turn me into Chris Read.'

He replied: 'No, no. You've got to do it your own way.'

But I insisted: 'Irrelevant. Just turn me into Chris Read please.'

So that was it. The road to Read had begun. To be honest, I could understand Frenchy's reluctance. He had one hell of a job on his hands.

We did start from scratch. I had to learn how to catch the ball. OK, I know I am a wicketkeeper and that sort of thing is rather important to my role. And I know admitting such a problem opens up all sorts of avenues for banter and abuse. But I did have a real problem with my catching. I was mixed up. I did not have a consistent method of catching the ball. Frenchy would throw me ten simple catches and I might catch them five different ways. There is no way that you can be consistent if that is the case. But it was. I needed to find a method that worked for me and then groove it.

I was confused. One minute I was an English-type wicket-keeper, the next I was like an Australian. That was because I'd been coached by an Englishman in Peter Moores (at Sussex, the Academy and with the full England team) and an Australian in Rod Marsh, who had been in charge at the National Academy before Mooresy took over there in 2005.

Mooresy had always coached me the English style, which is not to move your feet too much and catch the ball in front of you quite close to your body. It involved lots of diving and rolling. On the other hand Rod was always preaching the Australian method, which means moving your feet more but also taking the ball wide of your body with a big swing of the arms, often on the inside hip.

The problem with the Australian method is that if you try to catch the ball wide in England you can often look an idiot because of the wobble. By wobble I mean what the ball does after passing the bat, when its ducking and weaving can embarrass even the best keepers. With the Duke ball we use here it wobbles a lot in England, especially at Lord's where the ball can drop as much a foot just before it is about to go into the gloves. At Headingley it can wobble quite a bit too, and although The Oval generally swings the least of the England Test grounds, since the OCS stand was built at the Vauxhall End the amount of wobble has increased there, too.

And some bowlers are worse for wobble than others. For instance, whenever I see Graham Onions' name on an England team sheet I know I am in for a tough time. For a wicketkeeper, he is an absolute nightmare because he gets the ball to wobble so much more than any other bowler. You have no idea what to expect because the ball suddenly moves. He's not got any control over what it does after it bounces and comes through to me. Mind you, he has got plenty of control over where he pitches the ball. He must make batsmen's hearts sink, because he is a very fine bowler.

Steven Finn is another who can be difficult as well, especially at Lord's, but James Anderson is the best for wobble. Being a genuine swing bowler, I can generally see the position of the seam clearly when he is bowling, and the ball usually kisses the surface nicely before behaving itself into the gloves.

Because of this, Bruce made me realise that I needed to move my feet more. But my set-up was never going to allow me to do that. I was too low when the ball was released – in fact, I was still in a full squat position – so I was working my legs too hard. I was having to get up and then try to move sideways. It was little wonder that I couldn't move my feet. You can have the same problem if you're too high when the ball is released.

There was another issue. Frenchy pays massive attention to the posture of the keeper and talks about having a 'Z' shape in your body so you can use your knees and hips, using both levers. By doing that, it enables you to move sideways better. Before I worked with him, my posture wasn't right and it didn't allow me to move freely.

When people commented on my keeping to say that I didn't look particularly athletic, I found it really strange, because, if I was fielding at extra cover, I would be one of the more athletic fielders, able to move well and quickly. But when I was keeping that wasn't coming out.

Now when I'm getting ready receive the ball, I will step in and then go down and up – like a goalkeeper saving a penalty. I will never go all the way down into the squat position, but I will still have a strong position from which to push off. Essentially, I am getting myself ready to explode into action – I need to be able to move to a ball that's coming at me at 90 mph and so I have to feel comfortable, relaxed and then back my natural ability and hand-eye co-ordination.

Once we had got the start position sorted, Frenchy and I decided upon a method of catching that was a mix of the English and Australian approaches. So now I don't catch the ball as wide as an Australian keeper would, but I move my feet more than the typical English keeper.

We decided that there were certain basics you simply cannot get away from – that when you catch the ball your head, hands and the ball all have to be in a straight line – but after that it is up to you what you do. As the ball is going into my hands, the ball, my hands, my head and my left hip are in line. The further my head gets out of line, the more there is guesswork in taking the ball. The reason I try to keep my hip in line is to improve my balance and because it helps my footwork. I do like getting energy in my legs, so standing still like Jack Russell, Alan Knott or even Mooresy doesn't suit me. I like that movement.

And now I do this instinctively. I need to be instinctive. My view is that the brain is like a computer: if you have 20 windows open on your desktop, your computer is going to run slowly. You want to shut down those surplus windows and operate with a clear screen. I just have to keep it simple.

There are other things I look to do when I'm keeping. I open my hands to make the catching area as big as possible. But I mustn't be tense doing this: my hands, legs, arms and body have to be relaxed. When I am standing up to the spinners, I try to minimise the 'give' in my hands, so I can get the ball back to the stumps quickly. There will always be some 'give' but, as you practise, it gets less and less and your whole body absorbs the ball.

There has been a debate in recent times about where someone should stand when the ball is being thrown in to the stumps. Traditionally the advice was to stand behind the stumps, in case the ball hits the wicket and so you can see where the stumps are to take off the bails. But we now like to do things slightly differently. Taking the ball in front of the stumps and bringing it back to them will give you more run-outs – that is a fact. So now, as I run in to the stumps, I will find the line next to off stump and I'll put my right foot just there. With the stump just by my leg, I know that, as long as I brush my right leg when I've received the ball, I'll be hitting the stumps. If it is a tight one, this technique can get wickets. Try it, and see if you can see the difference it makes.

I certainly don't want to take anything away from Mooresy, because I owe so much to him, not least for igniting a love of keeping in that first-ever session we did together when I was 13. It was the most fun I'd ever had in sport. But his method, which of course works for many other keepers, wasn't quite right for me. I realised that only when I met Frenchy.

So the long road with Frenchy began. It has taken a while, but it has been so worth it. I can't thank him enough. He turned my career around, and in the process we have become really good friends. He has become part of my family, and he and his wife Andrea mean so much to me.

To start off with, it was just a question of grooving the exact technique I was going to use, and then honing it by catching hundreds of balls. It wasn't complicated at all. Frenchy would underarm the ball very slowly straight at me and I would make sure my movement was the same every single time. He would throw me 20 balls as if a right-handed batsman was facing, and then he would throw me 20 as if a left-hander was facing. Then we would start again. And again. And again.

It was long and, at times, it was tedious, but it was hugely beneficial. I just caught ball after ball so that gradually, over time, my technique became obvious and apparent. There was no confusion. I could catch the ball consistently. The minute I found that consistent method, along with the correct posture, my keeping was transformed.

When I first met Frenchy, I always had a bat in my hand. He told me that had to change. Of course, I didn't agree entirely because my batting is so important to me and to my place in the team, but I took his point. Before I met him I probably concentrated 80 per cent on my batting and left 20 per cent on my keeping. That has changed. The balance is much more equal now.

Frenchy made me realise how hard I had to work on my keeping and, whoever you are, how much work you have to put in to perform consistently at the top level. Only keepers will know how difficult it is to do all this, because you can have the best day that you have ever had with the gloves and most people might not even notice.

As I've heard people say: we're like surgeons. We get noticed only when we make a mistake. All we can do is strive for consistency. It is very difficult to gain instant credits on the marker board, like a batsman can for scoring a hundred or a bowler can for taking five wickets. It's possible to perform really well, and yet not pick up a single dismissal in an innings. So you must do it over a period of time and hope that after, say, a year people might say something like: 'You know what? He hasn't actually made any mistakes yet!'

So, once we had sorted the detail of the technique that Frenchy so craves, it was time to do what he had wanted me to when we first met: overload. That is at the basis of all the work he does with wicketkeepers. He wants to put you under so much pressure in training that anything you then encounter in a match seems easy by comparison. For example, he might work out that when I am standing back to a seam bowler, once the ball has hit the pitch it might be coming through to me at 40 mph. He would then set the machine (in essence a bowling machine on the floor, used for fielding and wicketkeeping) at 50 or 55 mph. Or he might do a practice where he hides the ball to eradicate any anticipation from me. He is trying to create the feeling that I have been wrong-footed, so that I can practise getting myself out of trouble if that does happen in a match.

Sometimes we'll do the session he tried with me the first time we worked together, using those reaction boards. He will make me move closer and closer to them to catch. It is not about taking ten out of ten. It is supposed to be so hard that that cannot happen. Five out of ten is actually pretty good in the circumstances. But we'll stay at the same distance apart and I'll look to get better and better until maybe I can get all ten. Then, of course, I have to move closer and try to get another perfect score.

While that might be fun, Frenchy has also devised a killer session, and it's the one I hate most. To do this one, I have to wear the all-over body armour protection that rugby players wear for their contact training. He then gets me to stand about a metre away from an old-style slip-catching cradle and he will launch balls at it. It is frightening how quickly the balls fly off. Basically, I will get hit eight times out of ten, but there might just be one unbelievable take that I manage that will make the session worthwhile. And my reactions always quicken as we go on.

I can empathise with rugby players when I do this one. It must be so hard for them to get themselves up for hard contact sessions in training, and that's how I feel with this exercise. It is so difficult to raise your adrenalin levels to those you will experience in a game situation, but that's what you have to try to do here.

Talking of rugby, Frenchy and I also do some sessions with Huw Bevan, our Welsh fitness trainer who was once a first-class rugby player. In these I might do some medicine-ball throws with Bevs and then go straight into a catching exercise with Frenchy. Or I might have a band around my waist, with Bevs holding it to provide resistance, while I do side-to-side drills with Frenchy firing balls out of the machine at the same time. I will then do the same sessions without the resistance. It is another form of overloading that I have found very useful.

Fitness is hugely important to me. It is vital for any wicketkeeper, of course. It goes without saying that you require strong legs, lower back and hip flexors in order to do the job day in and day out. But to be the England wicketkeeper these days I think you have to be very fit. As I mentioned earlier, you are expected to be the drummer in the band, and you are not expected to stop drumming throughout the day in the field. You are expected to run the shuttles in between the overs and generally buzz around all the time. You can't do that if you are unfit. And you've got to remember that the most important part of the job is to concentrate and make sure you catch the ball. If you cannot do that because you are tired from buzzing around, then you are in trouble ...

Fitness in cricket has changed massively. It has become ever more important, even if it is a game where some can get away with very little attention to it. It's not like athletics, where having a beer the night before a race might add a crucial fraction to your time and therefore lose you the race. But there is still no excuse for not trying your damnedest to be as fit as you can. That's what I've always tried to do. I've always been of the thought that if I am right physically, then there is a much better chance that I will be right mentally.

The mental and physical disciplines go hand in hand. I've got a huge belief in myself that I can perform, not only in the good times but under pressure too. Other people can't give you determination; you have to find that within yourself to want to be in the gym at six in the morning, to want to be able to do the extra bit of work after the day's training is over. It's about answering questions of yourself mentally and physically.

I do need to pay attention to my fitness as sometimes I can put on a little bit of weight. I'm not someone who just looks at a Mars bar and immediately puts on 5kg, but then I'm also not like Jimmy Anderson, who can eat three chocolate puddings a night and be lighter the next morning. I've never quite worked that out, but that's the way Jimmy is. I've learnt over time to listen to my body. There are always so many fads about fitness, but I think eventually you work out what is best for yourself.

In my early years I was quite small, and I wanted to get bigger, a little bit ripped, as they say. Yes, there may have been a bit of vanity involved. So I did that by using quite heavy weights, but I got a little stocky. I got too caught up in the weights at one stage and got a bit too heavy. So I made an effort to slim down. I changed the way I trained. I was no longer obsessed with lifting weights and I did a huge amount of running.

But I've now found cycling. All that running, especially on

treadmills in the gym, caused some problems too. I got an Achilles' tendon injury, which is quite a common problem for keepers. Alec Stewart had difficulties with his, and so did Andy Flower. He damaged his while we were warming up before an ICC World Twenty20 match in South Africa in 2007. But mine got so painful that I was banned from running towards the end of the 2012 summer.

I had to find something to make sure I didn't turn into a fat lump. I'd already done a 100-mile charity bike ride at the start of the summer, just after we returned from the tour of Sri Lanka. I'd gone on it with Bruce French for the Chestnut Tree House children's hospice, near Arundel, which cares for children with serious illnesses from across Sussex.

Frenchy is a massive fan of outdoor pursuits, and he'd always said that one day we should do something fitness-wise that wasn't in the gym and wasn't keeping wicket in the nets. He loves climbing (on our tour to South Africa in 2009-10 he, Andy Flower, Huw Bevan and Richard Halsall climbed up one of the huge floodlights at the ground at Buffalo Park, East London), and his initial idea was climbing Ben Nevis. And I'm not talking about walking up but going up the cliff. He's a proper mountaineer.

We talked seriously about doing that, and I even remember doing an interview about it with Dean Wilson of the *Daily Mirror* while we were out in South Africa. 'Frenchy is a mad-keen climber. He brought in a DVD for me called *Touching the Void* and I watched it in East London,' I explained. 'I then said to him: "Right, I want to see what it's like at the summit, but I want it to be a proper one, not just a hill." We discussed it and I queried how long it would take for me to get ready to do it, and he said, with three weeks behind me, I'll be fine. He then came up to me and said: "Ben Nevis, March, we're going." Now I've told the media, I think it's fair to say I can't get out of it. While I don't want to kill myself, I'd like to do something properly and so he said Ben Nevis is for starters. I want the full monty with the ropes and the crampons and ice picks to drag yourself up a mountain. He is keen to take me and I'd love to do it. Whether we get the time is another issue.'

Well, time was an issue and I did get out of it. There was also the pretty significant factor that I am absolutely petrified of heights. Oh, and I'm not sure the England management would have been too happy about it either. So instead I suggested mountain biking to Frenchy. I had done a bit of it with my dad back in South Africa where I grew up (I came to England aged 11) and we decided to cycle the South Downs Trail from Winchester to Eastbourne.

I'd been to the Chestnut Tree House a couple of years previously after playing a game for Sussex at Arundel. I was amazed that I'd never really noticed it before, as I had driven past it so often. But they gave us a tour and it was so impressive to see what they do there. Walking away that day I thought that was a charity I wanted to support in the long run. Anyone who has kids will know it is their worst nightmare that one of your children gets sick, so seeing what they do is something that always stuck with me. And I was delighted when I was asked to become a patron of the Chestnut Tree House.

It costs the charity £5,000 a day just to keep it running, and our initial aim on the bike ride was to raise about £10,000. As it was, we raised the incredible sum of £35,896, and I was a pretty proud bloke when I presented a cheque for that amount to the charity in June 2012.

In the summer of 2012, however, it was not mountain biking that was all the rage. It was road biking. Team Sky were doing their stuff in the Tour de France, with Bradley Wiggins emerging as the overall winner of the Tour, the first Briton to do so, of course. And then Wiggins won the Olympic time trial in London, as I sat watching on TV up in Leeds where we were preparing for the second Test against South Africa, totally transfixed. Huw Bevan, who has also found cycling as a love, sat on a bike in the gym and pedalled as hard as he could for all the time Wiggins was doing his trial. I don't think Huw got quite as far as Wiggins, or Sir Bradley Wiggins, as we should call him now after his deserved knighthood in the New Year's Honours List for 2013, but he didn't do badly.

One disadvantage of mountain biking is that it takes a bit of planning if you want to ride a decent trail. You usually have to put your bike in the car and drive somewhere to get started. It's enough to stop you doing it if you're not quite fully motivated on any certain day. However, road biking is simpler. You just get out there and go. And I quite like the idea of trying to beat one's best time over, say, a 20-mile course.

My other sporting love is golf. I play off seven – I'm pretty much the worst seven handicapper you will ever see on a golf course – but find the sport can be so frustrating. Andy Crumpton is a mate of mine with whom I go cycling. He works in the City and on a Saturday morning he used to go to play golf to relax, but he would come home more angry than when he left. So now he cycles.

I can see why he's turned to cycling. I don't want to get too deep about this, but there is something very therapeutic about it. It is a form of escapism. You can go out on the South Downs at 6.30am and be the only person out there – it is an amazing feeling. You're seeing things others can't. It is just so relaxing. It is also very good for the body. If you do 70 miles and burn 3500 calories before breakfast, you are going to feel pretty good about yourself.

When I had eight weeks off at the end of the 2012 summer before going to India, I did loads of cycling on top of all my other gym training, and the results were unbelievable. I lost about 5kg of fat. I've had periods like that before, when I've been able to train hard, but I've never had results like that. I honestly felt fitter than I've ever been before.

And the cycling was helping my Achilles' injury too. I was lucky that I had met a man from the cycling company Specialized at Lord's during the summer. He'd offered to help kit me out, but he said: 'If we're going to do it, we'll do it properly.' They knew all about my injury, so they measured me up for my bike and everything else to go with it. At first I was the classic 'all the gear, no idea' cyclist, but I've learnt. And the fitness staff have told me that the slow pedalling motion is actually strengthening my Achilles'. Lots of fun and a good workout – no wonder I'm addicted.

And I also know that I'm very lucky, as Team Sky have also been very kind to me. When I arrived back from the Test tour of India at the end of 2012, there was a brand new Pinarello Dogma bike waiting there for me, thanks to them. And before I went to New Zealand on tour (where I took my new bike so that I could train in between matches) this February, I spent three days training with the Team Sky group in Majorca. I did a time trial on the toughest climb on the island, Sa Calobra, which is about seven miles long with 26 hairpin bends and an average gradient of 7.1 per cent. That is very steep and very winding! To make matters even worse, when I took on the ride I had already done two and a half hours' training that day.

I was feeling pretty pleased with myself that I had done it in a time of 46 minutes and 39 seconds until I discovered that Sergio Henau, the Colombian member of Team Sky, had done it in 23 minutes and 56 minutes – almost exactly twice as fast. It will be a while before I'm a contender on the Tour de France! The whole experience with Team Sky was amazing. I even had dinner with Sir Dave Brailsford, the principal of the team, and picked his brains. It was fascinating.

I'm pleased to say that I don't get muscle cramps when cycling, not even on the long rides. It seems an age now since that problem so affected me in the early stages of my England career, especially when playing in one-day cricket in Asia in the winter of 2005-06. But they were a real problem.

The first thing to say about that, however, is that it used to really annoy me how people viewed cramps back then. It was massively frowned upon and seen simply as a sign that you were unfit. And that was not just from those spectators watching. I felt that was the impression, too, from inside the England camp. I received a lot of advice, not all of it helpful.

I've already mentioned that one-day international against India in Jamshedpur in 2006, which was the first limited-overs game in which I kept wicket under coach Duncan Fletcher – it was also the match in which I suffered the worst cramps of my life.

Geraint Jones was the first-choice wicketkeeper on that trip and Andrew Flintoff was the captain, but neither played in that match, the sixth of the series in which we were already 4-0 down, with the fifth match at a soggy Guwahati having been abandoned three days earlier, leading to crowd trouble. Because the outcome of the series was decided, I got my chance to keep wicket for England for the first time, and Andrew Strauss captained England for the first time. We both ended up on saline drips.

It was a ferociously hot day. While we were fielding, we received a message that in the city a mile away the temperature had been recorded at 43°C. I reckon it was hotter than that in the middle – maybe as high as 53°C. We'd lost the toss, but we did extremely well to bowl India out for 223 in 48 overs, with Jimmy Anderson and Sajid Mahmood taking three wickets each.

I was due to open the batting, but I returned to the dressing room in a right state. I remember sitting in a chair and my whole body was cramping, and by that I mean every single muscle. It was horrendous. I looked down at one of my thigh muscles and it was horribly deformed. It was bulging out, and I was in complete agony.

I'd seen Owais Shah in a similar state once on an England Lions tour. Sometimes those watching find people cramping funny, but it is not funny at all, I can tell you. Owais was there in Jamshedpur, too, but he was not playing. I remember him coming out as twelfth man when we were fielding, with a cold towel to put over my head, a drink and a sympathetic tap on the back. He knew what I was going through.

I was told to get into an ice bath. I felt that was the wrong thing to do, because I knew that once I got in there I would just cramp more. But I obeyed my instructions, and guess what happened? It got worse. I certainly couldn't open (Ian Bell did so, making 46), and ended up going in at six, making just three. Straussy had already set up victory by then, though, having made 74. He wasn't out. He'd had to retire hurt with cramps. It was that sort of day.

It's a shame that we are no longer allowed to be put on drips in these circumstances, because they can obviously rehydrate you so much more quickly. I remember another occasion in South Africa, early in my career, when I was told to drink the Gatorade energy drink all day as it was believed that if I did, I would not get cramps. I did as I was advised and drank the stuff all day, but still got cramps.

But thankfully there have been significant advances made in both the attitudes to and the prevention of cramps. Nowadays there is a lot more testing and monitoring. We are weighed at the start of the day and at every break. And we have regular sweat tests. Unsurprisingly for anyone who has ever seen me in action, they show that I sweat a lot (in the Test in Colombo against Sri Lanka in 2012, I lost 3.5kg in weight between the start of play and lunch on one of the days). But I'm not alone in sweating heavily: Kevin

Pietersen and Jonathan Trott both do so as well. By contrast the tests also show that Alastair Cook hardly sweats at all. That's just ridiculous. He doesn't know how lucky he is.

The tests we took also revealed something else: apparently I have a higher salt content in my sweat than is normal. By losing so much salt all the time, it was little wonder I was getting cramps. I realised that I needed to plan a lot better in terms of my hydration if I was going to be able to counter the problem.

So now I have a rigid routine. Every night before a playing day I mix up two litres of electrolyte drink. I aim to have drunk all of that by the time we start practising at the ground the next day. So I will be up early, and I will start sipping from one of my two bottles as soon as I wake up. Usually I will have finished one bottle by the end of breakfast, and then I can take the other with me to the ground. If I don't need to go to the toilet by the time we get to the ground, then I know I'm behind the eight ball. I'll also nip off at the end of warm-ups to relieve myself. Again that is a good sign!

I've also realised the effects that good nutrition can have on my performance levels. Again it comes from experience. When you are 21, you can eat and drink almost what you want. And I've always trained hard, so I thought that, if I ever did overindulge, I could then train any excess off. What I've learned now is that if I get my diet 100 per cent spot on, I actually don't have to train so hard or punish my body as much.

So now for breakfast I will have porridge, two poached eggs on brown toast, black coffee and orange juice with some creatine mixed in with it. I've recently started using creatine, not as a way of building more muscle bulk as quite a few athletes do, but more as a recovery aid. For those wondering, creatine is a popular sports supplement that is produced naturally in the body and is used to help the muscles recover more quickly after exercise.

Whereas power athletes might do a 'loading' phase of creatine, where they take maybe 20g a day for a short period, I just take 3g every day for 28 days. I'll have two days off, then I'll start again. This programme has, of course, been approved by the team doctor. All our tablets, supplements and medication are cleared, and certainly the odd anti-inflammatory doesn't go amiss after a day in the field.

Another part of my match-day routine is to have a bath for about 15 minutes every morning. No matter what time play is starting – and that can often be as early as 9.30am when we are abroad – I will make sure I do that. Having a bath at 6.30am is a little bit strange, but I simply have to do it. It is partly to loosen up my body and partly because I use it as a period to get my head right before going out to face the cricketing world.

Is it superstition or habit? I'm not really sure of the difference sometimes. I don't think I'm massively superstitious, but then again there are certain things that simply have to remain part of my set-up, as I detailed in the previous chapter when talking about my routines before keeping and batting.

Take my England cap as another example. I've always had a thing about cricket caps. Jimmy Anderson often talks about the first time we played together. It was at Abergavenny down in Wales against a Pakistan Under-19 team, I think, and it was for an ECB Under-18 team, a 'B' team no less. We weren't good enough to be in the first team in those days. I wasn't always keeping, and Mark Wallace, the Glamorgan wicketkeeper whose home ground is coincidentally at Abergavenny, was usually picked ahead of me. Carl Gazzard, who played for Somerset, was also in the mix for the position, too.

Anyway, Jimmy remembers what he calls my 'fetish' with the peak of the cap with which I was presented that day in Abergavenny. I spent a long time bending it to make sure it was the perfect shape. Why not? The peak is always the key to a good cap, isn't it? My cap must have looked pretty good anyway, because everyone else in the side suddenly wanted me to do theirs, too. And that's something that continues to this day. I am still obsessed with my cap and I can often be seen adjusting the peaks of my team-mates' caps to get them just right.

But I have only one cap. Or to rephrase that, I have only one cap I will wear for Test cricket, and I still wear that cap I was given on the outfield by Andrew Strauss and David Graveney on my debut in 2007. It's in a bit of state these days, with its sweat and champagne stains, and I get some grief about it from the boys. But even though I've received caps for my 25th (versus South Africa in Durban in 2009-10) and 50th (the third Test against Pakistan in Dubai in 2011-12) Tests, I keep them at home. There is only one England cap for me and that is the original one. I will wear that for the rest of my England career. I'll admit that at one stage I did ask the rest of the boys whether I should change it, but all I got in response was 'No chance!'

They consider it lucky, apparently. It's like the seating positions on the coach on the way to games. Now this is something I'm superstitious about. Maybe not as much as Graeme Swann, mind you. If you sat in his seat on the coach he would go absolutely mad. His seat, as you are walking down the coach and looking to the back, is the one in front of the back seat on the right-hand side. In the back right-hand corner is Alastair Cook. He stays there now even though he is Test captain. We've told him to move down to the front so that we can talk about him, but he won't have it.

In the middle of the back row is Jimmy. On the left at the back is Steven Finn. I'm in front of him and opposite me is Stuart Broad. That's the way it has to be every single day. It's the same in the changing room. Swanny, Cooky and Jimmy always change next to each other. And Broady and I are always next to each other.

Broady is my best mate in the England side. He's godfather to my son Johnny. I remember watching him make his international debut on TV, in a rain-affected one-day international in Cardiff in 2006. He bowled pretty well, taking one wicket – Shoaib Malik LBW – in his three overs, but he had these flowing blond locks and I just thought 'What a ponce!'

But then, not long afterwards, we were both selected that winter in the National Academy squad that spent time in Australia during the Ashes. I first met him up at Loughborough during training and we hit it off immediately. The thing about Stu is that, yes, he has all the good looks, but the guy works bloody hard at his cricket. There are a lot of people in cricket who want all the nice spin-offs, like the cars and the phones and so on, but are not prepared to put in the hard work to earn those luxuries. The thing I really rate about Stu is that he will put in the work. He knows those spin-offs are there, but they are not the most important things to him. He is such a genuine bloke, and a really good mate.

And so I was delighted that he was there when I returned to England colours. It was not a Test match, indeed initially it was just a warm-up one-day international against Scotland in Edinburgh that was abandoned. But it was some moment for me when, four days later, I walked out to play against South Africa at Headingley in a limited-over game at the end of the summer of 2008.

'It's incredible that the keeping position for England has become this big thing,' I said at the time, 'The way I try and look at it is that you can't take it too personally otherwise you put yourself under too much pressure and you can't perform. I learned a huge amount from being involved with England before and I come back now as a more mature person and cricketer – I'm really looking forward to doing the job and doing it better.

'I think it makes you stronger. I think an experience like that does change the way you think and your attitude towards a few things and you grow up a bit. My family stuck by me throughout and you learn who your friends are in that situation. I'm lucky a few people stuck by me, but I don't think I changed that much.

'It's very easy to become quite intense. I guess that's all about wanting to do well and no matter how it comes out on the field, you're just trying to do well and put your best performance in. I've never shied away from hard work and I've always worked hard on my game, but things like going back to your hotel and not thinking about anything else but the next day – you have to have your break away from it and your release. I think coming back older and wiser, I will have found a nice balance between the time when you're on and when you are off and let yourself relax a little bit.

'When I was first thrown out into the international scene there was a lot to learn. A lot of it was off the field more than on it and you don't know how you are going to deal with that until you are there. To have that experience behind me is massive and hopefully I will be able to deal with it better this time around. I feel proud of myself this time around, because when you are left out people give you stick and say that is the end and he will never be back. To come back and perform for Sussex the way I have, I am quite proud of. It shows a bit of mental toughness, too, and I am pleased with how I have done it, but there is a lot of hard work to come.'

Yes, there were so many people who had said that I would never play for England again. But here I was, just under nine months since I'd been dropped. I was back. I was a new man. I was clean shaven. I didn't have a stud in my ear. I was married. I was so proud, but I was also nervous. I needed to get this right. I'd worked extremely hard, and been through so much turmoil, that I just had to get this right.

I opened the batting in that first match with Ian Bell. We put on 77 and I made 42, including five fours and even a six off Jacques Kallis over long on. I was out the next ball, caught at point, but it was a decent return, and our new captain Kevin Pietersen made 90 not out so that our total of 275 looked useful as South Africa prepared to bat under lights. I then took two catches and stumped Mark Boucher as he lifted his foot. We won by 20 runs.

The next game was at Trent Bridge. South Africa won the toss and batted. They lasted 23 overs. Yes, 23 overs! They were all out for 83. I took a record-equalling six catches (Alec Stewart also took six against Zimbabwe at Old Trafford in 2000) and Stu took five for 23 from his ten overs. Belly and I knocked off the runs in just 14.1 overs. I made 45 not out off only 36 balls, including a six down the ground off Makhaya Ntini. It was some day.

KP texted me after that match. It meant the world to me. I'm not sure if KP pushed for my return to the side, but I do think he has always rated me as a player. He likes the way I play, being so aggressive. He was doing things differently as captain, but he was also doing things aggressively. He was preaching and talking about a kind of assassin's temperament – perform, win, go home. And we were doing that. He said in his text: 'Mate, fantastic, I'm really proud of you. You did very well.'

We won easily at The Oval where Samit Patel picked up five wickets, and then even more easily at Lord's where not even a duck could dampen my spirits. We were winning 4-0 in the series and it would probably have been 5-0, had the last match in Cardiff not been abandoned after just three overs. I really did think I was back now – but I knew I had to push on again.

3

Keeper or Umpire?

The wicketkeeper's role is so often overlooked. But, quite simply, he is one of the most important players on the field; as I said earlier, he is the heartbeat of the team. I would say that, of course, but I do think his importance is downplayed too often. In my opinion, it's about time he was 'bigged up' a bit more.

There are always specialist coaches for all other facets of the game – batting, bowling, fielding – then you have fitness coaches, masseurs, physiotherapists, psychologists to name more than a few, but how often do you see a wicketkeeping coach with a team full time? How often is it planned during a training session that there will be time for the wicketkeeper to do his work? There's always time for batting, bowling and fielding … It just doesn't make sense.

The appointment of Bruce French to work with England has, of course, changed that, and it has helped me enormously. All he has to do all day is look at how I am doing. He can examine and analyse every tiny part of my game, and at practice we can go off to our own little corner and do our work quietly.

But in recent years the role of the wicketkeeper in international cricket has become even more important. Apart from having to concentrate on catching every single ball, we now have to be umpires as well. The Decision Review System (DRS) has changed the game in many ways. For example, it has made batsmen play spin very differently (no longer can they just pad the ball away and assume they will get the benefit of the doubt). But people often forget that it has also put a lot of pressure on the keepers. We have the best view of possible edges or LBW shouts, and can give the most objective assessment of whether we have a chance of getting a wicket through DRS. This is something that escapes a lot of bowlers a lot of the time – they just think everything is out!

Even though we may have the best view of anyone in the team, it is obviously not as good as the umpires' view. For a start, a keeper can't be exactly behind the stumps all the time and directly in line like the umpires. You wouldn't catch much if that were the case. And in terms of LBWs, as a keeper you can lose the line of the ball if it tails in late to the pads of a batsman. But since the DRS (first known as the Umpire Decision Review System and before that trialled as just 'referrals') has come in, it has certainly made me respect the job of the umpires much more. Making those split-second decisions is not easy.

I actually played in the first county match in which a referral system was trialled. It was a Friends Provident Trophy match between Sussex and Somerset at Taunton in late April 2007. Nobody really understood how it was going to work. It had been decided that in the televised matches in that competition that year, sides could make two appeals to the third umpire if they thought a decision was wrong. And so on that day in Taunton our captain Chris Adams became the first player to challenge a decision when he was given out LBW by umpire Jeremy Lloyds off the bowling of Peter Trego.

I hadn't really been able to challenge my earlier decision (I had opened and was clearly caught behind for 17 off Charl Willoughby), but Grizzly, as he is known to almost everyone in the game, thought that he was far enough down the pitch to challenge the call, even if he felt very uncomfortable about doing so. 'I went through fifteen seconds thinking I'd better get off, but then I thought "Hang on, there's a referral system now,"' he said afterwards. 'It was quite an awful situation – but nothing ventured, nothing gained.'

That was the problem all the players had at first: they did not like the idea of challenging the umpire's decision. From a young age, we had always been taught that his decision is final. Now suddenly it wasn't. As it happened, Grizz still had to go on his way anyway, but only after a two-minute delay which resulted in the crowd slow hand-clapping. Barrie Leadbeater was the third umpire and he said that he could find 'no obvious error' in the original decision.

In the FPT that year there were nine televised matches in which there were 11 referrals. Not once was the decision changed, so it is fair to say that it didn't go down well with the players. And exactly the same can be said of its first experiment in international cricket when an England team was involved. It came in the away four-Test series in West Indies in 2008-09.

It was the third rubber in which it had been trialled, after series between India and Sri Lanka, and then New Zealand and West Indies. And for our Test matches the number of reviews per innings per team had been reduced from three to two, just like we had used in those county matches. At that stage even India were in favour, before their senior players expressed doubts about it and they soon refused to use it, even though by then everyone else had realised the benefits it can bring to the game.

At the time the ECB were keener on the system that had been used in the Stanford Super Series (we will come to the subject of that man Stanford later) in Antigua the previous year, where the umpires were allowed to use TV replays for all contentious decisions and the TV umpire was also allowed to intervene when he spotted an obvious error made by the on-field umpires. The crucial difference was that there were no challenges from the players; it was all done by the umpires. But the worry with that was that it would take too much time, with the umpires constantly asking for decisions to be reviewed.

As players we were in an awkward situation as regards this new review system. What did you say? I remember that Steve Harmison came out and blasted it. 'There doesn't seem to be any consistency or clarity,' he said. 'That means umpires are in danger of being isolated on the field and terrified to make a decision. And I have to say, such is my continuing confusion, that I fear the new system is in danger of making a mockery of the time-honoured authority of the officials on the field.'

Mind you, Harmy had reason to be unhappy with the system because, in the first Test in Jamaica, a match which became infamous because we were bowled out in our second innings for just 51 (Jerome Taylor taking five for 11) to lose by an innings and 23 runs, he had had an LBW decision against Ramnaresh Sarwan overturned. Having said that, later on he also had a catch I took off Daren Powell upheld and no one was sure whether Powell had definitely hit it.

The Sarwan decision, made by Tony Hill but overturned by TV umpire Daryl Harper on account of height, was interesting. He was on just 5 at the time, but went on to make 107, so it was certainly costly. The way DRS works today, it would still have been given out: using Hawk-Eye's results which produce automated responses to three questions – Pitching in line? Hitting in line? Hitting the stumps? – it would have been termed as an 'umpire's call', and the decision would have stood, whereas Harper was able to give him the benefit of the doubt, overturning the original verdict.

I was interviewed after that day's play and said: 'Steve Harmison's one with the use of Hawk-Eye looks like it is hitting the top of the bails, which is out. So from that point of view you can get a bit frustrated. But it's not easy. The third umpire is making a guess decision as much as anyone else. If you are trusting Hawk-Eye to track the ball three-quarters of the way or longer, then why not all the way?'

That is what happens now. Hawk-Eye is used to track the ball all the way to the stumps, and this has changed people's perceptions. We've all had to recalibrate our minds as to the judgement of what is out or not. But back then it was still confusing us.

'From my own point of view, it's very much an instinctive call,' I said. 'You see it and you either feel it's out or you don't. But when a decision like the Harmison one is given not out, you almost start second-guessing yourself a little because I thought that was pretty close.'

The time taken to reach the result of a review was, and still is to a certain extent, a bone of contention, and I was asked about that too. 'Do you sacrifice that to make sure you get the right decision?' I responded. 'There is a huge amount at stake at the minute and big decisions have to be made. Traditionalists will say it does take quite a bit of time out of the game, and why shouldn't the umpires have the right to make their decision as they always have done?'

I was being careful about what I said. Sportspeople, and most especially cricketers in my experience, are always averse to change. We can be a cynical bunch. 'I think a lot of the players have some sympathy with the umpires, because they are making tricky decisions,' I said. 'We've just had an afternoon of having to try and make decisions in a split second and it's not easy. Everyone makes mistakes, players will make more mistakes than umpires in a day's play. If an umpire makes a mistake it's not because they are trying to. If the decision is changed then so be it.'

The truth is that when it first came in, we saw the referral system as a way of burgling a wicket. We didn't respect the fact that it was there to rectify the howlers that umpires occasionally make. So if Chris Gayle was going well and there was a appeal turned down, we might risk a review just because we desperately wanted him out. And if there was a referral remaining and one of our tail-enders was given out, we thought we'd give it a go just in case. We were using it as a tactical move rather than in the way in which it was really intended. As time has gone by, and we've got to understand how to use it better, our thought process has changed completely and now it has to be an absolute howler for us to review.

As such, I've become a big fan of the DRS now. If you've got the technology, why not use it? There is so much at stake these days, why wouldn't you use it? Ultimately people's careers are on the line. But if you are going to use the technology, then you must use all of it, and you must use it in every series. Otherwise you are playing a different game in every series in which you play.

The situation with India refusing to use the system has been particularly disappointing, but then you have moments like the second Test at Trent Bridge in 2011 where Stuart Broad's stunning hat-trick changed the game and you know that it might have been so different had the DRS been in place. Upon replay it was obvious that his second wicket of the hat-trick, that of Harbhajan Singh LBW, was not out because Harbhajan had got an inside edge, but at the time all you could do was laugh when the Indians complained. 'Don't blame us,' we said.

On our victorious tour to India in 2012-13, in the second innings of the first Test at Ahmedabad, Alastair Cook would probably have been given out LBW sweeping to the left-arm spinner Pragyan Ohja for 41 if the DRS had been in place. As it was, the original not-out decision of umpire Aleem Dar stood. Our new captain batted for over nine hours and, although we lost that Test (and I made 91 in a partnership of 157 with him) by nine wickets, Cooky's innings was vitally important in that it proved to everyone what could be done in India. We'd been bowled out for 191 in our first innings and, having lost 3-0 in the United Arab Emirates to Pakistan, as well as a Test in Galle that year, the commonly held view was that we could not, as a team, play spin. That innings altered perceptions and was the springboard from which we won the series.

Sometimes the DRS works for you, and sometimes it works against you. For instance, during the 2010-11 Ashes series in Australia, Cooky would have scored many fewer runs than the 766 he ended up with, if the DRS had not been in place. When he'd made 64 in the second Test at Adelaide, he was given out caught behind off Peter Siddle by Marais Erasmus, but it was overturned on review, and he went on to make 148. Then, in the fourth Test at Melbourne, Tony Hill gave him out LBW to Ben Hilfenhaus when on 27, but replays showed that he had clearly inside-edged it. That decision was overturned, too, and he made 82. The key thing for me about DRS is that more correct decisions are achieved, and that has to be right.

After that trialling of referrals in the Caribbean, we did not then use it for the following summer's Ashes series, but it was in operation that winter when we went to South Africa. Again it caused controversy, never more so than in the last Test at the Wanderers in Johannesburg, where the South Africa captain Graeme Smith was given not out off Ryan Sidebottom when he had made only 15. In attempting a cut, Smith had edged it through to me. There was a huge noise. To my mind, it was out for all money.

It was not given, though. But then we thought we were OK because we knew we could review it. There may have been no

HotSpot technology in use during that tour (apparently there were only four such cameras at the time and they were all in Australia and New Zealand), but we knew that stump microphones were going to be used in determining reviews and were confident that would sort it.

We had no hesitation in reviewing, but then word came back from TV umpire Daryl Harper that the decision was going to stand. Smith was not out. We could not believe it. It appeared to be an outrageous decision, and we felt seriously wronged. Our team director Andy Flower went into Harper's room to complain. Almost inevitably Smith made a century, and we were hammered in the Test, and South Africa ended up drawing the series 1-1. It was only later that we discovered that Harper had received a poor sound feed from the host broadcaster. To say it was frustrating was an understatement. But there had already been other frustrations in that series.

In the first Test, I had been sure that A.B.de Villiers had bottom-edged Graeme Swann to me. Umpire Steve Davis did not think so, so we reviewed immediately. But, of course, without HotSpot – and that is not always 100 per cent accurate anyway – and the Snickometer, which takes too long to be used, no edge was detected and de Villiers remained.

We had already wasted a review on Jacques Kallis, when we thought he was LBW to James Anderson, but he wasn't and went on to make 120. And then when we batted, Stuart Broad was upset when it seemed to take the South Africans an awfully long time to decide to refer an LBW decision against him. He was eventually given out off J.P.Duminy and made it clear to the umpires, Davis and Aleem Dar, that he thought it had taken too long. Because of those experiences, among other reasons, Andy Flower declared himself 'not a fan' of the system, and there were teething problems all round.

But quite apart from the technological issues of trying to make sure that the technology will prove that a decision should be changed, there is the problem that I mentioned earlier: most bowlers think that everything they appeal for is out. Swanny is certainly like that, and so is Broady. Paul Collingwood at slip wasn't much better, either. He thought everything was out as well. So that left me and captain Andrew Strauss at first slip as the mediators. You try telling a bowler he is wrong! It is never easy. They are fired up and usually don't want to listen.

What you've got to try to do is take the emotion out of the situation and make a logical decision. Eventually, we decided that there would be only three of us involved in the deliberations – myself, Straussy and the bowler – and that if two of us agreed, we would go with the majority verdict on whether or not to challenge the decision.

In fairness, Straussy and I were always pretty much on the same page on most decisions, but we definitely got better over time. I certainly learned to be more aware of the different surfaces we play on. During the Ashes of 2010-11 in Australia, I was convinced that a number of LBW decisions against their opener Shane Watson were plumb, but in fact they were going quite a long way over the stumps. It took me some time to get my head round the bounce you can get on some of those Australian pitches. And Watson takes a big stride when he plays forward as well.

What we have had to become more aware of is that, in terms of an LBW decision, the protection given to the umpires is still quite big. For instance, if the umpire gives an LBW out and the ball is shown to have been clipping the stumps, it is still out. But if he gives the decision not out initially and the ball is hitting in exactly the same place, then that will remain not out. You need to be absolutely certain that a ball is hitting the stumps hard before challenging a not out LBW decision. It might seem unfair to some eyes, but what it means is that the original decision by the umpire is upheld until it is shown to be definitely wrong.

Of course, we have got plenty wrong ourselves. I can't begin to think how many we have thought were out, but then have been proved to be not out on replay. But what about the other way round? The one where we decide that it is not out, and then replays show it is out? That is the one guaranteed to rile a bowler more than anything else.

Fortunately, I can remember it having happened only once but, needless to say, I get reminded about it very often. It involved Swanny. It had to, really. So now, every time I say to him that I think an LBW off his bowling is not out, he will say something like 'Yeah, but remember that one in South Africa? I was right and you were wrong!'

My only comeback on that is usually: 'One time in hundred, Graeme!' I might also just blame Straussy for that particular decision, too.

In my own mind, I thought that the LBW decision that Swanny keeps going on about was against one of South Africa's top batsmen, but, after checking on it, it was in fact Dale Steyn who was reprieved, in the second innings of the Test at Durban, which we won by an innings and 98 runs. Now Steyn may be a quite brilliant bowler, but he is hardly a top batsman. What's more, Swanny got him out soon afterwards anyway, LBW again for just three, as he ended South Africa's second innings with five wickets, and nine in the match altogether. So it wasn't exactly a costly error, or one that we would expect still to be hearing about years later.

In fairness to Swanny, you can see why it did involve him, because the DRS has changed his game and for a lot of other spinners, too. He now gets the LBWs that he once didn't, especially against left-handers who used to be able to pad him away off the front foot without being punished. Now they know that they have to try to use their bat, otherwise they are in big trouble. But in fact all batsmen, whether right-handed or left-handed, have had to change their approach. It used to be that if you got well forward, you were unlikely to be given out LBW, whether the ball looked straight or not, because the umpire would tend to give you the benefit of the doubt. Now that won't suffice, because the DRS will show if it was going on to hit the stumps, and onfield umpires have also learned to give more decisions, because they've realised that more would hit. Where we used to go with bat and pad together, this is no longer the way in case the ball hits the pad first. Now it usually has to be bat out in front of pad.

Swanny had a superb time out in South Africa, and it was little surprise when he was named as our man of the series. He passed 50 Test wickets in the first Test at Centurion and kept getting out left-handers (Ashwell Prince was his 'bunny' in this series – I think he faced five balls from him in the series and was out three times) and kept getting wickets in his first over.

But his success was no surprise to me. I've always rated him, as a great character and, of course, as a bowler. I had to, really, after he got me out with that 'Cheese ball' in 2008, didn't I? But seriously, I have always thought he is the best spinner in England. I know it's easy to say that now, but I truly did think that all along. It was based squarely on personal experience.

You can only judge a bowler, I reckon, on what he is like when you face him. There are some bowlers you hear and read about, and then you face them and you do not think they are up to much. That was never the case with Swanny. I always struggled against him. He always spun the ball – and tried to spin it – much more than the other spinners in county cricket. And because he tried so hard to spin the ball, it meant that he got really good drift and shape on the ball.

The moment you start getting that drift as a spinner, it makes you so dangerous. For instance, Shane Warne got so much drift because he tried so hard to rip the ball. And however much he actually got the ball to spin, it was the drift as well that helped him become so special. For Swanny, as the years have passed, he has just got to know his game better and better. There are some spin bowlers who, even if you are not necessarily dominating them by attacking them, you always feel in control against. Swanny is never one of them. You always feel that he has some trick up his sleeve to unveil against you. You just never feel comfortable, which is why we hope he makes a swift recovery from the elbow operation he had during our series in New Zealand earlier this year.

4

Big Decisions: Stanford and Mumbai

Graeme Swann's debut was my return Test after being dropped. It was at Chennai in December 2008, and he took two wickets in his first over – Gautam Gambhir and Rahul Dravid, both falling LBW. Andrew Strauss scored centuries in both innings, while I made 53 not out in the first innings and 33 in the second innings, which was pretty respectable. However, we lost by six wickets as India made 387 in their second innings to win.

So much had happened before that, though, both personally and in India. As far as I was concerned, I'd made my one-day international comeback at the end of that 2008 English summer. I came back vowing to keep my head down and to make sure that all that fuss in the media would never be repeated. I just wouldn't let it happen. If anything did happen, I wouldn't be reading it; I'd read it all before.

However, you could be sure that if I didn't read it, somebody would be telling me about it. I'd have mates – or supposed mates –

texting me to say things like: 'Have you heard what Bob Willis is saying about you on Sky? He's absolutely tearing you to pieces!' Thanks for that. On one occasion, I actually texted back to a friend and said: 'What good do you think that is doing? You're supposed to be a mate of mine. What good is that doing my confidence by telling me about such things?'

But now I was going to ignore it all. I was going to worry only about what my coaches and fellow players thought about my performances. I'd decided that no good could come of paying too much attention to what the critics and commentators were saying on TV and in the written press. As Mike Atherton once told me: 'You're never as good as they say you are, and you're never as bad as they say you are either.'

Despite my good intentions, the trouble was that something huge and unprecedented was about to hit cricket. It was not going to be easy to keep my head down. We were about to play a match where we could each earn $1 million – just for winning a 20-over match. It was to be winner takes all. Yes, Allen Stanford had arrived – by helicopter at Lord's, of course – and England were to play his West Indies SuperStars team in Antigua on 1 November 2008.

As I said at the time: 'Cricket has never seen anything like it, so it's enough to get anyone's head spinning. You get the feeling cricket will never be quite the same again. We have to be careful about the way the game goes, because Test cricket is still the ultimate form, where most players want to make their biggest mark. If we were playing the West Indies in a Test, we could be more confident. But in Twenty20 one guy can change the whole match in a few overs. So it's a fifty-fifty call. One team will scoop the lot and the other will walk off empty-handed. That's why people who aren't interested in cricket might watch this game.'

When the match had first been announced, I hadn't even been

in the England squad, of course. And when I first read about it I thought the figures were a misprint. I honestly thought that they'd added on an extra zero or two by mistake. Then, when I saw it was for real, I thought: 'Ah well, I'm not even in the squad so I'm happy for the guys – if just a little jealous.'

At the time, Tim Ambrose was the England wicketkeeper. He'd gone to New Zealand instead of me at the beginning of the year, and then played against the same opponents at home that summer and then against South Africa in the Tests. But then I'd come back for the one-dayers. The rivalry that had begun at Sussex was continuing. We'd both made our first-team debuts in 2001, after Tim had originally been spotted by Peter Moores, playing league cricket for Eastbourne, and we battled for the keeping gloves until Tim left for Warwickshire at the end of the 2005 season. Now, here we were, fighting over the England keeping spot, too.

But I want to clear something up. We were never enemies, as some have tried to suggest. I remember one article in particular in the Brighton local paper that was saying as much. That has never been the case. It was always a friendly rivalry between us, or as Tim said when he was first picked for England ahead of me: 'You can call it rivalry, but it has always been healthy competition. I'm friends with Matt and I'm sure he'll be very disappointed.'

Tim and I have always been good friends, and we always will be. He's one of my best mates in cricket. He's a fantastic bloke and someone I respect hugely as a cricketer. The truth is that the two of us being at Sussex together was one of the best things that could have happened to me. We came to an agreement early on that we would work together to get the best out of each other, and then whoever was best would end up playing. And that is an attitude I've carried on throughout my career. I see other keepers as providing me with an opportunity to get better. They are always going to be there, whether you talk to them or not. My whole international career I've been under pressure. There's usually been someone else, someone they reckon is better, so it's part and parcel of professional cricket for me. It's like it is another day, another name. It's something I've been used to, and have decided to use to my advantage rather than worrying too much about it. Having said that, sooner or later either Tim or I was going to have to leave Sussex as it didn't make sense for one or other of us to be missing out. I think we both understood that. I just had the determination that it wasn't going to be me. There were no hard feelings when he left.

So, did I feel awkward when I took Tim's place just before the Stanford match and all the money that was on offer from that? If I am honest, no. Tim will know where I am coming from when I say that. I've always believed that if you want to be playing in the England cricket team, then you've got to be the best cricketer in England for that spot. That is certainly the case as the wicket-keeper. You live and die by the sword.

No one was feeling sorry for me when I was dropped. You've just got to dig deep and fight your way back. That might sound a bit cruel, but that is sport. The minute I stop performing to the best of my ability, there will be another young guy waiting to come in. That is what drives me; that is what keeps me on my toes.

I was certainly on my toes before the Stanford match. With so much money at stake, all sorts of thoughts were going through our heads. Nobody wanted to make a mistake that might cost his team-mates so much money. I remember I was asked in one interview how I would feel if a high catch went up to decide the match.

'You'll probably see me pulling the gloves off and shouting to someone else to take the catch,' I joked. 'These are things you do think about, because you could end up in that situation. If you mess it up, you'd feel terrible but the only way not to regret it your whole life is if you've done everything possible to prepare yourself. Anyway, I prefer to think about one of us hitting a four off the last ball or making a flying catch to win the game.'

The truth, however, was that we were never winning that match. It was an absolute debacle from start to finish. It really was that bad. We got our attitude wrong from the very start. I'll admit that it wasn't easy, because this match came at a time when the recession was beginning to bite, but I think we tried to play down the money situation too much. Fair play to Swanny. He was the one who said that we couldn't just say that the money was irrelevant. It wasn't. This was a life-changing amount of money we were talking about; money that could be won in just one match of Twenty20. He talked about what he would do with 'three hundred grand after tax' and laughed that he might buy 'a bright pink Ferrari or something like that'.

That's the route we should have all gone down. We should not have been scared of what people thought about us instantly earning such a huge amount of money. Ultimately, around the world, there are other sportspeople who play for these sums of money all the time – think of baseball, football, golf, tennis and so on.

It was the only time in my career I can remember players making hourly checks on the exchange rates from US dollars to pounds. That's why the situation became so ridiculous that the night before the match against Stanford's SuperStars team, Andrew Flintoff called a meeting of the England players who had been selected to play the next night in Antigua. For the record they were, in batting order: Ian Bell, myself, Owais Shah, Kevin Pietersen, Flintoff, Paul Collingwood, Samit Patel, Luke Wright, Graeme Swann, Stuart Broad and Steve Harmison.

But it wasn't any of us that Fred was worried about. He was

more concerned about the four players in the 15-man squad who had been left out of the starting line up: James Anderson, Alastair Cook, Ravi Bopara and Ryan Sidebottom. That was because the deal with Stanford was that, while each man in the winning team got $1 million each, the non-players in the squad would share $1 million and the management and coaching staff would share another $1 million. The boards of each country (the England & Wales Cricket Board and the West Indies Cricket Board) had already decided to share the remaining $7 million for cricket development, whatever the result. The losing team were to get absolutely nothing.

Fred was feeling particularly sorry for Jimmy, who had been such an integral part of the England limited-overs side for so long. He had been picked for all four Twenty20 internationals that year (three of which had been won, with one abandoned) and had played in all of the matches in the 4-0 one-day series victory over South Africa at the end of the English summer. In fact, he had been an ever-present in the previous 14 months where he had made 27 consecutive limited-overs appearances and taken 138 wickets for England in all forms of the game. Fred's point was that Jimmy had been left out only because of the conditions and not because of his worth at the time. The pitches at Stanford's own ground next to the Antigua airport were slow and uneven.

We had played two warm-up games beforehand against the county Twenty20 champions, Middlesex, and the winners of the Stanford domestic Twenty20 tournament, Trinidad & Tobago. Both were tight matches. We beat Middlesex by 12 runs after scoring just 121 for four, and then we had a real scare against Trinidad, eventually scraping home by one run in defending our 141 for six. They needed three off the last ball, but Ravi Rampaul managed only a single. But it had become obvious that we had to play two spinners in Swanny and Samit, and therefore a seamer had to miss out. Unfortunately, it was Jimmy.

Suddenly, from nowhere, Fred was coming up with a solution. He was proposing that each of us should donate $100,000 from our winnings into the team pot, and that would then be shared among the four who were going to miss out on playing. Now Fred was obviously a big character in the team. He may not have been captain, but he was still a huge influence. So when he said this, nobody argued. There was no debate about it whatsoever. He just said that was what he was proposing, and that was that. There wasn't a word from anyone. I just remember looking around the room and thinking: 'I wonder if anyone else is thinking what I'm thinking?'

I'll tell you what I was thinking. I was thinking that $100,000 is an awful lot of money. I was a young cricketer who had been dropped by England and had fought my way back into the side, and now someone was telling me that I had to give $100,000 away. Some people were obviously earning a lot more than me if that didn't seem to matter to them too much. But the other, more important, thought going through my mind was that we had not won yet. We were doing all this worrying about the money when we hadn't even won it yet. We were tempting fate.

I wish I'd been brave enough to say these things, but I wasn't. And, of course, we then lost the next day. As I said, that was always going to happen. We didn't just lose; actually, we got hammered by ten wickets. We made only 99, and that was mainly because Samit made 22.

It was not just money that was preoccupying our minds. The black bats we had to use were spooking us, too. We just couldn't get on with them. There had been a bit of a fuss about them beforehand. They had been a trademark of the Stanford domestic Twenty20 tournament, but just before the deal for this SuperStars match had been announced, the MCC had introduced a clause to the laws of the game stating that all bats had to be of a natural wood colour.

Eventually, as this was not an official international match, a compromise was reached, but it didn't stop us all looking very quizzically when these black things turned up for us to use. Normally, when a bat arrives you examine the willow carefully, checking its grains. But now you obviously couldn't see a thing. They could have been made of anything. And the ball certainly didn't go off them like it did off our usual bats. In fact, as soon as we started netting, we knew we were in trouble. The boys were doing their range hitting, and they couldn't clear the ropes. The bats were just woeful.

Luke Wright tells a funny story about this. Now, Luke hits a long ball, as he's shown plenty of times. And in the match against the SuperStars he smashed one off Kieron Pollard over his favourite area of long on. Having hit the ball, he took a few strides down the pitch in admiration of his shot, expecting to see the ball disappearing way over the boundary. The next thing, he realises that he might have to start running because there is a chance of a brilliant boundary catch. Then, horror of horrors, he now sees that the fielder is actually running in from the edge. The ball is going nowhere near the boundary. And then it is caught by Darren Sammy. Luke is out for one and he walks off looking at his bat, thinking, 'I couldn't have hit that any sweeter!'

The problem was that when the West Indian boys came out to bat, they smashed it everywhere. They didn't seem to have any trouble with their bats. Captain Chris Gayle made 65 not out, hitting five sixes, and Andre Fletcher made 32 not out as their team cruised past our target in just 12.4 overs.

Now, of course, it was a blessing in disguise. With Stanford sentenced in June 2012 to 110 years in jail for defrauding investors of

$7 billion, it saved us from a lot of questions to answer. But, in truth, it was a week to forget anyway. All that stuff I had promised myself about keeping my head down and maintaining a low profile went spectacularly out of the window during the match against Middlesex.

We were fielding when I looked up at the big screen and had to do a double take. I thought I saw my wife Emily sitting on Stanford's knee! I looked again. That was what was happening, and obviously quite a big deal was being made of it. I could not believe it. I just thought: 'Oh my God, here we go again. I'm in it again!'

I was so angry. When I saw Emily later, the first thing I did was have a real go at her. But then I found out the true story. And I should have known, really. I should have known that it was not Emily's fault. It was, of course, Stanford's fault. This whole week was about him. It was his show. He did what he wanted. He got what he wanted.

The floodlights for the warm-up games were terrible. You could barely see a thing, and as a result some ridiculously simple catches were dropped. The reason for this was that the lights had had to be dimmed so as to not to blind the pilots landing their planes on the adjacent runway. But, for the big match, the caps used to dim the lights had suddenly been taken off. The lights were fine. Stanford had decided what he wanted and he had got his way.

There were cameras following his every move. And he moved wherever he wanted. He even came into our dressing room. They might be allowed to do that in American sports, but for us in cricket that is a complete no-no. So during that game against Middlesex, he went and sat near the England players' wives. Emily was standing near him and he just suddenly grabbed her and said 'sit here', knowing full well that the cameras were on him. It was a clear publicity stunt.

Poor Emily was five months pregnant at the time and she just got caught up in something that was never of her making. She was just in the wrong place at the wrong time. She absolutely hates the fact that it happened. If she was some sort of football WAG, who liked the attention, then she might not have minded. But one thing I can tell you about my wife is that she is not a WAG. In fact, she is as far at the opposite end of the scale from a WAG as can be. Alastair Cook's then girlfriend and now wife, Alice, was with her and was also in all the photos of the incident, and those two are two of least pretentious girls I've ever met. For both of us, it was a shocking thing to happen. We were both so unhappy about it.

The next morning my phone – the one given to us with a West Indian number just for that trip – rang. It was a young American woman. 'Mr Prior, it is Sir Allen Stanford's PA here,' she said. 'Sir Allen would like to have a word with you.'

'OK,' I replied, and all the while different things were spinning around in my head. You have to remember that throughout this week we had been told that we had to treat Stanford as if he were royalty. It was his ground, it was his event and it was his money that he was giving to the ECB. The deal that had been signed was for a five-year period. There had already been a lot of rumblings during the week that it must never happen again, but at this stage nothing had, of course, been decided. And we were still to play the big match.

What was I going to say? I was still very, very angry. Stanford came on to the phone and said: 'I just want to apologise. I didn't know that they were the England players' wives sitting there, and I didn't want to be disrespectful. I didn't know that the cameras were on me.'

He went on in that vein, while I contemplated what my response was going to be. I just felt that I couldn't let it lie. Yes, he was apologising, but I also thought that he was feeding me a lot of – if you'll excuse the word – bullshit. I had to have my say. I had to tell him I thought he was lying. Given what has happened since, it's hardly a heinous accusation.

'Look, mate,' I eventually replied. 'I accept your apology, but please don't lie to me. You knew exactly where all our wives were, because you left them their tickets. And you say that you didn't know that the cameras were on you, but they've been on you all the time so far.'

My quiet reintroduction to international cricket was not going too well. And it didn't get any quieter. When I said earlier that Graeme Swann's debut coincided with my return to Test cricket, it is worth mentioning now that we both very nearly did not play in that match in Chennai. Not because our place in the side was under question, but because of the fact we initially did not want to go on that tour.

Our reluctance was hardly without foundation. After Antigua we had returned home briefly before leaving for India and a series of seven one-day internationals and two Tests. We knew it would be hard, but we soon realised how hard when we lost the first game at Rajkot by 158 runs after India made a massive 387 for five in their 50 overs. After that, we went to Indore where Yuvraj Singh followed up his 78-ball 138 in the first match with another century and then four for 28 with the ball. Opening the batting again, I did at least manage 38, but we lost by 54 runs.

In Kanpur, I was dropped down the batting order. It was a much closer match that was shortened by bad light, but we suffered another defeat nonetheless. There was rain in Bangalore, where the match was reduced to 22 overs a side, but still the result was the same. We lost again. This was getting bad. So when we made 270 in Cuttack, with Kevin Pietersen scoring 111 not out, things appeared to be looking up. Not so. India knocked the runs off with 6.2 overs remaining. It was 5-0. Really bad.

We jumped on the bus to take us back to our hotel in Bhubaneswar. It was a journey that none of us will ever forget. At some stage during it, some shocking news started filtering through. I remember one of the boys saying something like: 'Something's happened. It looks as if we could be going home.'

At that stage I didn't know any more so I'll admit that my immediate reaction was relief that at least we couldn't get beaten 7-0, as looked likely. We were getting absolutely pumped. But then it started to become clear what had actually happened. There had been a series of horrific terrorist attacks in Mumbai. We returned to our hotel, the Mayfair Lagoon in Bhubaneswar, where there were players running from room to room asking each other: 'Are you watching the TV?' The scenes being shown were graphic and frightening. They were not censored, as they would have been in the UK; we could see the blood everywhere.

And there was the Taj Mahal Palace Hotel in the middle of it, the hotel where we had stayed just under two weeks before and where we had left our white kit for the Test matches in Mumbai and Ahmedabad that were supposed to follow the one-day series. It was so scary to think that we had been there such a short time before. The Japanese restaurant, Wasabi by Morimoto, where the terrorists apparently had a stronghold, was where we had eaten more often than not during our stay there.

The rumours began to fly: that the terrorists were specifically targeting westerners; that they had been staying in the hotel while we were there. We may have been many hundreds of miles away from Mumbai, but still this felt so close and so real. We didn't know what was happening in the rest of the country. Nobody did.

We had to go home. There was no doubt in my mind. The remaining two one-day matches in Guwahati and Delhi were duly cancelled. And we did go home. But for how long? That was the question. Was the whole tour off? Or would we go back for the two Tests?

I didn't want to go back for the Tests. I'll admit that now. And I wasn't the only one. There were the obvious well-publicised ones, such as Andrew Flintoff and Steve Harmison who thought that way, but there were others as well, and I was one of them. We were being promised extra security, a 'ring of steel' it was eventually called. But what I did not like was the fact that these security people could get injured or killed while protecting us. How could that be right? That did not sit at all well with me.

But the other consideration at the time, of course, was my position in the team. I hadn't actually yet been recalled to the Test side for my comeback. Tim Ambrose had been selected for this tour as well. He had played in the last Test of the previous summer, against South Africa, after Michael Vaughan had resigned as captain in the wake of defeat at Edgbaston. KP had taken over at The Oval, scored a century and England had won by six wickets, even if it was only a consolation win after South Africa had already taken a 2-0 lead in the series. I had a feeling that I was going to be reinstated under KP's captaincy, but that was going to be the case only if I was actually there.

It is so easy to talk about moral stances and safety issues when considering whether to tour – remember that my first trip with England was to Zimbabwe in 2004 when there were political and moral issues to consider – but often it simply boils down to how secure you are in your position in the team. So, in 2004, the likes of Fred, Harmy and Marcus Trescothick felt that they could miss that Zimbabwe trip. Their places were safe. Some might think that you should be stronger than that, but can you when cricket is your livelihood?

The only time I have ever been oblivious to cricket and my position in the team was when I returned home from the West

Indies tour later that winter when my first child, Johnny, was born. Since then, Emily and I have become the proud parents of two more children, Zac, who was born in 2011, and Finn, who was born in early 2013.

Tim played in the Test that I missed in Barbados and actually made 76 not out. It was a flat pitch, with the match ending in a draw after we had scored 600 (Andrew Strauss made 142 and Ravi Bopara 106) and West Indies replied with 749 (Ramnaresh Sarwan made 291 and Denesh Ramdin 166). Indeed, it was so flat that the boys still joke about it today. But, to be honest, it would not have mattered what the pitch was like or how many Timmy made – I was so happy to be back in England and be there just after JJ was born. I remember sitting there with my little baby boy in my arms, watching Timmy bat and not for one second did I ever think I had made the wrong choice. Cricket was irrelevant then.

When I returned to the West Indies, I said to the press: 'I'm not going to lie, it's been pretty amazing. Any father knows that the birth of your first child is fantastic and it was a great feeling. I was really happy that I was able to go back for that week and spend it with my family.'

Beforehand, deciding to leave the tour to go home for the birth hadn't been a decision I had taken lightly by any means. I had spent a lot of time thinking it over and speaking to people who I thought were the right ones to talk to. My family had obviously had a huge say, but so did my team-mates. And I was hugely backed by all of them. Most of them said that I should go home. When you are backed by your team-mates it makes it a lot easier.

When I returned to the Caribbean, I knew I had to perform and get back into the groove pretty quickly, which I did, scoring a century – my second in Tests – in Trinidad and making sure I celebrated it in the rightful manner by rocking my bat in my arms. That was for Em and JJ.

But if I found that decision to leave the Caribbean difficult, this earlier one about returning to India was even tougher. With Em pregnant, it gave me much more to think about than just my career. We returned to England for only five days, but it was a long five days full of phone calls and much agonising. Eventually we were persuaded to go to a holding camp in Abu Dhabi. From there, Hugh Morris (the managing director of England cricket) and Sean Morris (then the chief executive of the Professional Cricketers' Association) went to Chennai (as the first Test had been moved there, with the second now to take place in Mohali) to meet the ECB's security adviser Reg Dickason.

Hugh and Sean then returned to Abu Dhabi to address us and reassure us that all the necessary security arrangements had been put in place. Quite a few of us were still unsure at this stage but, when I look back now, once we decided to get on that plane to Abu Dhabi, we had essentially committed ourselves to going back to India. There was no turning back.

And so we did return to India to play those two Tests. When we got there, we knew we had made the right decision. We could see what it meant to the people of that country. They were so grateful to us for coming back, and they gave us an amazing reception. It felt like we had made a difference, even if it was only a small one. We had praise from all quarters. Even the prime minister, Gordon Brown, called us 'brave and courageous'.

For me personally, it was just great to be back in Test cricket. That it was against India, where all the trouble had started for me the previous year, was testing and I had some ghosts to exorcise. But I think I did that. I got runs immediately, which always helps the confidence, and I thought I kept well in the difficult conditions that Asia always throws up.

As I mentioned, we lost in Chennai. And then we drew in Mohali, where it was distinctly chilly, and fog curtailed a lot of play, but KP made 144 and for India Gautam Gambhir made 179 and 97 in his two innings, with Rahul Dravid making 136 in the first innings. So I went home for Christmas pretty happy with myself. As well as having a new baby, I was back in the one-day and Test sides. It was time for a quiet festive period before the tour of the West Indies in the New Year.

Quiet? As with my return to international colours, there was nothing quiet about this festive period as the news of a split between KP and Peter Moores became public. You'll probably be wanting me to spill the beans on the shocking inside story of this episode, of the hatred I saw every day between KP and Mooresy. Well, sorry to disappoint you, but the honest truth is that for the whole tour in India I was oblivious to the fact that there was anything going on at all. It just wasn't apparent.

I found out about it when everyone else did: when it came out on New Year's Eve. I was shocked; I had no idea. And so days of a bewildering news story began. It was everywhere, and everything about the England dressing room was suddenly big news. There were articles about which players were in which camp. In one piece, I was in the neutral group. In another I was in Andrew Flintoff's gang. As far as I can remember, I wasn't in anyone's gang. I was just the wicketkeeper who'd been dropped desperately trying to re-establish myself in Test cricket. It was all madness.

And the madness of the situation was emphasised by the fact that KP and Mooresy both soon lost their positions. I was shocked that in such a short space of time they were both gone. To me it seemed such a shame that it had to turn out like that. It just didn't make sense. But for KP there was still a place in the side and I knew he would provide his response with the bat. That's what he does when he is cornered. He comes out fighting with runs. And as for Mooresy, he was and still is the most positive person I know. So I knew he would be OK in the end. I knew that he would accept this setback as part of a learning curve in his career, and use it to spur him on. I thought he handled the whole scenario with massive dignity. He has never been bitter about it and that is a great credit to him.

5

Sussex by the Sea

'Come with me, young man,' said the legend with the beard. Mushtaq Ahmed had arrived at Sussex at the start of the 2003 season and immediately asked coach Peter Moores who the wicket-keeper was. My battle with Tim Ambrose was still raging, but at that point I was the Sussex wicketkeeper. Mooresy pointed me out and Mushy came over to introduce himself. And then he led me to the nets. It was the start of a quite remarkable learning experience for me. There he bowled six overs to me. Just the two of us. No batsman.

Mushy wanted to see if I could pick his googly. He soon had his answer: no. I was clueless. He would bowl it and it would be blindingly obvious that I hadn't picked it, and Mushy would laugh that infectious laugh of his and say: 'I done you!' 'Done' is one of his favourite words in the English language, I reckon. He uses it in the present, future and past tenses. And he had certainly done me on numerous occasions. I was going to have to learn to pick him.

So that's what I did. And Mushy helped enormously. After every team net session, we would work together on our own. 'Just me and you, one on one,' he would say. He was such a good pro, always wanting to practise. And gradually I learned to pick him from the hand. Every session we did, I got better. It was only occasionally when he really tried to rip his leg-spinner that I sometimes thought it was a googly. Those were the only times I got confused thereafter.

It was so good for me, and not just for my keeping. It helped my batting against spin immeasurably. It is no coincidence that now that Mushy is spin bowling coach with the England team, I use him for my batting as much as any of the other coaches. Kevin Pietersen is the same; you'll often see him having throw-downs with Mushy.

Some people might try to pick a spinner through the air, but I always look to pick him from the hand. It's just like facing reverse swing in that I try to gain as many clues as I can and as early as I can. When I was on tour with England in Pakistan in 2005, Mushy invited me to his house for dinner one evening. Inzamam-ul-Haq was there, too, and Mushy said that I should ask him anything I wanted about cricket. He was, after all, one of the greats of Test cricket, eventually making 8,830 runs at an average just under 50, with 25 hundreds. I was in awe of him to be honest, and the best I could come up with was: 'So how do you play reverse swing please?'

Inzy sat back in his chair and laughed. 'It is easy,' he said. 'It is very easy. All you do is pick the ball in the bowler's hand. Then you know which way it is going to swing, and then you hit the ball.'

'Ah right,' I said, while chuckling to myself. 'If only it were that simple,' I was thinking. But it was a good tip, really. If you can spot which way the bowler is holding the ball in his grip (in other words which side is shiny and which side is rough) then he is giving you a huge clue as to which way it will swing. Say

Receiving my England cap (the one I still wear) from Andrew Strauss in front of the pavilion at Lord's, before making my Test debut, against West Indies on 17 May 2007. *(Getty Images)*

All thoughts of coolly acknowledging the crowd went out the window when I reached a century on my debut – I was jumping around like a schoolkid. *(Phil Brown)*

I rarely kept for England in my early days in the limited-overs side, but one experience in Jamshedpur in April 2006 showed just what hard work it was in the heat of the subcontinent – it was over 50°C in the middle and I suffered the worst cramps of my life that day. *(Getty Images)*

I found out just how much I still needed to learn during our tour of Sri Lanka in 2007–08, and I lost my place after a disappointing performance in Galle, where I missed two very costly chances. *(Phil Brown)*

Peter Moores, who had helped me get started at Sussex, was an enormous influence in the early stages of my career. This exercise was designed to improve my reflexes. *(Phil Brown)*

More recently, England have employed the wonderful Bruce French as a specialist keeping coach, and there is no doubt that he has helped me to improve immensely that area of my game. *(Getty Images)*

Back in the England side. Against South Africa in 2008, we won the one-day series 4-0 including this ten-wicket victory in Nottingham, when I also took a record-equalling six catches. *(Phil Brown)*

Not long after came the controversial game against Allen Stanford's West Indies SuperStars. Pretty much everything went wrong for England that day. *(Getty Images)*

Not your average nets session. A military guard watches over us as we leave our coach to train in Chennai in December 2008, soon after the Mumbai atrocities. *(Getty Images)*

Action from my first season at Sussex, back in 2001, when we won the second division title in the county championship – it proved to be the start of a very successful run. *(Getty Images)*

Celebrations for Mushtaq Ahmed after he took his 100th wicket of the season in 2003, helping us on our way to our first-ever county championship title. I learned so much from working with him, and am delighted he has become part of the England set-up. *(Getty Images)*

Alastair Cook and I contemplate one of the First World War graves, near Ypres, ahead of the 2009 Ashes series. It was a humbling experience.

(Getty Images)

Nathan Hauritz leads Australia's celebrations in Cardiff after I was out before lunch on the final day to leave us in a seemingly hopeless position at 70 for five. But Jimmy Anderson and Monty Panesar saved the day.

(Getty Images)

Meeting the Queen at Lord's on the second day of the Ashes Test in 2009. It was a great honour, and we went on to take a 1-0 lead in the series, helped by Andrew Flintoff bowling the quickest spell I've ever kept to.

(Getty Images)

'The Cheese ball'. I'm off to celebrate with Graeme Swann after he'd bowled Ricky Ponting at Edgbaston.

(Getty Images)

You can see the pain on my face as I warm up ahead of the fourth Test at Headingley, when a back spasm almost forced me out of the match.

(Getty Images)

I don't get too many stumpings, but this one to dismiss Marcus North in the final Test at The Oval helped us towards a 2-1 series victory – a wonderful moment!

(Getty Images)

Zaheer Khan and umpire Ian Howell study the pitch during the 2007 Test at Trent Bridge. He was angry that Jelly Beans kept on appearing on the wicket – and I wrongly got the blame.

(Getty Images)

Players on the England balcony look to see what is happening as one of the windows in the Lord's pavilion shatters – it was a freak accident during the Test against Sri Lanka in 2011.

(Phil Brown)

it is a right-arm bowler bowling. If he is using conventional swing and wanting to bowl an away swinger to a right-handed batsman, he will position the shiny side of the ball on the right of his forefinger and middle finger that are holding the ball's seam.

The ball might start reversing after some careful work on it from the fielding side after, say, about 50 overs. First of all, you need to keep the ball very dry and as one side roughs up naturally the other is kept shiny and soft. Now, if that same bowler has the shiny side on the right, it will duck into the right-hander rather than swinging away from him. So you watch first to see if the bowler shows you the ball when putting it into his hand at the start of his run-up. If not, then you can try to look for it as he runs in. This is quite hard at first and can be very off-putting, but you can do it if you try really hard.

Of course, bowlers are not silly. They have wised up a bit. Some of them flick the ball over after putting it in their hand so as to fool you, and most of them try to hide it when running in. Zaheer Khan of India is one who does this really well. But there are usually other clues, if you look closely enough. Most bowlers will struggle to hide the ball in their load-up, although Jimmy Anderson is particularly good at continuing to hide it then.

Keeping to Mushy helped me so much. Having had my own problems picking him in the nets, it was comforting to watch batsman after batsman have the same troubles against him. They would go back to cut the ball and I'd be thinking: 'Ha! Ha! He hasn't picked the googly here, he's in serious trouble.'

Don't cut the googly is a very basic piece of advice, but we've all tried and failed in that respect. We've all done that because we haven't picked it. So what do you do if you are not picking the googly? Play for it, I reckon. With Mushy, his danger ball was always his googly. So if you played for that and it turned the other way as a leg break, then the chances were that it would miss the bat by a considerable distance.

That was the theory we used when we faced South Africa's Imran Tahir in the summer of 2012. His danger ball is also his googly. He got hatfuls of wickets in county cricket because batsmen couldn't pick it. But he'd actually come to Hove and bowled at us in the nets once upon a time, so I knew a bit about him. I knew that if we played for his googly, then he might not have much else to fire at us. Australia's batsmen must have been picking his googly reasonably well in Adelaide later in 2012 when he recorded match figures of none for 260, the worst in Test history.

If I do play spin quite well – and some observers have very kindly said as much – then it is because of the work I did with Mushy. It was why I could pick Muttiah Muralitharan relatively well. When we played Sri Lanka away in 2007-08, I remember that I downloaded a video to my iPod on which there were six balls of Muralitharan bowling his normal off break and six balls of him bowling his doosra (the other one). On every coach journey or flight, I watched that video religiously, and soon I was able to pick up a key difference. I just watched his fingers. When they were horizontal and you could see the palm of his hand, that was a normal off break. When his fingers were pointing towards the sky, that was a doosra.

Of the current spinners in world cricket, I would say that Pakistan's Saeed Ajmal is the hardest to pick. He caused us all sorts of problems in the United Arab Emirates in early 2012 when we lost the series 3-0. Everything that happens in his load-up happens so quickly that it is really difficult to spot whether it is an off break or a doosra.

What about Shane Warne? Well, I played against him only in county cricket. But, as much as it pains me to admit it, he dealt with me. He chewed me up and spat me out. He is undoubtedly the best bowler I have ever faced. There was a match between his side, Hampshire, and Sussex at Hove in 2005. It was in April, and therefore before the Ashes of that year began. At that stage, there had been a little bit of chat – only a little – that I might have an outside chance of making the side for that series. So I saw this match as a huge opportunity; I wanted to prove myself against Warne. When I walked out to bat, I did so with the intention of taking him down. The problem for me was that Warney obviously had the same idea. He was going to take me down.

Sadly it didn't end up being much of a competition. I walked out with my usual confidence. Some would call it a strut, of course. Warne certainly thought it was a strut. He wasn't bowling at the time, but he was standing at slip. After I had got to the wicket, he stopped the whole game. And he mimicked my walk to the wicket by walking up and down the pitch, with his arms out as if he was carrying a water melon under each arm. That was what he was calling me: 'Water melons.'

It seemed like he stopped the game for about half an hour. He absolutely rinsed me, totally annihilated me. At first I tried to ignore it. But then I did the only thing I knew. I went back at him. We had a right old war of words. Simon Katich, another Australian, was also playing for Hampshire, and he joined in too. I actually thought I was doing OK. That was until Warne came on to bowl. I was so wound up by then that I thought: 'I'm going to take you apart here.'

The ball was a slider. The shot was a huge sweep slog. The result was inevitable. I was LBW for four, departing with a flea in my ear from Warne, Katich and the rest, just as you would expect. It took me some time to calm down, but, when I did, I realised that I had been outdone by the master. I had learned an important lesson there.

'I will one hundred per cent admit that Warne and Simon

Katich got under my skin in the first innings,' I said to our local paper, the *Argus*, afterwards. 'I spoke to [umpire] Ian Gould and [team-mate] James Kirtley and they both told me to treat it as a back-handed compliment.'

Did I say I had learned a lesson? Well, I thought I did, until I was out LBW to him again in the second innings, this time for 12.

There was another incident in that match. When Katich was batting he was continually standing in front of me when throws came in from our outfielders. I was having to run round him and was generally getting myself into a tangle just because he was in the way. So I asked him if he would move out of the way. I was firm in what I said, but I don't think I was overly aggressive. He was in the wrong, I thought, after all.

His response? 'F*** off!'

That was it. As I'd done with Warne when I was coming out to bat, I did the only thing I knew: I went back hard at him. The next time he got in my way, I made sure that I moved him out of the way. Yes, there was physical contact, but that was the only solution in my eyes. Obviously he wasn't happy, but I just said to him: 'I asked you to move last time.'

What followed was disappointing. Our coming together blew up in the press. I think my captain Chris Adams was trying to stick up for me, but his public comments were not really what I wanted. 'Playing hard on the field is fine by me, but to try to pub-licly humiliate young players in the opposition is disappointing,' he said. 'Matt Prior came in for quite a lot of verbal abuse. Because of what he has done in the game, Shane Warne will always be con-sidered a great. Off the field, he was outstanding and the first person to congratulate us and say what a great game it was [the match was drawn], but I have lost a lot of respect for him because of the way he behaved in this match.'

Inevitably, Warney had his say back. 'It is disappointing the way

Chris Adams conducted himself. I think it's a bit hypocritical the way he did it and I'm sure he regrets it now. The reason you only hear about Australians sledging is we don't say what happens out on the field. We just have a beer afterwards. If people want to talk about what happens out in the middle and they don't like it, I can't control that. I'm not going to apologise for it, either.

'I play the way I play, and I'm not going to apologise for the way Hampshire play. Anyone who comes up against us is going to be tested, mentally, physically and technically. If they don't like it we'll win easily, which is good and what we want to do. I'll make no apologies about the way we play. The game was a hard one, everyone enjoyed it, there were no reports, no nothing.

'As I said before, it's always Australians being accused of sledging, generally, because we don't say what other people say, we leave it out in the middle. If anyone says what goes on in the middle, it's up to them and their right to do that if they want to, but if I get sledged out in the middle you won't hear me saying what anyone said to me.'

As I said earlier in the book, that is actually what I believe. What happens on the field should stay on the field. Yes, I've gone into detail about this incident, but only because it happened a long time ago and much of it has already come out into the public domain. If I had had my way it would never have come out at all.

'I thought cricket was a non-contact sport,' Warne wrote in his column for *The Times* in reference to the incident with Katich. And he's right, it is a non-contact sport. That is how it should be. I would never condone such behaviour, but it's just that sometimes tempers flare. Katich was out of order in my opinion, and this was my way of sorting that out.

Sussex versus Hampshire fixtures have always been a bit fiery, and this served only to fire them up a bit more. But I have to he honest and say that I felt Warne owned me a little bit after that. He had a psychological hold on me that I could not break free from. I remember after one match when we played against him at Hove that I went up to him in the Sussex Cricketer pub just by the ground and spoke to him about our clashes. We got on fine and talked about cricket for quite a long time. But I still got the impression that he didn't necessarily rate me.

That was borne out by some of his comments in the years that followed. For instance, when I was picked for that match against the Stanford Superstars in 2008 he said: 'Every team wants an Adam Gilchrist – someone who can bat like one of the best in the world while also keeping wicket well. But a wicketkeeper should be able to keep wicket first and foremost – runs with the bat are a bonus. For me, the wicketkeeping art is being lost. These days it's simply a case that if they can bat, they will get picked.

'When I see Matthew Prior in the team I think "Are you serious?" OK, he can slog a few at the top of the order with the bat. But if I'm Steve Harmison or Andrew Flintoff and you get a top batsman to edge one, I'd be holding my breath to see if he catches it. He is that bad.'

A little harsh, Warney! And it's only usually my mum who calls me Matthew, although I have since discovered that he called me 'Wayne' to the journalist in question, who saved his blushes by altering it to 'Matthew'. But in fairness we get on well now, and I hope I've proved to him that I can keep and bat. I actually wish I could have played Test cricket against him. That would have been some battle.

I have to say that I've always loved the way that the Australians play their cricket. And I had got a sharp taste of that on my first-class debut. It was in 2001 that I was selected as a 19-year-old to play against Worcestershire at New Road. In the opposition was Andy Bichel, the Australian fast bowler. For a lad just out of school, he was the fastest bowler I'd ever seen live. He was some-one I had watched on TV and considered him a giant in the game, and now I was playing against him.

I remember watching our innings – I was batting at nine – and seeing one shot in particular, from our Welsh batsman Tony Cottey, who pulled Bichel in front of square for four. And I just thought: 'I could never do that. He's too quick!'

It was a match that was badly affected by the weather. In fact, the first two days were rained off. And on one of them I recall an inci-dent that summed up our coach Peter Moores. It showed just how enthusiastic he was, and still is; how much he always wanted – and still wants – there to be cricket played on every scheduled day.

The outfield was saturated, as, sadly, it often is at Worcester. And there was a particular problem at gully if a right-handed bats-man was facing a bowler from the Diglis End of the ground. There were puddles there that weren't going. But, having spoken to the two umpires, John Hampshire and David Shepherd, Mooresy came bouncing back into the changing rooms. We were expecting him to say that play had been called off for the day and to announce what he thought we should do to entertain ourselves. But, no, Mooresy had other ideas.

'I think we might have a game on here, lads,' he said. There was a lot of surprise within the room, but our left-arm seamer, Jason Lewry, was the first to pipe up, saying: 'What are you on about, Pete? It's soaking out there!'

'Well,' replied Mooresy, 'the rule is that you can't run to gully. And if the ball goes in a puddle there and gets too wet, it can be changed.'

There was a little more than surprise now. I, as the young debu-tant, wasn't saying anything, but plenty of others were. 'What are you on about, Pete?' they asked. 'Listen to yourself. This is first-class cricket. You can't do that.'

And, of course, we didn't do that. It was one of Mooresy's most ridiculous ideas ever, but you just had to admire his enthusiasm. It was, and always has been, infectious. But we did eventually start play on day three, and in due course it was my turn to bat for the first time in first-class cricket.

I was facing Bichel. In he raced and, unsurprisingly, the first ball was short; very short, a bouncer. It hit me in the ribs as I tried to fend it off, and the ball dropped down next to me. From there it was picked up by the short-leg fielder, Anurag Singh, who piped up with the words: 'Welcome to first-class cricket!' Such poor and predictable banter.

I wasn't worried about him, but I was rather worried about Bichel. He came very hard at me, just as you would expect. There were lots of short balls, and lots of words. And what did I do? I went back at him. As I mentioned, that was my way. That's what I would have done had I been playing schools cricket, so that's what I did now, first-class cricket or not. I edged one for four and, as I ran past Bichel, he caught me with his elbow. What was Shane Warne saying about it being a non-contact sport? And, if you think I'm telling tales out of school, please bear with me.

So the next time I ran past Bichel, I dug my bat into his shin. Again, this is not something any cricketer should do, and certainly not something I would do now, but I was young a little bit hot-headed. In my mind, Bichel had started it. This was getting serious, and I think quite a few of my team-mates were rather taken aback by what was happening. I certainly know that Jason Lewry was. He was batting with me at the time. We've joked about it since, but he was not happy with my antics. Tail-end batsmen never like it when opposition fast bowlers are wound up, and, boy, was I winding up Bichel.

We got to lunch anyway, and off to the lunch room I went. I was keeping my head down, minding my own business, when suddenly I realised that the bloke waiting to get his food in front of me was none other than Andy Bichel. There he was, the blond muscular Australian fast bowler. He'd looked quite big on TV. He looked even bigger now. He had a reputation for being very fit and a bit of a gym monkey, and I could see why now. He looked massive. My heart started pounding. I looked around to see if there were any of my Sussex team-mates nearby who might be able to help. There were none. I was on my own.

Bichel started to walk towards me. I honestly thought: 'He's going to crack me one here!' I thought I was going to get laid out there and then by this huge Australian fast bowler. To say I was nervous would be an understatement. He was now right next to me. Instead, he smiled, thrust out his hand to shake mine and said: 'Great battle, mate!'

I loved that. Not just because of the relief it brought me, but because of the attitude it epitomised. That was, and is, the Aussie way. And that was the way I played my cricket and have always played my cricket since then. When you walk off the pitch, it's over, as far as I am concerned. Win or lose, it's how you look your opponent in the eye and shake their hand that counts. It is by that philosophy that I have tried to live my whole career.

I ended up making 25 not out on my debut and felt pleased with how I had coped, but there was then a return fixture at Horsham to be negotiated. And this was on a pitch that was much faster and bouncier than the one at a wet Worcester. And, worse still, Bichel had not forgotten what had happened at New Road.

As soon as I walked out to bat (this time I was up the order at seven), the battle began again, verbally and physically. Bichel began to bowl faster and faster. And as he did so, I went back at him harder and harder. This time my batting partner was James Kirtley. He was even less impressed than Jason Lewry had been. In fact, he was so unimpressed that he felt moved to come down to the middle of the pitch and reveal his feelings to me. 'Will you just shut the f*** up!' he shouted at me.

'Sorry, Amby,' I replied. (He was known as Amby because his surname is pronounced exactly the same as Curtly Ambrose's first name.) But it was little surprise when Amby was bowled by Bichel for one. I hadn't done his cause much good, if I'm honest. But I made 40 in that first innings, and we went on to win the match by 33 runs.

That year, 2001, we were second division champions in the county championship. Given that Sussex had finished bottom of the division the year before, that was a fine achievement. And in my first season I felt that I had played a part even if, as a foretaste of things to come, I had been pushed hard for my place by Tim Ambrose. I made just one fifty with the bat but took 39 catches and two stumpings.

The title was clinched with a three-day, ten-wicket win over Gloucestershire at Hove – the only match of the season I missed – with the winning runs being scored by Murray Goodwin, who had had such a good season in his first year at the club, scoring over 1500 runs with six hundreds. Richard Montgomerie and Chris Adams had excellent seasons too, with Monty making seven centuries and Grizz three. Robin Martin-Jenkins chipped in with bat and ball, as he always did, and with the ball Mark Robinson, James Kirtley and Jason Lewry all took more than 50 wickets, Amby being the most successful with a superb haul of 75.

Robbo, the likeable Yorkshireman who had joined Sussex in 1997 after spells at Yorkshire and Northamptonshire, was my room-mate that season. I remember him saying to me after we had won the second division title: 'Really savour this moment because some people go through their whole careers without winning anything.'

He added that I would be very lucky to win the county

championship in my career. I've the utmost respect for Robbo, who is now head coach at Sussex and one of the most committed and enthusiastic people I have ever met in cricket – just like Peter Moores, really. Sussex have been very lucky to have had those two men in charge. But at the time I did find that comment rather strange.

The way I had always been brought up was to win. Whether I was playing cricket, football or whatever, it was all about winning. Some people say that it is all about taking part – and, yes, it is important that as many people as possible participate in sport – but that was never how I saw it. My mentality has always been to win.

So I felt a little sad when Robbo said that. Trying to win is why you play the game, and then to enjoy the celebrations afterwards. You want to be spraying champagne around and lapping up the adulation of the crowd. That is what you should strive for. It's certainly something that we are very aware of in this current England side. We make sure that we celebrate our successes properly. We work hard and then we celebrate hard, whether it is personal or collective success.

It's funny looking back now, because since that win in 2001, Sussex have won trophy after trophy, and Robbo has been a big part of that, too. That title was the first of ten trophies in ten years, and as for the county championship, we won that three times – in 2003, 2006 and 2007. There have also been National League titles in 2008 and 2009, as well as a second division win in 2005. We won the second division of the county championship again in 2010 and the C&G Trophy in 2006, as well as the Twenty20 Cup in 2009. That's a lot of winning and a lot of celebrating.

Of course, winning the championship in 2003 stands out among all those achievements. Yes, 2006 was special too (because of England commitments, I played only three matches the following year in 2007 when we won it again), mainly because things had moved on quite a bit from 2003. Mooresy had left to become the ECB academy director, with Robbo taking over from him, and Tim Ambrose had moved to Warwickshire, so that I was definitely the first-choice wicketkeeper. And we had a very different team from 2003, with the emergence of local lads such as Michael Yardy, Chris Nash, Carl Hopkinson, Luke Wright and Ollie Rayner.

But 2003 was the one. It was the first time Sussex had ever been county champions. There had been a rather long wait – 164 years to be precise – and I was privileged to be part of the victory that ended it. It is not often in sport that you are part of something that is happening for the first time. This actually shaped my thinking for the rest of my cricketing career. Mooresy had always talked us creating a legacy, and this was what we were doing.

It was something Mooresy talked about a lot and it was then the idea was lodged in my mind. It has now become the biggest part of why I play cricket. I want to be a part of a team that leaves a legacy. So when I play for England, I want to be part of the best England team ever. And I felt fortunate to be a part of that Sussex team, because it could well be remembered as the best Sussex team that has ever played. Because we were the first, our achievement will never be forgotten, and for me that will always be more important than any individual statistics. It is the legacy that I will be most proud of.

So when, just after lunch on the second day of the last game of the season, Murray Goodwin pulled Leicestershire's Phil DeFreitas for four, it meant that we had secured a sixth bonus point of the match. It meant that Lancashire could not catch us. It meant that we were county champions. The game stopped. Muzz and his batting partner at the time, our captain Chris Adams, embraced, while the rest of us charged onto the field to join them. The game stopped, suspended in time. That's not really supposed to happen, but fair play to the umpires, Trevor Jesty and Merv Kitchen, and the Leicestershire captain DeFreitas, they all accepted it. It was a very special moment. We did a lap of honour in front of a crowd that was near a full house, while 'Sussex by the Sea' blared out on the loudspeakers.

Just before lunch on the previous day, the first day of the match on which Leicestershire had chosen to bat, something else very significant had happened. Mushy had bowled Brad Hodge with his googly to record his 100th first-class wicket of the campaign. Not since 1998, when Somerset's Andy Caddick achieved the feat, had anyone done that in an English season, and, so I'm reliably informed, not since 1967 had anyone done it for Sussex, when Tony Buss was the man to do so. Mushy would repeat it in 2006, when we won the championship again. In 2003, he finished the season with 103 wickets, taking ten or more wickets in a match five times, and on each occasion we went on to win the game.

What a signing he had been. He hadn't played much county cricket since that 1998 season, when he had lined up alongside Caddick for Somerset, and he had had very little international cricket in the meantime. But, in 2002, he had appeared in a few games for Surrey and one of them had been against us at Hove. Indeed, I'm not even sure he was our first choice, as I think Mooresy and Grizz initially wanted to go for either Stuart MacGill or Harbhajan Singh as the overseas spinner, but those two signed for Nottinghamshire and Lancashire respectively, instead. But Mushy impressed in that game, and soon after the end of that 2002 season he had signed for Sussex.

I still get stick to this day from England team-mates who say that the only reason we won the county championship was because of Mushy. And, yes, of course Mushy played a huge part. He was probably 80 per cent of our success that year. But most successful sides require an outstanding individual to perform. Take Andrew Flintoff in the 2005 Ashes, and what about Alastair Cook in the 2010-11 Ashes? It's rare that one man doesn't stand out among many other good performances.

But successes are rarely down to just one man. For instance, spinners need runs on the board, and that season in 2003 we got plenty of them on the board for Mushy to bowl at, so that he was able to set attacking fields. In fact our first-innings average total was 423. No other team was anywhere near that. We scored 19 centuries between us – spread between Muzz, me, Tony Cottey, Robin Martin-Jenkins, Grizz, Richard Montgomerie, Mark Davis and Kevin Innes. In that final match against Leicestershire, Muzz went on to make a record 335 not out, and then Jason Lewry finished them off in the second innings with eight for 106.

Just to show how strong we were, that list of century-makers doesn't include Tim Ambrose, who played in 15 of the matches and batted at five, but still averaged more than 40 with the bat. That's a man who went on to score a Test century. We had a strong batting line-up, that is for sure.

Tim and I shared the wicketkeeping duties that season. We actually ended up keeping in eight matches each, and we received our county caps on the same day when the match against Surrey at Hove fizzled out in a draw and we both made unbeaten fifties. And we kept the same positions in the batting order, whether we were keeping or not. Tim was at five and I was at seven. When I was not keeping, I reckon I had one of the most comfortable jobs in cricket – batting at seven and fielding at silly point to Mushy, where there were always plenty of chances.

I still got over 1000 runs for the season, which I don't think many people have done from seven, making four hundreds and ending up second in the Sussex averages behind Muzz. This was a breakthrough season for me with the bat. I played with real freedom, hitting a lot of sixes – twice I went to a century with maximums – and I'd like to think that I played some innings that really mattered. Certainly the 148 I got against Middlesex at Hove in the match that was third from the end of the season was an important innings. We were in trouble at 82 for five and looking like we might follow on, but Mark Davis (who made 168) and I turned things around and we ended up winning that match.

It was such an enjoyable season. And it was the first time I saw how powerful it can be when you have 11 players (or the 15 that we used that season) pulling so strongly in the same direction.

That experience with what happened at Sussex in 2003 was behind why I called Kevin Pietersen in 2012 after his infamous press conference following the second Test against South Africa at Headingley, in which he hinted at retiring from Test cricket and said: 'It's tough for me in this dressing room.' I believe that no side can be consistently successful if everyone is not pulling in the same direction all of the time.

I'd learned that lesson at Sussex in 2003 and it has stuck with me throughout my career. It was exactly the same ethos that team director Andy Flower and captain Andrew Strauss preached since they had been thrown together in 2009, and it had been the backbone of our success under those two. We'd worked extremely hard to build a team culture and we had got to a good place – top of the ICC rankings in fact – by 2011. So when it seemed it was going awry in 2012, I really felt that I had to try to do something about it.

It had all been kicking off that week in early August. Kev had just made a quite brilliant century in Leeds, but he was obviously not happy in some way. Then, when I heard that he was saying that he wasn't happy in the team, and that it was tough for him being in our dressing room, then it suddenly became a players' issue. It all changed then.

I interpreted what he said that he was having a go at the dressing room, and that he wasn't happy with what was going on there.

As much as the management, the coaches and the ECB have a responsibility to sort out contractual matters and other issues at that level, so the players have a responsibility to sort out matters in the dressing room. It doesn't matter whether it is KP or Joe Root (who made his Test debut in late 2012), we need a situation where everyone is happy and relaxed in the dressing room. If they can be those two things, then they will obviously perform better out on the field. That is the theory behind any talk of team spirit.

When KP made his comments, I'll admit that I actually took it quite personally. What had made this England Test team, who had got to number one and were fighting to retain their status at the top of the rankings, brilliant was we always had 11 players pulling in the same direction. It was a team. No one person had done more than anyone else. It is a very powerful thing to have 11 blokes pulling in the same direction. Kev had been a big part of that. Of course, he is a player you want him in your team. You watch a bloke bat like he has and, of course, you want him in your team. Who wouldn't?

I like everything out in the open, and we as players all thought it was fine and rosy, but obviously it wasn't. I didn't want to believe what was said in the press without speaking to Kev. And I got the impression that he wanted to speak to me. I'd had a small niggle after the Headingley Test and he had sent me a text asking me how my injury was. In the circumstances, it felt like a very strange text message to be getting at that time. It gave me enough of an inkling to text him back and ask if I could give him a call in two minutes' time.

So that's what I did. I called him from the train I was travelling on back to Brighton. If that situation arose another 100 times, I would phone Kev another 100 times. It wasn't done for any other reason than that I saw a team-mate struggling and, as far as I'm concerned, that becomes the responsibility of the players. If someone isn't happy in the dressing room, then you have to go out of your way to find out what the issue is and do as much as you can to make it right. Sometimes when you do that, and hear what they have to say, you can see their point and say: 'You know what, mate? You're right.' On other occasions, it might be a case of being honest and saying: 'You need to sort a few things out.'

Kev and I are both pretty straightforward and honest guys who don't mince our words. I've played with him for a long time since before he was a superstar, before he made 158 against Australia at The Oval in 2005. We've been on Academy tours together, in fact we were at Loughborough for the first Academy intake there in the new facility. We spent six months there in the winter of 2003-04, before going to Malaysia and India with players such as Graeme Swann and Owais Shah. A young lad called Alastair Cook was a part-time student at the Academy that winter, if I remember correctly, too.

In that situation, I got to straight to the point with KP. I said to him: 'What's going on, Kev? What's up buddy? You tell me and I'll tell you.' I asked him if what had been reported had been correct. He said it was, so then I asked why he felt that way and what the main issues were. What followed was a refreshing and honest conversation. I think he respected me for making the phone call, and I also think he was pleased to hear from me and, from what I've heard him say, I think he was pleased someone made the call. Sometimes, you need to say tough things to your mates in order for them to improve and, more importantly, for the team to move forward.

But the most important lesson that came out of the phone call was how fragile team spirit can be if you don't look after it. It was little surprise that we lost our number one ranking at the end of that 2012 summer. If you don't look after that team spirit, it can disappear very quickly. What I soon realised during the hour I was on the phone to Kev was that there were certain values we had let slip as the England cricket team. It can be hard to monitor such things when you set such high standards, and we had set some really high standards in terms of our team spirit.

It's not the big things that go first, it's the little things. We could have handled that parody Twitter account better. By that I am referring to the fake account called KP Genius, which basically took the mickey of Kev and his personality. First, I should say that I genuinely believe that no England cricketer was involved in that account. It was eventually revealed that it was the work of a lad called Richard Bailey, who is a mate of Stuart Broad's, but Broady was not party to anything that was going out on Twitter from that account. He was nothing to do with it and quite rightly put out a statement via the ECB to say as much.

I was one of those who followed that parody account, and, if I'm totally honest, I found it quite funny. But I was wrong in doing that. So I had to hold my hands up to KP and admit that I was wrong. I apologised to him for that. That parody account was one of the areas where we let our standards slip in terms of team spirit. But, don't get me wrong, there were also areas in which Kev had to come towards the team, areas where he had to make changes. He had to buy into being one of the 11, rather than it being a case of ten players and one other. But on the other hand, it was not a case of us not having done anything wrong and Kev being the big, bad monster.

At the end of the conversation I was confident that, if he was prepared to do the things he said he was going to do, then he was going to be back as part of the England set-up very quickly. But the problem was that the very next day the story broke alleging that he had been sending messages to members of the South Africa team. That news scuppered any power that the conversation I'd had with him had. I didn't speak to him after that, because it became an issue for Andy Flower, Andrew Strauss and the ECB. There was nothing the players could do about that. We couldn't get ourselves involved in that. We had to concentrate on playing cricket.

Of course, Kev did return to the side and played in the incredible Test series victory over India before Christmas 2012. It was his magnificent 186, along with 19 wickets shared between Monty Panesar and Graeme Swann, that allowed us to beat India in Mumbai in the second Test, after we had lost the first Test in Ahmedabad. After that victory I took a picture on my mobile phone of a smiling Kev sitting on a chair holding a signed stump from the game and below I wrote: '"Re-integration" complete! Well played @kevinpp24.' I told Kev what I was going to do and what I was going to say, and he loved it. He thought it was a great idea.

Sometimes I think that we take sport so seriously that there are times when we should instead sit back and just have a giggle at what's gone on. That was why I tweeted that photo. I didn't mean anything other than I thought Kev was totally re-integrated. I hadn't even heard the word 're-integration' before this business – we'd had a bit of a row with a team-mate and we had got past it, but now we were going to play cricket. The guy is either in the team or he is not.

Some suggested that I might have been having a go at the ECB with my tweet, but it wasn't anything like that. He was brilliant on that tour. He had just made a century to show what a class player he is, but the way he was off the field in India was as important as how he was on it. And in both respects he was awesome. It brought me back to the motto we had pinned up in our dressing room throughout the 2003 season at Sussex: 'United we believe, together we achieve'. It was very much the message Mooresy lived by, so it became our message, too. It is funny that writing this book has brought back memories of things like that. I haven't heard that motto for years, but I think it is rather good. I might have to give Mark Robinson a ring and talk to him about it.

I once read something Nasser Hussain had written about team spirit. He said: 'I have never been a big fan of the concept of team spirit. That usually comes with winning matches.' That is very similar to the view once expressed by Steve Archibald, the former Spurs footballer, who once said that team spirit was 'an illusion glimpsed in the aftermath of victory'.

I can't agree with either of them. As regards Nasser, I wonder if he ever played in a cricket side that actually had a truly great team spirit, otherwise he wouldn't say that. That's not having a go at Nass, for whom I have a lot of respect, but maybe it is a case that great team spirit is a truly rare thing and harder to find than you might think. However, I have no doubt that this current England side has it, and that is one of the major reasons why we have been so successful.

And the Sussex side has always had it. In 2003 we knew that we didn't have the strongest side on paper, but we made a collective decision that we were going to work harder than anyone else. We decided to be the fittest side on the county circuit. And I think we achieved that aim. Some of our fitness results were extraordinary. In those days, the bleep test was all the rage – that is a running test whereby you run shuttles over 20m to a series of bleeps that get closer and closer together until you are sprinting flat out to keep up. You run until you drop, and then you are given a score according to the level at which you pulled out.

The minimum score we were supposed to achieve was 12.5, so consider my joy one pre-season when I turned up and chalked up 13.6. I thought that was unbelievable. I was so happy with myself, and I thought the coaches would be equally happy with me. That is until I discovered that the squad average on that test was 13.8!

For a cricket squad, that is a seriously high level of fitness, and it was no wonder with guys such as Jamie Carpenter, Tony Cottey and Richard Montgomerie in the squad, all of whom were up around the 15 mark.

Once the season was under way, Mooresy would always make sure that our fitness levels were topped up with his infamous 'fitness fielding' sessions. Those two words should never be put together when Mooresy is in charge. 'Time for some fielding fitness,' he would say. 'We're just going to have a jog around the field to warm up and then we'll get a sweat on.' We just knew that we were in a whole heap of trouble then!

His ten catches routine was a killer. Essentially, all you had to do was catch ten catches without dropping one. But it wasn't quite as easy as that, because Mooresy had this remarkable knack of making sure that every catch was ridiculously difficult, involving a full-on sprint where you might just about get your fingertips to it, usually after a dive. After ten of them, your lungs were crying for mercy.

Then it was immediately on to another station, where you might work for a minute taking catches from two of your team-mates positioned about 15m apart. One would drop a ball just in front of him, which you would dive to catch, then you'd have to get up, turn around and run over to take the same kind of catch from your other team-mate behind you. The up and down movements for a minute made sure that your legs were burning.

There were other team-building exercises that Mooresy used to bring us tighter together. I've always believed that team hardships do bring you closer, so that when you are in a tough situation in a match you draw on those shared experiences. And that was certainly Mooresy's thinking. For instance, I know that before I was on the staff at Sussex the players arrived at Hove one morning for practice and found themselves instead confronted by a whole load of pots of paint. So they painted the ground together that day.

Another ritual was that on the first day of every pre-season we would all have to go for a swim in the sea. We all had to walk in slowly until the water was up to our necks, and then we had to walk back out. That was not too bad for someone like Tony Cottey, who is not the tallest (sorry Cotts!), but for the rest of us, with no running allowed, it was murder. It was freezing.

On away trips we would always go for a team meal (they seem to have been replaced by protein shakes these days) and there would be a series of toasts made. One of them was to 'Good Old Sussex by the Sea'. Another was repeating that motto – 'United we believe, together we achieve' – and then, after 2002, most poignantly, there was one to 'absent friends'.

That was because we had lost one of our own. In 2001, Umer Rashid had been a regular member of that side that won the division two county championship title, bowling his left-arm spin tidily and chipping in so usefully with his left-handed batting that he scored a championship hundred against Durham. Umer was ready to play his part in 2002, too, but he died in a tragic accident while we were on a pre-season tour to the island of Grenada in the West Indies. He was just 26 years old.

We had had one of those team meals the night before. And, with a day off the next day, I have to admit that quite a bit of alcohol was consumed. On that rest day, Umer had arranged to go to Concord Falls, a local beauty spot, along with his younger brother Burhan (who was 18), who had come out to Grenada on holiday with his girlfriend. Umer had invited us all to go with him and most of us had agreed. But the next morning, as the hangovers kicked in, people gradually started to pull out. I think I, along with Jason Lewry, was one of the last to do so, about ten minutes before they left. I said to Umer: 'Sorry

Umes, I feel rubbish. I'm just going to chill out by the pool today.'

Umer wasn't upset. He wasn't that sort of guy. 'No worries, buddy,' he replied. 'Hope you have a good day.' And off he went. To this day I still think about that moment. I was going. What would have happened if I had gone? Should I have gone?

We were all sitting around the pool that day when a phone call came through. The waitress said that it was an urgent call for one of the players from Sussex. Richard Montgomerie took it. I can still see him taking that call now. It was Burhan's girlfriend. Monty's face just dropped. You could tell immediately that something terrible had happened. He came off the phone in some distress, as we all asked him what was the matter. 'There has been a terrible accident at the falls,' he said. 'They think that Umer and his brother have drowned.'

Sadly, as Peter Moores confirmed to us later, the story was true. Burhan had got into difficulties, and Umer had gone to assist him. They both went under and they never resurfaced. There was utter shock and heartbreak among our squad. Just ten days earlier we had been equally shocked by the news that the gifted and universally well-liked Surrey and England all-rounder, Ben Hollioake, had been killed in a car crash in Perth, Australia. Now this. It just didn't make sense.

The tour, arranged by two former Northamptonshire players, Nigel Felton and Allan Lamb, which was to have included matches against that county and Yorkshire, was cancelled immediately. We went to the ground where we had been practising, and I just remember our press officer, Francesca Watson, coming up to me and asking if I was OK. I wasn't. I don't think anyone was. I burst into tears and sat there sobbing for about half an hour.

It seemed so unfair. Often when there are tragedies, those who pass away are made out to be much better people than they actually were. But that could never be the case with Umer, nor with Ben for that matter. Umer was such a lovable character. He was fun-loving and bubbly, the life and soul of the dressing room. He just got on with everyone. Nobody would have a bad word to say about him, because he would never say a bad word about anybody else. He was a wonderful team man, who did not have a selfish bone in his body.

The one thing I will say about Umer, though, is that sometimes he could be a little frustrating, a little too relaxed, especially when he was next in to bat when he would often not even have his pads on. I remember one occasion when this really wound up James Kirtley. They were at the opposite ends of the intensity scale those two. Umer was so laid back as to be nearly horizontal, while Amby was so professional and motivated that everything had to be in place and on time. So on this one day Umer was next in to bat, and, yet again, he didn't have his pads on. He was oblivious to any worry about this, but Amby wasn't.

'You're next into bat and you have not got your pads on again!' shouted Amby.

'It's safe, man,' replied Umer, as he often did.

'No Umer, it's not safe!' screamed Amby. There may even have been a swear word in there, too.

But it was safe. And everybody laughed about it later. Everybody loved Umer. Sadly on that fateful day of 1 April 2002, it was not all safe for Umer and his brother.

We decided that before returned home to England we had to travel to the falls to pay our respects. It was strange. You imagine them being something like Victoria Falls, with its huge thundering and dangerous waters. But it was nothing like that. It was a small, trickling, peaceful waterfall. And the pool in which Umer and Burhan had died was so small. You could probably get from one side to the other in three strokes. But Burhan could not swim at all, and Umer was not a strong swimmer. It was all so terribly sad, but I am sure that Umes would have been proud of what Sussex have achieved since. I know that he has been in our thoughts throughout it all.

6

Ashes Regained

'What are you doing? Get out of here!'

It was Alastair Cook who was screaming at me. That he was sitting alone in the shower area of the dressing room (with no shower on) and had already been there for some time will tell you everything you need to know about this rather bizarre situation.

This was Cardiff 2009, my first Ashes Test. This was a nerve-shredding finale, as James Anderson and Monty Panesar tried to survive to salvage a draw. When Paul Collingwood had been out at 6pm, caught at gully off Peter Siddle for a brave and defiant 74, our last man Monty had gone to the wicket, ten minutes into the final hour of play, with a minimum of 11.3 overs remaining.

I don't think Monty will mind me saying that I thought it was all over. I suspect that I wouldn't have been alone in feeling that. It was just too long to survive. It's always such a horrible feeling waiting to lose. You almost want to get it over and done with, to pack your bags and move on. I hate that sort of slow death in a cricket match.

I was playing with a tennis ball at the time, walking around the dressing room, bouncing it off the walls and catching it. I was still frustrated and a little angry at having got out for 14, caught at slip off the spinner Nathan Hauritz. The ball had turned and bounced, but I had been trying to cut it and had gloved it to Michael Clarke. Yes, it was a decent ball, but it was not a good shot in the circumstances. It was a bad way to get out.

Our task had always appeared a stiff one. We had begun the last day on 20 for two, with Cooky and Ravi Bopara already out. We were still 219 runs behind Australia. We just hadn't played quite well enough throughout the game. We had won the toss on a very slow pitch, with a bit of 'tennis-ball' bounce. We'd made 435, but the fact that no one scored a hundred tells the story that we might have done so much more. I had made 56, which was pleasing in my first Ashes innings, especially as I had scored at nearly a run a ball (62 balls) before inside-edging Siddle to be bowled just before the close of day one. But it did at least make me think 'I can do this' in Ashes cricket.

But, like the others who scored half-centuries – Kevin Pietersen with 69 and Colly with 64 (Graeme Swann chipped in with 47 not out and Andrew Flintoff made 37) – there was a feeling of 'what might have been'. KP was out sweeping at Hauritz to a ball that was a long way outside off stump and was deflected via his helmet for a simple catch to short leg. He was absolutely crucified in the press for it. It was an immediate wake-up call for all of us about how closely scrutinised the Ashes is. The media coverage goes up to a different level.

But it was harsh on KP. He'd played really well, and had played patiently. It was also obvious that he was struggling with an Achilles' tendon injury, which was eventually to put him out of the series after the second Test at Lord's. The shot he played was on, because there was no fielder on the leg side at 45 degrees. As he himself said afterwards, if the ball had not clipped his helmet it would have been easy runs down to fine leg. As I mentioned in the lead-up to my century on Test debut, I like to play that shot, too, so you won't find me criticising it. But in fairness, Hauritz had also seen what KP was trying to do and had thrown the ball wider of off stump.

Australia's batsmen did not make the same mistakes as us in failing to convert their starts into big scores. They made 674 for six, with centuries for Simon Katich, Ricky Ponting, Marcus North and Brad Haddin.

We had decided to play two spinners in that match – Monty and Swanny obviously – mainly because there had been some turning pitches for Glamorgan there earlier in the season. In a one-day game against Essex, they had actually been docked points because the pitch had turned so much. But the truth was that the pitch for this Test match was just too slow. Any spin there was relatively easy to counter. At one stage, we even ended up getting Colly to bowl some off-cutters. I obviously wanted to stand up to him, but two consecutive balls to the left-handed North spat out of the rough outside his off stump and sped away for four byes. I wasn't happy, to say the least, especially when Colly suggested that I stand back about four yards, just like they do in club cricket. 'I'm not standing in "clubland",' I told him in no uncertain terms.

On and on went Australia. I kept trying to keep the guys' spirits up, as I always try to do, but it wasn't easy. When you are in the field for so long (Australia batted for 181 overs in the end – two whole days), it becomes very hard work. You can feel the guys getting quieter one by one, and you've got to try to find a way of keeping them going, as well as yourself. We hung in there, but there wasn't a lot of banter. I was very aware of those issues I'd had before about people calling me a big mouth. So I restricted myself to straightforward comments like 'Come on lads! Keep going!' But deep down we were all thinking: 'How long are we going to be out here?' At one stage, I thought we were going to be fielding for three days.

But eventually, half an hour before tea on the fourth day, Ponting declared with his side 239 ahead. Rain had been forecast for most of the day, but it looked at its closest as the skies darkened and the floodlights were called into action (the previous day they had been used for the first time in a Test in England or Wales). We limped to tea on 20 for two, but there was no further play that day.

By lunch on the last day, I was already out. The night before I'd said to myself: 'Right, tomorrow's a big day. Someone's going to have to be a hero tomorrow – can you be the man?' I'd batted so fluently in the first innings that I felt I could be that man. But the truth is that I got too far ahead of myself. I stopped worrying about what I was doing to every ball and started thinking things like: 'Let's get to lunch, and then let's get to tea.' I wasn't concentrating on the there and then, and that is always dangerous for a batsman to do. Suddenly Hauritz got that one to turn, and I was gone. I really felt that I had let the team down, if I am totally honest. I was gutted. The rest of the day was agony.

We were 102 for five at lunch and the close seemed an awful long way away. But Colly was still there and it was mainly thanks to him that Monty and Jimmy were able to have some sort of chance of saving the game, with 11.3 overs left when they came together. I should mention Swanny as well, because, after being hit by some short stuff from Siddle, he decided to lash out and made 31 valuable runs that helped whittle down Australia's lead.

As I said earlier, it wasn't much of a chance. Monty could so easily have been out to his first ball, poking at a length ball from Siddle. But he wasn't out and he didn't get out as Siddle and Hauritz naturally went hard at him. He actually started looking quite solid. Then Jimmy hit a couple of fours off Siddle, the first of them putting us ahead. Australia would have to bat again now. The change of innings would take two overs (ten minutes) out of the equation. This was getting serious.

Suddenly there were guys in our changing room looking at each other and asking: 'How long have we got left here?' But others were countering with: 'Hang on, we've only got one wicket left. Let's not get too carried away.'

But still it was time for cricketing superstition to kick in. In such circumstances, you genuinely believe that because you have been sitting in a certain place or engaging in a certain activity that is the sole reason for a wicket not having fallen. It is madness, but it is true. That is why Cooky would not move from the shower. That was why Swanny would not move from his seat out at the back of the dressing room where he was watching the German Grand Prix on TV. And that was why I had to keep bouncing my tennis ball off the walls. And that was why I couldn't drop it either (and why, to this day, I still have that tennis ball in my cricket bag). That was the deal with the Big Man upstairs who looks after us cricketers.

One of the team management, it may have been Andy Flower, was absolutely desperate for the toilet. But he wasn't allowed to go. He could not leave his seat. He'd have to wet himself. Nobody was allowed to leave their seats. Well, OK, maybe not everybody. I think our team operations manager, Phil Neale, was moving about. He went into the umpires' room to check how long we needed to bat to make it impossible for Australia to have a chance of batting and winning the game. He came back with the news that we needed to bat until 6.40pm. That was great, as it was knocking on for 6.30pm, but, just because we knew, it didn't mean that the two batsmen in the middle did. It was time to send a message out to tell them.

Bilal Shafayat, who has played for Nottinghamshire, Northamptonshire and Hampshire, was our twelfth man and he was dispatched to take a message out. Of course, you can't just do that in cricket. You have to have some supposedly ulterior motive – like a change of gloves. So off he went with some batting gloves and a drink for Jimmy so that he could inform him of the news that he and Monty just needed to survive until 6.40pm.

Jimmy certainly needed a drink. He's never batted that long in his life. Only joking, Jim! And I think it is only fair to say that Jimmy was joking when he tipped some of his drink on the batting gloves that Bilal had taken out for him. So Bilal had to go back out with another pair. And, in a flurry of so-called confusion, our physio Steve McCaig was also summoned out onto the field.

Ponting, understandably, wasn't happy. He thought we were time-wasting, and he was probably right. At times like that, you have to do what you have to do. People can claim it was bad sportsmanship, and plenty did so back in Australia apparently, but to my mind it would have been very English not to have done so. Every other side in the world would have done it against us.

You know what? I actually think we could have wasted more time. But this was enough for Ponting, who, surprisingly, had just decided to bring on Marcus North, with his part-time off spin. Ponting was shouting and screaming, and in particular sent a volley of abuse towards McCaig, who was only standing in as our physio that day. He was absolutely gutted, the poor bloke. He's an Australian, you see, and Ponting is his hero. He'd been abused by his hero. He woke up the next day and discovered he'd been all over the Australian press, too. Even his own family were having a go at him. I felt sorry for him, I really did.

Throughout all this, the crowd had been fantastic. The noise was incredible. They were all cheering for England – a Welsh crowd cheering for England. That was strange, for certain. But they were cheering. The place was going mad. To be honest, when I'd discovered that I was playing my first Ashes Test in Wales, I'd been a little worried. I asked myself: 'How will the Welsh people accept the England cricket team?'

I'd played at Cardiff only once before and I'd been out first ball for Sussex against Glamorgan in a C&G Trophy match in 2006. But I'd played against Glamorgan a couple of times in Swansea, and the National League match I'd played there in 2001 stood out in my mind. It was one of the most hostile atmospheres in which I'd ever played cricket. From my experience, it was immediately obvious to me that the Welsh don't particularly like the English. But I need not have worried. The crowd was better than we could ever have imagined. The way the locals took to Ashes cricket was phenomenal. They loved it, and we loved it, too.

And, as 6.40pm approached, they loved it even more. Now the problem was the exact time. Whose watch was correct? Was it the one on the pavilion? Or was it the one on umpire Aleem Dar's wrist? It came to 6.39pm and we were 12 runs ahead. Hauritz began another over. He was bowling from around the wicket to Jimmy. Five balls were blocked. And then this was surely it: the last ball. It was wide and it went off wicketkeeper Brad Haddin's pads and away so that Monty ran through for a bye. That was it.

Or was it? Monty and Jimmy met in the middle to have a chat. And then Ponting came in from extra cover with his hand outstretched. It was over now. Australia knew that they could not win. We'd salvaged a draw. Jimmy and Monty had survived 69 balls. We went berserk, but not so that anyone could see. Andrew Strauss was big on making sure that the Australians didn't see us celebrating. 'You can shout and scream in the dressing room,' he said. 'But don't let the Aussies see you.' He stressed to us that we had only drawn. We hadn't won.

At the time we were all thinking 'Cheer up Strauss!' but, of course, it was sound advice. And he was probably thinking back to the Ashes Test at Old Trafford in 2005 when Australia, mainly thanks to Ponting's brilliant hundred, had grabbed a dramatic draw. Their players celebrated wildly on the balcony, and the England captain Michael Vaughan gathered his team together (including Strauss, of course) on the outfield and made a point to them about how the Australians were celebrating a draw. It was a huge psychological advantage to England.

But the truth was that this did feel like a victory. My first taste of Ashes cricket had not been a let-down. It had been everything I expected, and more. I'd been told that there is nothing like the hype of an Ashes series, that it catches the imagination of the country like no other series, and I had not been disappointed. But, until you have experienced it, I am not sure you can totally understand the difference from ordinary Test cricket.

It was already very apparent to me that, on and off the field, Ashes cricket is very special. It was crazy, like nothing I've ever played in before. More so for the off-pitch goings-on than for what happened on the field. I did a press conference at Lord's for the second Test and I've never seen so many people and cameras crammed into one room. It was quite daunting. I even started to be recognised in public for the first time.

On the field, it tests you like nothing else. It puts you under pressure and in an uncomfortable position most of the time against a very good team. It's always sink-or-swim time. You have to ask yourself some tough questions. You just hope you can answer them and come out the other side.

We'd certainly been asked some questions in Cardiff, but the score was still 0-0 in the series (Cardiff had been chosen because the first Test was usually at Lord's, where we often lost). The Ashes was under way after a long build-up. It seemed years ago since we had been beaten in the first Test of our tour to the West Indies, where we'd been bowled out for just 51 in Jamaica and the new leadership regime of Strauss and Flower had decided to stamp their authority.

There was a meeting in Antigua after that Test where some home truths were told. We needed to sort ourselves out. Individual players had to take more responsibility. And, although we did not win a Test in the rest of that series – the pitches were ridiculously flat – we did not lose another either. We had shown some steel. And when West Indies came to us for two Tests at the start of that 2009 season, we had beaten them easily. First at Lord's we'd beaten them by ten wickets, a match we had really targeted because, remarkably, we had not won the first Test of a rubber for 14 series. Not since 2005 and the first Test of the summer, against Bangladesh, had England won the first Test of a series.

It was also a match remembered for the debuts of Tim Bresnan and Graham Onions, as well as from a personal point of view my passing of 1000 runs in Test cricket in my 17th Test. With Andrew Flintoff having been injured in the Indian Premier League, I was picked to bat at six, as we played five bowlers. And I made 42 before, somewhat annoyingly, hitting Fidel Edwards to cover. But our 377, thanks to Ravi Bopara's 143, was made to look very good once West Indies were skittled for 152, with Onions – Bunny to the boys – taking five for 38. It was some start from him, even if it was also a rude awakening for me as to how much the ball wobbles after passing the bat when he bowls.

It was also a match in which Graeme Swann, in seaming conditions, opened the bowling in West Indies' first innings. That caused some comment. I'm used to standing up to spinners early on in Twenty20 (for instance, in 2012 for Sussex Michael Yardy would open with his slow left-arm, and in 2011 it was often Ollie Rayner or Chris Nash with their off spin), but in a Test match? This was different. But I thought it was clever work from Andrew

Strauss. There were a couple of reasons behind it. The first was that Devon Smith, the West Indies left-handed opener, had gained a reputation for being uncertain against spin, as Swanny had often got him out in the Caribbean.

And secondly, when West Indies had bowled, the ball had not swung immediately, so it was worth giving Swanny a couple of overs before our main swing bowler, Jimmy Anderson, could come on. As it was, Swanny didn't get a wicket in those early overs, but he still won man of the match for his six wickets in the match (including Shivnarine Chanderpaul for just nought and four, which is always a bonus given his propensity to hang around for such long periods of time), along with his 63 not out.

The second Test was at Chester-le-Street, and again we won easily, this time by an innings and 83 runs. We racked up 569 for six, with Alastair Cook making 160 and Ravi Bopara 108, his third century in successive Tests. Jimmy Anderson then bowled with remarkable skill as he took nine wickets, with his swing unplayable at times. But I had my problems in the match. I'd scored 63 with the bat, but on the fourth afternoon when keeping I tried to take a ball from Tim Bresnan that bounced in front of me. I didn't take it every well.

It hurt! God, it hurt. I'd done some damage to the ring finger on my right hand and although, after some treatment, I carried on, I didn't reappear after the tea break, or at all on the final day. Paul Collingwood took over. X-rays revealed no fracture, but it was an injury that was to trouble me for some time afterwards. I was, however, able to play in the three-match one-day series (the first game at Leeds was abandoned without a ball being bowled) that followed the Tests, and was also able to bat at three in the absence of Kevin Pietersen, who was resting his Achilles' injury. And at Edgbaston I made my highest one-day score of 87, a best I still haven't passed.

That angers me just writing that. It should be so much more. Who knows, by the time you read this, I may have forced my way back into the England one-day set-up, but at the time of writing it doesn't look likely. It's why I left England on Christmas Day 2012 to go to play for Sydney Thunder in the Big Bash in Australia (I also played for Victoria in the same competition in 2010-11 at the end of the Ashes tour, before being called into the England one-day squad) and also entered the auction (without success, as it happened) for the Indian Premier League. I hadn't been required for the two Twenty20 internationals that followed the four-Test series in India and I wasn't selected for the five one-day internationals that took place in India after Christmas. I began to get tired of people asking me if I had retired from international one-day cricket. I hadn't and I haven't!

But those runs at Edgbaston weren't enough to merit selection for the ICC World Twenty20, which was being held in England that year, and began with England losing their first match to the Netherlands at Lord's. We actually beat the eventual winners Pakistan to qualify for the Super Eights, but were knocked out of the tournament by West Indies at The Oval after rain had brought Duckworth/Lewis into the equation.

Again I was disappointed to miss out. A World Cup in your country? Of course, I was gutted to miss it. I'd be daft to say or think anything else. But it did at least give me a rest period to get my finger right before the Ashes, even if the performances of the selected England wicketkeeper for that tournament, Essex's James Foster, set people talking about him. As I've said before, I'm used to that. There is always someone else barking at your heels, always someone else the critics think is better. But I was indebted to Alec Stewart for his kind words to the press at this time.

'Foster's the better keeper, but as a package Prior plays,' he said, 'Andrew Flintoff isn't a number six and then we're only going in with five batsmen, which we can't do against this Australia side. Brad Haddin and Matt Prior are pretty similar cricketers. Matt Prior's going to bat one place higher at number six, they're both capable of getting Test match hundreds and their glove work is good enough. James Foster, I think everyone would agree, is the best keeper, probably in the world, and Prior is the best batsman-keeper for the balance of the side.

'I think we're ultra-critical of Matt Prior,' Stewie continued. 'People might think I'm biased or whatever, but all we seem to do is highlight any error he makes. When he kept wicket at Lord's against the West Indies and the same at Durham, no one wrote a word about Matt Prior, because he kept wicket well. If he misses something then it's headlines, Foster – two fantastic stumpings (of Yuvraj Singh and Dwayne Bravo) and it was headlines. It's how we interpret Prior and we interpret Foster. I've always said Foster is the best . . . but Prior is still a decent keeper and a very, very fine batsman.'

In fairness, I'd like to think that I'd done enough to guarantee my spot for the Ashes, and I was duly picked in the 16-man training squad, as well as in the team for a three-day warm-up match against Warwickshire at Edgbaston. Having rested my finger for a period of time, I'd then played in three county championship matches for Sussex against Yorkshire, Worcestershire and Somerset, making a couple of fifties, and in a Twenty20 match against Surrey at Whitgift School that was abandoned before we batted. But before that match against Warwickshire, we had something else planned. On Friday 26 June, the England squad was told to meet at St Pancras station, from where we caught the Eurostar to Lille. We then went to Flanders Field to visit the First World War battlefields. With us were some active soldiers and a war historian.

We visited Tyne Cot cemetery, attended a memorial service, laid wreaths and went on a tour of trenches that have been preserved from the war. We were told about Colin Blythe, the former England and Kent left-arm spinner who took 100 Test wickets, who died aged 38 on the Forest Hall to Pimmern military railway line at the Battle of Passchendaele in 1917. Stuart Broad was chosen to lay a specially made stone cricket ball as tribute at his graveside.

It was a humbling experience. To see what these men did for our country and what they did to protect us sent out a very strong and powerful message to us. It was a reminder of the saying 'You don't know where you're going until you know where you've come from'. It may be clichéd, but it is so true.

You obviously can't compare cricket to war, but this was about taking us out of our comfort zone and about us being patriotic and finding a special togetherness, about getting the England team united again after some troubles around the start of that year. That is why it was a little disappointing that one of our top players couldn't get out of bed on the Saturday morning. Yes, we had had a bit of a night out, but still . . .

We had been to a restaurant in Ypres and then later to a nearby bar where we had been tempted by some Belgian beer that turned out to be rather potent. I think it is fair to say that there were some seriously sore heads the next morning. But most of us managed to rise in time to catch the bus, indeed all of us except Andrew Flintoff. There was no moving him from his bed. We banged on his door, but he just wouldn't wake up. Straussy had to admit later in public that Fred had 'stuffed up', and he had. Sadly, it was the first sign that his behaviour was becoming a little bit individual, and that the team had begun to move on from him.

That said, Fred's contribution before the second Ashes Test at Lord's was much more positive. When we arrived at the ground for practice on the Tuesday after Sunday's dramatic conclusion in Cardiff, we all sat on the square – just the players, without any coaches – to review the first Test and look ahead to the second. Fred spoke for a long time. He stressed the point that in the other Ashes series in which he had appeared, England had always been 1-0 down after the first Test. Now we weren't. It was still 0-0, and he was confident that we could win this series.

There was, though, some serious history counting against us. England had not beaten Australia at Lord's since 1934. And that was the only occasion in 27 Tests going back to 1899 on which a victory had come. But the thing with this current England team is that, when there are records to be broken, more often than not we break them. And that was our aim here. We were determined to break that duck. We were determined that Lord's was going to be our ground, and the fact that eight of the Australia team were making their first appearance at Lord's was an undoubted bonus.

There was another reason for Fred to speak to us on that Tuesday morning – he had to tell us that he was indeed intending to retire from Test cricket at the end of the series. Much had been speculated upon in one of that morning's newspapers, and here was Fred telling us that it was true. He was struggling with his right knee and had decided to concentrate on the shorter forms of the game after this series. We were told that he would tell the world the next day. So while we practised over at the Nursery End of the ground on the Wednesday before the Test, Fred conducted a packed press conference behind the pavilion.

The Ashes media frenzy suddenly got even more intense. By the end of an extraordinary match, it had somehow managed to move on to yet another level. But first there was a lot of work to be done, and winning the toss helped. We batted, and we batted well. Very well. So well in fact that Andrew Strauss and Alastair Cook put on 196 for the first wicket. What a statement that was after Cardiff. Straussy went on to make 161. It was, in my opinion, one of his best knocks. Cooky made 95, but, disappointingly, no one else made a fifty, so that we were bowled out for 425. Decent, but it could have been so much better.

However, when Australia were bowled out for 215, with Jimmy Anderson taking four for 55, it suddenly didn't look such a bad score. The ball hadn't swung in Cardiff, but now it was hooping considerably, and Jimmy was causing all sorts of problems for the Australia batsmen.

At lunch on the second day Australia were 27 for two, and the break was extended while players from both sides met Her Majesty the Queen. I'd met her a couple of times before – once when she came to Loughborough to open the Academy, and also on my debut at Lord's against West Indies in 2007. So, as I joked to someone at the time: 'We're in regular contact!'

She didn't say anything to me this time, but HRH Prince Philip did. I obviously had my wicketkeeping pads on at the time, so he asked me if I was the wicketkeeper. 'Do those pads actually work?' he asked, and I replied 'Well, you're meant to use your hands most of the time, but every now and then, the ball does get you on the shin, so, yes, they're OK.' Then he saw that I had some strapping on the finger that I'd been struggling with and he said: 'Well, the pads may work but the gloves obviously don't!'

Having bowled Australia out for 215, there was a decision to be made – should we make them follow on or not? The Australians had begun day three on 156 for eight, and I think at that stage it had been Straussy's intention to make them follow on. But Nathan Hauritz and Peter Siddle didn't look in too much trouble that morning and, as time went on, it became clear that it was a good day for batting. So that's what we did. We batted positively in extending our lead. The only downside was the way in which Kevin Pietersen was so obviously struggling with his Achilles' injury. He'd had an injection in it after Cardiff, but it clearly wasn't right as he hobbled around in a partnership with Ravi Bopara, and they weren't able to take quick singles.

But everyone contributed, and it was set up for me, when I went in, to bat with real freedom. Those are the situations I like best and I really enjoyed myself here, making 61 off just 42 balls. I was run out going for a second by a direct hit from the boundary by Marcus North. What a way to go! I walked off thinking: 'I've thrown away an Ashes hundred there, and at Lord's too.' Ashes centuries are special and so rare. Yes, there was some way for me to go and time was running out, as we looked to declare, but I felt so good that day that I thought it was possible.

We eventually declared before play started – 15 minutes late due to rain – on the fourth morning, setting Australia 522 to win. It seemed a lot of runs and it is indeed a lot of runs, but the flip side of that is that the Lord's pitch gets only flatter as any game there goes on. We knew it would not be easy, especially as there was growing concern about the state of Flintoff's knee. How long could he last?

We were soon to find out. He immediately took two wickets, both with an element of controversy. The first was Simon Katich, caught in the gully by KP, but TV replays showed that it was actually a no-ball. And secondly Phil Hughes was caught at slip by Straussy diving forward. He was sure that he had caught it, but Ricky Ponting at the non-striker's end stopped Hughes on his way off in the hope that the catch would be referred to the television technology. Umpire Rudi Koertzen consulted with his colleague at square leg, Billy Doctrove, and they agreed that the ball had carried cleanly to Straussy, so Hughes had to go.

I had the best view in the house of that catch, looking straight down to my left. And I just thought that it went straight in, that there was absolutely no doubt. But then, looking at the television replays, I did think: 'Crikey! That actually looks a bit dodgy.' But so many of those types of catches do, and the key point to make is that Straussy is just not the type of character who would claim a catch if there was any doubt. If he had had any doubt, he would have let the umpires refer it. He caught it cleanly. I didn't doubt it then and I don't doubt it now.

When Graeme Swann bowled North to make it 128 for five, there was a possibility that the match could be all over on that fourth day, but Australia rallied. Michael Clarke and Brad Haddin put on 185 in 47 overs, so that by the close they were 313 for five. It was going to make for an enthralling last day.

As it was, it was an unforgettable day. Andrew Flintoff, despite the problems with his knee, bowled ten unchanged overs on that final morning, taking three of the remaining wickets to end with a five-wicket haul and ensure victory by 115 runs. You simply couldn't get the ball out of his hands.

It was unforgettable because I have no hesitation in saying that it was the quickest spell I have ever kept wicket to. At the start of the morning, I had placed my marker where I would normally stand to Fred, but with each over it was going further and further back. The pace was almost scary. But then I've always thought that Fred was the most frightening bowler I've ever faced as a batsman or wicketkeeper. On his day, he was simply outstanding. How he didn't take more five-wicket hauls in Test cricket is amazing (just three of them in his 79-Test career). It's probably because of the length that he bowled, which might have been a yard short, but it also meant that he hit the splice of the bat more often than not and was always economical.

Here at Lord's, because the ball was reverse swinging, he actually pitched it up a bit more. And that was also the reason why it was the best spell of bowling I've ever kept to – there was that searing pace but also the skill of the reverse swing, too. In my experience there is only one other spell that comes close to it, and that came from two bowlers operating together, and, bizarrely, it didn't even claim a wicket. It came in the Ashes series in Australia in 2010-11. It came in the first session of the third day in the first Test at Brisbane. Stuart Broad and Jimmy Anderson bowled 11 overs between them against Mike Hussey and Brad Haddin, conceding just 17 runs. There was loads of sideways movement, loads of playing and missing, unbelievable accuracy. Broady was at his aggressive best and Jimmy had his 'wobble-seam' ball going really well.

That wobble-seam was something he had developed for that tour, for when the ball stopped swinging. I think it was something he picked up from watching Pakistan's Mohammad Asif, who bowled it so well. The theory behind it is that, if he doesn't know which way the ball is going to go, then the batsman shouldn't have a clue. He spreads his fingers slightly wider either side of the seam and does not use quite as strong a wrist action as he does when swinging the ball.

But, as I said, there were no wickets in this remarkable spell. Although saying that, Hussey was actually given out LBW by Aleem Dar from Jimmy, but he reviewed the decision and it showed that the ball had fractionally pitched outside leg stump. Four overs later, Jimmy had a very similar appeal on Hussey. But this time Dar said no, and we could not review it, because we had already used up our two referrals – one against Simon Katich and the other against Michael Clarke, whom I'm sure I had caught off Steven Finn but it could not be proved by the available technology. The Snickometer, not used in the Decision Review System because of its time constraints, later seemed to suggest that I was right.

At the end of that series over a cold VB beer, I spoke to Hussey and Haddin about that spell from Broady and Jimmy. Hadds said to me: 'Mate, we were walking to the middle of the pitch at the end of each over and we were shaking our heads. I would ask Huss what we were going to do – "What have you got for me?" I would ask – and he would reply that he hoped that I had an answer to that! We would wish each other good luck and go back to our ends to start playing and missing again.'

Anyway, although we had won at Lord's, a historic triumph, there was some bad news for us in that Kevin Pietersen was out for the series. It had been decided that he required an operation on his Achilles' and that was that. How much would it affect us? That was the big question.

'Losing KP is obviously a big blow to us,' I said in an interview. 'But that is all it is. It is not series-ending or defining, it is an injury to a top player and it is something we'll have to get over. I'm absolutely convinced we can win the series without him. Yes, we'll have to work extremely hard to do it, but that is exactly what we've all been expected to do and nothing changes that.

'As batsmen it is our job to score big runs, whether Kev is there or not. The rules and the game-plans haven't changed for us. We've still got to get the runs that will help the side get into a position to win the Test matches. It is always great to have batsmen of KP's quality in your side because the runs he scores and the way he scores them can have a huge influence on a game. But there are a lot of other guys in the dressing room who can score match-winning hundreds.'

Before the next Test at Edgbaston, I had another engagement – the Friends Provident Trophy final at Lord's for Sussex against Hampshire. I'd played in only two group matches – and we'd actually lost both of them against Gloucestershire and Yorkshire – but I never feel apart from the Sussex team. It's never difficult going back to play, even if I know that I am taking someone else's place. They always make me feel very welcome, and I think that's because they know how much I care about the club. I am Sussex through and through.

But sadly on this occasion I could not reproduce the sort of form I would have liked, being out caught behind second ball to Dominic Cork (and I could easily have been LBW first ball) as we lost by six wickets, despite a brave 92 not out from skipper Michael Yardy. Our total of 219 (this competition was still 50 overs then) was never going to be enough. Sadly, there was not another trophy to add to the cabinet at Hove, but, as I said in the earlier chapter about Sussex, at least there have been quite a few of them in the last decade. Indeed, there was another one added just three weeks later when we won the Twenty20 Cup at Edgbaston, beating Somerset in the final, and then a second one at the end of the season with the NatWest Pro40 League title.

I say 'we' but I didn't play in that finals day or at all in the Pro40 competition. With the finals day coming just before the last Ashes Test, it was decided by the ECB that it was best if I was rested. As I said at the time: 'All my energy and all my thinking is obviously going towards the Test, so first and foremost I think it would be unfair on myself or on my Sussex team-mates, if I were to turn up if my head was not fully on the white ball and Twenty20 cricket – slogging and what not – when really I'm thinking about building a long innings of Test cricket.'

Before any of that it was off to a very soggy Edgbaston, where play didn't start until 5pm on the first day. Ricky Ponting won the toss and decided to bat, but after he had decided to do so, Brad Haddin broke a finger. He had obviously already been named in their line-up. We would have been well within our rights to have made him play, but we didn't, allowing Graham Manou to take his place, and that was actually to have an advantage for me when it came to the next Test at Headingley. Good sportsmanship does have its rewards.

With further rain during this Test, it was always going to be a draw, but there were still plenty of moments that are remembered from it. I've already mentioned one, Graeme Swann's self-proclaimed 'ball of the century' that bowled Ricky Ponting in Australia's second innings – the delivery that spawned 'the Cheese ball', because he could remember only bowling one as good as that, and that was to me. But I also took a pretty spectacular catch to dismiss the left-handed Marcus North off Jimmy Anderson, diving high to my left in front of Andrew Strauss at slip.

It was one of those moments where you see a catch and just go for it. There can be no half-measures in those circumstances. I saw it, went for it and it stuck. I'm glad it did stick, because I'd nicked it out of Straussy's pocket and he wouldn't have been best pleased if I'd grassed it. I'll be honest, though, and say that, even though those sorts of catches look the best, they are often not the hardest. That catch off North is certainly not one that Bruce French always raves about.

Instead, he often talks about a catch that I know no one will remember. It was against Bangladesh in Dhaka in 2010 off Tim Bresnan's bowling. Because of the low pitch I had to stand quite close and the catch came low to my right. It was one of my best catches. Frenchy loved it. He loves the craftsmanship of keeping, and to him that was a great example. It keeps appearing on his laptop screen for me to see.

The other thing that stood out from this Test was the bowling of Graham Onions on the second morning. Australia began it on 126 for one, and it was a little bit of a surprise when Andrew Strauss decided that Bunny should bowl the first over of the day. It was some decision, though. His first ball nipped back and trapped Shane Watson, who had been brought in to replace Phil Hughes at the top of the order, plumb LBW. What a start to the day. In walked Mike Hussey. And out walked Mike Hussey, as he shouldered arms to his first ball. Michael Clarke survived the hat-trick ball – a bouncer, rather surprisingly, but that was the idea and

Clarke very nearly got a touch on it – but not long afterwards Ricky Ponting succumbed to the same delivery and Bunny had had an incredible morning.

Jimmy Anderson took over then, dismissing Clarke, North, Manou and Mitchell Johnson in the space of 13 balls. He later got Peter Siddle to bring up a five-wicket haul. He bowled quite superbly. With the whole of the third day lost to rain, we tried to bat aggressively to make up for lost time, and Andrew Flintoff and I ended up putting on 89 in only 15 and a half overs. Fred made 74, I made 41, and Ian Bell, who had come in to replace Kevin Pietersen, made 53, Straussy scored 69 and Broady also made a fifty.

Australia were 88 for two going into the final day, still 25 runs behind, so I suppose there was a faint chance of victory, especially as Swanny had just bowled his wonder ball to Ponting. But the truth is that the pitch was still pretty flat, and Clarke made an unbeaten hundred and North chipped in with 96.

We were still 1-0 up with two Tests to play. And there was even time for me to play golf at The Belfry with Straussy and our bowling coach Ottis Gibson before heading north to Headingley for the fourth Test. It was to prove an eventful one.

It began at 4.50am on the first morning when a fire alarm was raised at our Radisson Hotel in the centre of Leeds. At first you think you're dreaming. Then, when you eventually wake up, you hope it will stop and that there really is no need to leave your room. Sadly, that did not happen here. There was actually a small fire in one of the rooms, apparently caused by some clothes being left too close to a lamp, and the guest had tried to put out the fire in his bathroom sink. So at 5am the hotel was evacuated. We had to go outside at that hour, on the first morning of an Ashes Test. And it was raining. It was horrible. We were probably outside for only 20 minutes, but it seemed like a lot longer, as we shivered grumpily until two fire engines arrived. Soon the clothes in the offending room were doused and we were allowed back into the hotel.

I thought my day couldn't get any worse. When we got to the ground and were beginning our preparations for the match, there I was enjoying our warm-up game of football when suddenly a back spasm struck. I stopped running immediately in the hope that the full spasm wouldn't come out, but it was too late. I knew what was happening because I'd suffered a similar problem before a Sussex match against Hampshire in 2006. But I have no idea where this one came from. I'd had no warnings that it might happen. I hadn't had a stiff back or anything like that. It just happened from nowhere there on the Headingley outfield, and down I went. I simply couldn't move.

It is like having extreme cramp in all the muscles around the spot, so basically what happens is that you're paralysed. You just can't move your arms or legs. And because all the muscles around your ribs tighten up too, it impedes your diaphragm. So you struggle to breathe. You really do feel as if the wind has been taken out of you. It is scary. And at that moment I thought: 'I'm out of this Test match.'

I was taken into the dressing room where I was given a Voltarol injection (in my backside), anti-inflammatory tablets and the physios began working on my back. I was comforted in some small way from my experience in 2006, because then I had kept wicket the next day. They do get better, these spasms, but it is a question of how quickly. Here it was a question of whether I could get moving enough to be able to declare myself fit enough to play.

Time was running short. This had happened at 10am. The toss was supposed to take place at 10.30am. As I'd gone inside, I'd apparently left a trail of confusion behind me, not least because almost straight afterwards our masseur Mark Saxby had been hit flush on the head by a stray cricket ball hit by one of the Australians.

If I couldn't play, who would? Paul Collingwood was straight into my kit bag to take my inners and keeping gloves out. Remember that he had taken over from me at Durham earlier that summer. He was quite excited, apparently. I think after keeping for a whole Test he might have had a different point of view. Bruce French got his gloves out, too. I'm told that he'd been involved in something similar against New Zealand at Lord's in 1986, albeit when he got injured during the game, after being hit by Richard Hadlee while batting. At first Bill Athey took the gloves, then he was replaced by Bob Taylor, who was working at the time in a hospitality tent, and then Bobby Parks was called from a championship match with Hampshire to deputise. And here at Headingley I think there might even have been calls for Alec Stewart to come down from the commentary box. He would have loved that. He probably would have scored a match-saving century as well.

It was at this moment that Andy Flower decided that he would ask if the toss could be delayed, just to give me some more time to see if I could play. And this is where our sportsmanship at Edgbaston came in handy. We had allowed Australia to change their team there when Brad Haddin was injured, so they could hardly say no when Andy went to see his opposite number Tim Nielsen and ask that the toss be delayed. It was for only ten minutes, until 10.40am. But before that I had to go back outside and test myself. I had to take a few balls. So that's what I did at 10.25am. I was able, just, to move and take a few balls. I even made a couple of tentative dives.

The physios had done a great job. It was certainly much better. It wasn't 100 per cent, of course, but I thought that it would only loosen off. The decision was made that I would play. 'I'm OK,' I said. I didn't want to miss a Test match when I might be fit to play a few hours after the start. But I don't think I would have made it if that toss had not been delayed. Now all I wanted was for us to be batting, so I could rest up then. And Straussy, having announced that Steve Harmison would replace Andrew Flintoff, whose knee had not looked at all fit at nets the day before, did win the toss and bat. I might just have punched the air in delight.

It was time for me to relax. If only. It was probably a good toss to lose, as it was only a good toss to win if you could get through the first session relatively unscathed. It could have been worse, because Straussy probably should have been given out to the very first ball of the game from Ben Hilfenhaus, but umpire Billy Bowden somehow turned down the LBW shout. But, still, our captain was gone in the fourth over and I was batting by the 19th over of the day. By lunch I'd lost two more partners and we were in disarray at 72 for six.

Not long afterwards we were all out for 102. At the first day's close Australia were 196 for four. It was little surprise that I was put up before the press. In addition to all the pre-match drama, I'd actually top-scored with 37 not out from 43 balls. I had to be positive in my assessment of the match looking forward.

'We can get out of this,' I said. 'It's not been a good day, and we're behind the eight-ball, but this game turns around so quickly and there's still enough in this wicket. It's still moving around, still swinging, and we've got four days to come back, which is good for us. We're annoyed with today, but we're raring to go for tomorrow to put things right.'

I was also keen to stress that all the pre-match stuff should not be used as an excuse, nor should the absence of Fred be overstated. 'We're a very, very tight unit, and we know that every single player in that squad is as important as any other,' I said. 'Whoever is spoken about most is irrelevant to what goes on in the changing room. Each member of the squad is a match-winner in our eyes.'

The truth is, though, that we had batted terribly on that first morning. We just didn't play the conditions well enough. We had talked beforehand about how you had to be very careful about driving at Headingley early on, about how you had to look to leave as much as you could. Because of the tennis-ball bounce, sometimes even if the ball looks like a long half volley, it is best to leave. But we ignored all that and paid the price.

Australia scored 445, with Marcus North making a hundred, Michael Clarke 93 and Ricky Ponting 78. By the end of day two we were 82 for five, and I was not out on four. The next morning I made it to 22 before edging Ben Hilfenhaus, but that did set the stage for Stuart Broad and Graeme Swann to have some real fun together. They put on 108 for the eighth wicket in just 80 balls.

It was interesting that here Broad was at seven as we, in the absence of Flintoff, opted to play five bowlers. That is always a hot topic, and is usually entwined with the debate about whether I should bat at six or a place lower. Me? I'd like to bat five or maybe even four if I can. I've always wanted to bat as high as possible.

There is no difference for me personally between six and seven, and my record in Tests between the two is little different. As I write in early 2013, my Test average at six is 45.66 with one century (131 not out against West Indies in Trinidad in 2009) and at seven it is 46.06 with four hundreds (my debut 126 not out in 2007, 102 not out against Pakistan in 2010, 126 versus Sri Lanka at Lord's in 2011 and 103 not out against India at Lord's in 2011).

For me, the balance of the team is the most important thing. But what I will say is that often in England a fifth bowler simply does not bowl enough, so it is rarely worth playing him. Of course, Flintoff balanced the side neatly, as, say, do the great

Jacques Kallis for South Africa and Shane Watson for Australia, but those sorts of cricketers are obviously rare.

Anyway, Broady and Swanny call themselves the 'engine room'. I'm not sure I'm part of it as I haven't reached that high honour yet, but, all joking aside, they have made some vitally important runs over the years. The runs from that part of the order – I'm not going to call it the tail, that is for certain! – can often win matches. That was not the case here, but it was fun to watch as they clearly egged each other on.

Stuart Clark was hit for 16 in an over by Broady and then his next over was hit for 16 again, this time by Swanny. It was remarkable stuff – whatever one did, the other tried to match – but it had to come to an end, and it did. Broady made 61 off 49 balls and Swanny made 62 off 72 balls, but we were all out for 263 and lost by an innings and 80 runs. Ouch! It was as painful as a back spasm.

During and after the Test, I had received some texts from friends mentioning my ego. They were all in jest, but what they were referring to was a leaked dossier from Justin Langer, who was then still playing for Somerset, but had been asked to give his thoughts on the England team by the Australian management. It had been published by a Sunday newspaper during the Test. Apparently, among other things, Langer said that I have a 'massive ego'.

I didn't read the dossier. I know it caused a bit of a fuss, but it wasn't something I lost any sleep over. As I said earlier, in relation to all my initial problems in international cricket, it is important whose advice and whose opinion you listen to. That was not something I would take seriously or listen to. If my team-mates or my friends had started saying something like that, I might have listened to it, but otherwise it was just not something that concerned me. I had an Ashes decider to concentrate on. It was 1-1 with everything to play for at The Oval.

At the end of the Headingley match, Andrew Strauss's leadership had really shone through for me. Firstly, when he was given a grilling in the post-match presentation by Sky Sports' Mike Atherton, I thought he handled the questions with real calmness and clarity. That certainly rubbed off on me, and I'm sure it did on the rest of the team. It reassured me that we weren't about to make a load of changes to the team or that all hell would break loose ahead of The Oval. We'd had a bad game but it didn't make us a bad team. You talk about what makes a good leader and here in this situation I thought Straussy showed as much. It was the first time I thought: 'This bloke is really special when it comes to that side of leadership.'

As the last rites of the match had been enacted it had been terrible. It felt like everyone was thinking: 'That's it now. We've had it.' It was almost as if we were 3-0 down. That's how bad it felt. I felt so low. We were then told that we had to go back to the team hotel for a meeting. I think most of us just wanted to go home. But in truth and on reflection, it was the best thing that we could have done. In that meeting we collected all the negative stuff, all the crap, and dug a great big hole and shoved it all in. We left it knowing two things for certain: one, that we were going to cop a heap of criticism in the press and, two, we were going to be strong and stick together.

We admitted that we had got ahead of ourselves. That had been our biggest problem at Headingley. It hadn't been all the distractions on the morning of the match. It had been the fact that we were 1-0 up, with two Tests to play. We had been thinking about winning the Ashes. Win at Headingley and it would have been all over. We would have won the series. That's what we were thinking, and that is always dangerous.

I know the media get frustrated when we say things such as 'We'll take each ball as it comes' and 'The first session is the biggest', because they are such horrible clichés, but the truth is that is how you have to approach every game. Outcomes take care of themselves. We as professional sportspeople have to focus on the processes and the smallest details. We didn't do that at Headingley, and it was a huge lesson to us. Instead of going our separate ways, parting for a week and reading and hearing stuff about 'What direction should they go?' or 'Who should they pick?', we all knew.

We knew that Andrew Flintoff would return from injury. And we knew that, unfortunately, Ravi Bopara was also going to be left out. His form had gone, and he had made only one and nought at Leeds. In his place came Jonathan Trott, with it easily forgotten now that Trott was already in the squad for the Headingley match and was very disappointed to be left out when it was decided to play five bowlers rather than an extra batsman.

But still there was an amazing build-up to this match. It was going to be a Test in which dreams could come true. It was difficult not to recall 2005 and the feeling that series, and especially its climax at The Oval, had generated around the whole country. I remember thinking back then: 'Crikey! Imagine being on that open-top bus or being in that changing room when you have won the Ashes in England. What a fantastic feeling that would be and any cricketer in England would give a right arm for that.'

Now we were the ones with that opportunity, and it was hugely exciting. We just had to make sure that we did not get carried away. It was important to remember that the game never changes. It's still a game of cricket, it's still a ball coming down at you or you bowling at a batsman.

I'd watched the US PGA golf on TV before the match and it had struck a chord. I often try to look at other sports to see if there is a close correlation with cricket, and I could see it here. On television, they said the first day of the golf is about setting it up for the weekend. You can't win on the first day, but you can lose it. I thought that made a lot of sense and about how you can relate that to cricket. You can't win a Test on the first day, but you can go a long way towards losing it (just as we had at Headingley). Each shot is important. Each ball is important.

It was time to get on with it. So, on the first morning, I drove to the ground with Stuart Broad and he said: 'By the end of today we will have a fair idea of whether we are going to win the Ashes.' On the second day, I also drove to the ground with Broady, and he said exactly the same thing. And on the third day we drove together again and I think he said the same thing again (and again on the fourth), but I also think we knew the answer by then because on the second day he had produced one of the great Ashes spells to turn the match on its head.

We had won the toss, and it was a good toss to win, because it was a dry pitch that was always going to turn; however, Australia again did not play a spinner. They hadn't played one at Headingley either, where conditions rarely suit spin. But we were sure that Swann would have a heavy workload at The Oval. We had made 332. Ian Bell, now at three, with Bopara dropped and Trott making his debut from five, made 72, and Andrew Strauss 55. Trott scored 41 and looked very composed in his first innings before he was freakishly run out from short leg by Simon Katich.

When someone makes his debut, the question always asked beforehand is: 'How is he going to step up?' And, if he is a batsman, the next question is usually: 'How is he going to play the short ball?' Trotty had no problem on either of those fronts. He immediately came through with flying colours. His temperament was phenomenal, as evidenced by his calmly taking 12 balls to get off the mark. He wasn't fazed at all.

Because of all his mannerisms and rituals, he came into the game with a reputation as probably the most sledged player in county cricket, and I think that actually stood him in good stead. He was totally unaffected by everything that was going on around him. Once he goes into that little Trotty bubble, no one can get him out of it, and that is his greatest skill.

And Broady's greatest skill is that he can seize situations. That's what he did on the second afternoon after rain had extended the lunch break, which Australia had taken at 61 for nought. Bowling from the Vauxhall End, he roared in and exploited the uneven nature of the surface with some wonderfully aggressive bowling. In no time Australia were 93 for four. First, he had Shane Watson LBW. Then, the big wicket: Ricky Ponting was bowled off an inside edge. Next, Mike Hussey was LBW, too, and then finally Michael Clarke was caught at short extra cover by Trotty, placed specifically there for that purpose. Later, Broady would bowl Brad Haddin to complete his five-wicket haul. It was magical stuff, and Australia were all out for just 160.

We just had to bat well now. And, though we lost three early wickets, Straussy and Trotty batted magnificently, the skipper scoring 75 and Trotty making a century that announced him on the international stage. What a match in which to make your debut, and what a match in which to score a century!

We declared nine wickets down, setting Australia 546 to win. They were never going to get those runs, even if they did go comfortably to 80 without loss on the third evening. It was, unsurprisingly given the pitch, Graeme Swann who did the damage, taking four wickets, and there was even a run out for Andrew Flintoff (of Ponting no less) on his last day in Test cricket. Steve Harmison took three late wickets, too.

And for me there was a stumping off Swanny. I've got only 13 in my Test career (to the end of the series in New Zealand in early 2013, that is) and I can remember every single one of them, but this was special. I stumped Marcus North as he attempted a big sweep and his back leg dragged out just enough, and I could swivel and whip off the bails. North's foot was on the line. By the time he looked back, I was already off on a jig of celebration.

In my wicketkeeping career it was a huge moment. In that one act, I felt as if I was proving a point – both to myself and to all those watching. At last I felt that I belonged in the Test arena as a wicketkeeper. I felt that I had had a good series with the gloves, and that stumping was now confirming as much. I belonged. That's how I felt. It was again a result of the hard work I had done with Bruce French. We had been practising getting my hands back to the stumps quickly. It was work that was at times arduous. As I have already said about a lot of the work with Frenchy, there were times when I was thinking: 'Why I am doing this? What is this all about?' And then an incident like this occurs and you realise. The ball had turned and bounced, so I took it high and to my left and, because of all the work I'd done with Frenchy, I automatically brought my hands straight back to the stumps.

But you don't just take the bails off. You can't do that every time the batsman plays and misses. That would really annoy everyone. The game would grind to a halt. So it was only when I realised that North's boot was just – about an inch probably – out of his ground that I knew I had to whip the bails off quickly. But having stopped the motion, I now had to get my hands moving again. It was almost like one of those bad dreams, where you're telling your-self to move your hands but they just won't budge. I've watched replays of that stumping and it looks as if I just nonchalantly took the bails off, but I can tell you that inside my head it was a very different story. I was screaming to myself: 'Move your hands!' Of course, I eventually did and I knew North was out, because he still had not moved his foot.

I'd had my problems in the Caribbean the previous winter,

where I'd conceded 35 byes in an innings in Trinidad. But what I will say about that match in Trinidad is that the pitch was a stinker for keeping. It was keeping so low, and Amjad Khan was a little wild on debut too, that I reckon I would let through as many byes if I were to keep on that pitch now. At the time it was just assumed that I was a rubbish keeper. And it is forgotten that I was man of the match at the end of that game. I did score 131 not out and 61, after all.

Now, with that stumping, I felt that I had gone from just hoping to catch everything to someone who could make a half-chance out of nothing. I felt a change of attitude towards me after that stumping. I started getting some credit for my keeping.

Swanny picked up the final wicket as Alastair Cook took the catch from Mike Hussey at short leg, and the celebrations began. We had won the series 2-1. We had won the Ashes. We had regained the Ashes. It was some feeling. The Ashes had been everything I hoped and dreamed it would be.

There were some special moments afterwards. Firstly, our families came into the dressing room for an hour. It was wonderful and touching that they could share the moment. And then the Australians came in to share some beers with us. It was awesome. If I'm totally honest, I couldn't believe I was sitting there in the same dressing room as Ricky Ponting. I have always had the utmost respect for him, both as a batsman and as a competitor.

I'd seen just how fiercely competitive he was when I'd arrived for my second innings in this match. Marcus North had dismissed Straussy just before lunch and I arrived with three balls to go. The third of them I hit hard into the ground and it bounced up and hit Ponting, who was at silly point, straight in the mouth. It was a nasty blow and I heard it crunch as it hit him. 'You all right, mate?' I asked him. He looked at me hard, spat a load of blood out of his mouth and replied: 'F*** off!'

I was a little bit shocked, to be honest. But I just thought to myself: 'We are dealing with a very different animal here.' He was saying to me: 'We are in a battle here and I do not need anything whatsoever from you.' That's how he played his cricket. You weren't mates. You were out there to kill each other. There are certain players in the game who carry an aura and Ponting was definitely one of them. I just sat there in The Oval dressing room listening to him talking. It was really special. It showed the great thing about Test cricket. You can hate each other for five Tests, and then at the end of them you can have a beer. And what you realise then is that you are just normal blokes who are representing your countries and trying to win games of cricket. I discovered that Ben Hilfenhaus and Mitchell Johnson, two blokes I'd had a few digs with on the field, were two of the nicest people you could wish to meet. That is what Test cricket is about.

The only downside of that day and its aftermath? We didn't celebrate more. Yes, I know Andy Flower and Straussy, both being pretty reserved types anyway, were keen that there was no repeat of the excesses of 2005 with the open-top bus and the very public drunkenness of some of the team, but still.

As I said earlier, it is part of my philosophy that you work hard, then you play hard, and then if you win, you make sure you celebrate properly. And we didn't really do that here. Things were not helped by there being a one-day international fixture against Ireland in Belfast just four days after we'd finished (and remember that we finished a day early, too).

More popular was a trip to Wembley to watch England's footballers play Slovenia, which England won 2-1. We'd been invited as a squad, and it was only later we were told that we had been asked to do a lap of honour at half time, but the request had been turned down. A lap of honour at Wembley in front of all those people? You don't get a chance to do that too often. It was a little disappointing, to be honest. But not even a 6-1 drubbing in the subsequent one-day series could dampen the joy of my first Ashes experience.

7

A Broken Window
and Two Bricks

The summer of 2010 is not easily forgotten. It would be nice if it was remembered for our 3-1 Test series victory over Pakistan, with maybe a little mention for my 102 not out at Trent Bridge, but sadly it will be recalled only for the spot-fixing storm which erupted during the final Test at Lord's.

It came on 29 August on the fourth day of the Test when the now-defunct *News of the World* newspaper published its scoop about small details of the Test being fixed. It claimed that it had paid a middleman, Mazhar Majeed, for details of three no-balls that were subsequently bowled by Mohammad Amir and Mohammad Asif exactly as predicted. But I'd actually heard about the story the night before (the Saturday night at the end of the third day) when Stuart Broad sent me a text saying something like: 'Oh my God, the **** is about to hit the fan!' I texted back saying: 'What are you on about?' He then came round to my room to tell me what he had heard.

There was talk of the game being called off. But the truth is that none of us really knew what was going on. What we did know was that we all had a phone call telling us not to say a word if anyone from the media called us to ask about the story. I couldn't quite believe it. We were all totally shocked by the news. It was difficult to get our heads around the fact that this was happening in a game in which we were playing.

But I have to say that, in the back of your mind, you often see things on a cricket field and wonder for a second if there was something wrong with them. Any sport will throw up such incidents. So when Mohammad Amir bowled his one no-ball on the first day that was so far over the line that it was almost comical, we were actually joking in the dressing room that he might have got paid to do it and just made a whole lot of money. But it was no more than a bit of fun. However, it turned out that this wasn't funny at all, and in the *News of the World* there was an allegation that three no-balls had been bowled for money.

It was a horrible business, but in February 2011 an International Cricket Council tribunal found Amir, Asif and their captain Salman Butt guilty of spot-fixing, and banned them for five, seven and ten years respectively. Butt and Asif had five and two years suspended. Then in November 2011 at Southwark Crown Court in London all three players, along with Majeed, were jailed for terms of between two years eight months and six months.

However, on that Sunday morning, I felt really sorry for my buddy Broady. He'd just played the innings of his life, making his maiden first-class century and going on to finish with 169 (which beat his dad Chris's highest Test score of 162), having been involved in a world-record partnership of 332 with Jonathan Trott (184) for the eighth wicket. He had helped Trotty drag us out of real trouble after we had been 102 for seven. But now everyone was asking whether it actually meant anything.

Had their batting been devalued? It was so deflating for him, and for Trotty.

Despite what was in the morning papers, we still needed six wickets to win, and Pakistan duly slipped from 41 for four to 147 all out, for us to win by an innings and 225 runs. But it was the most unusual atmosphere that day. We weren't even sure whether we should play, but we did, and, understandably, I have never known a frostier atmosphere towards an opposition team. There was a huge amount of anger towards them for putting us in this position and also for what they had done to our great game, the damage they had caused. The truth is that we did not really want to be on the same pitch as the Pakistan team that day.

The overwhelming feeling was almost one of sadness. There we were playing a Test match at Lord's, the home of cricket; we were representing our country, but no one wanted to be there. Now that is sad. Graeme Swann ended with five for 62 in that second innings (to add to four for 12 in the first innings), taking four wickets on that morning, but it was one of the most hollow five-fors he will have ever taken. We couldn't even bring ourselves to celebrate each wicket. The after-match presentation had to be held inside, and we didn't know if it was appropriate to smile or clap. And we'd just won a Test series. It wasn't good.

Up until then it had been a really hard-fought series. With the ball moving around a lot on some pitches that helped the seam bowlers, it had not been an easy summer for batting. So I was pretty happy with the fact that I averaged 58.50 and was second in our averages to Trotty, who averaged 67.33. My century in the first Test at Nottingham was especially pleasing. We had been in a spot of bother at 72 for five when I came in, and then that became worse when Eoin Morgan, playing in just his third Test and having made 130 in the first innings, was run out.

I hate being involved in run outs. But anyone who has followed my career with a little bit of interest might know that already. I was, after all, involved in an incident at Lord's in 2011 during the second Test against Sri Lanka that attracted rather a lot of publicity. Yes, 'window-gate'!

It happened on the last day as we were looking to make a declaration, so we were looking to pick up every run possible. I was batting with Ian Bell, who was facing. He swept at left-arm spinner Rangana Herath and the ball just missed leg stump before cannoning off the pads of the wicketkeeper, Prasanna Jayawardena, who ran towards square leg to retrieve the ball. I thought there might have been a tight single there and called for one. But, in fairness, it was always going to be difficult for Belly to make it, because he was still down on one knee having played that sweep shot. So he sent me back and Jayawardena hit the stumps at the non-striker's end with a direct hit, and I was gone for four from two balls.

So I returned to the dressing room feeling very frustrated. As I said, I don't like being involved in run outs. I was in good form at the time (I had made a hundred in the first innings) and to be run out is always such a waste of an innings. I wasn't blaming Belly, for certain. It was my own fault.

When I got back to our dressing room, I wasn't in a huge rage, as some batsmen are when they get out, in whatever manner. But, yes, I was frustrated. At no stage did I think I was going to put a bat through a dressing-room window. I may have thrown gloves and shouted and screamed with the best of them when I have been out, but I would never have thought that I would put a bat through a window. It wasn't even as if I had been run out on 99 or anything like that. What happened was a complete accident, and there was no more or less to it than that.

Whenever I do Q&A sessions, I get asked about this incident a lot, and the problem is that the truth is rather less exciting than some people want to believe, so for a bit of fun I'll say something like: 'Yeah, I threw my bat through the window; I had Andy Flower in a headlock and kicked Andrew Strauss in the balls and then had a wrestle with the security manager.'

What really took place was that I walked into the dressing room and went to the spot where I always change, next to the window looking out onto the pitch, on the left as you go into the dressing room or on the right as you look in from the outside. My bats (I usually have four with me at any given time) are always placed on the ledge against the window – the one that is now always shown every time I get out at Lord's! So when I'm out, I always place my bat back there among the others. But this time I did fling my gloves into my bag first and then I slammed my bat down on the seat. I thought that was it. I had vented my frustration. Everyone now knew that I wasn't happy at being run out.

Then I went to put my bat down next to the others on the ledge. And I'll admit that I probably didn't put it down as gently as I might have done on another day. But it was only because I couldn't quite reach that I threw it a very short distance, rather than placing it down more carefully. What happened next was remarkable. Or so I'm told anyway, because I didn't actually see it. Apparently the bat bounced off the wall, and then went into the window. And it must have hit dead centre. The next thing I knew, the window had exploded and glass had gone everywhere. Talk about a shock. The shattering of glass can do that.

But now I was staring at big broken window, with pretty much everyone in the ground looking at me because it had made such a noise. I'd made a scene and I was thinking: 'Oh no, what are people going to say?' It didn't look good, obviously: run out, then a smashed window, but the problem was that people were putting two and two together and coming up with five, seven, nine and ten.

The first thing I saw was a replay on the dressing-room TV of

Straussy getting up from his seat on the balcony, looking across to see the damage and then shaking his head like a disappointed headmaster. Then I looked up to see Alastair Cook and Graeme Swann. Well, all I could see were their shoulders moving up and down as they were giggling so much. I still wasn't in the mood for laughing, though. I just sat in my seat with my head in my hands, not worrying about having been out now, but rather worrying about what was going to happen about the broken window.

My mood wasn't lightened either by the sight of MCC member after MCC member taking photos of the broken window with their mobile phones. I was about to kick off with a couple of them when I thought to myself: 'Hang on! You've probably caused enough trouble as it is.' At that moment, a dressing-room attendant appeared, complete with broom and dustpan, to clear up the mess. For some reason, it wasn't our usual guy and the poor chap obviously had no idea what was going on. 'Which window is it then?' he asked.

Well, that was it. Swanny and Cooky could contain themselves no longer. Their giggles turned into loud laughter, and soon the whole dressing room joined them. Even I could see the funny side now. Right in front of this bloke was the biggest hole you'll ever see in a window, and he was asking which window was broken!

I still felt stupid, though. We went out to field soon afterwards and every time I looked up at the pavilion during Sri Lanka's second innings (the match ended in a draw, by the way), I just saw this broken window. To make it worse, a young lady had been cut by the glass, and there was understandably a bit of an uproar among the MCC members sitting down below the dressing room. Straussy said that we should go down downstairs and apologise immediately, but I'll admit that I wasn't keen to do it then. Yes, I wanted to apologise, but I thought it would be better to do it at the end of the game. I wasn't sure about making such a big fuss while the game was still going on.

However, Straussy was adamant that we go immediately, and, as ever, he was right. So I went down with him and apologised profusely to everyone. And I'm glad to say that my apology was accepted. I specifically went to see the girl, who was with a doctor in the pavilion, to check that she was fine, and I think that I have just about been forgiven.

Not that it was quite the end of the matter, though. I was warned by the match referee, the former India seam bowler Javagal Srinath, because I had breached the International Cricket Council code that relates to the abuse of cricket equipment or fixtures and fittings during an international match. Luckily for me, though, Andy Flower had been in the dressing room when this happened and had seen everything clearly. I'm not sure he would have believed me if he hadn't seen it. He'll know what I mean by that. I'm only jesting. But because he had seen everything, he could back me up when we went to see Srinath.

'I was two metres away when it happened and there was no real malicious intent at all,' Andy said to the press later. 'Matt was a little frustrated and shoved his bat in the corner and it knocked around, bounced off one or two other bats, and then hit the pane of glass. It was a freak accident, but definitely an accident. It is not a major incident by any stretch of the imagination, and it is a shame that people will think anything other than that. If there was more to it, then of course it should be taken further. But there really is not.'

Thankfully, Srinath accepted our story. 'Matt knows that his action was in breach of the code,' he said. 'And he should be more careful in the future. That said, it was clear that the damage he caused was purely accidental and without malice. It is also noted that he apologised to the ground authority for the incident.'

Anyway the run out at Trent Bridge against Pakistan the previous year hadn't attracted the same amount of attention. And not just because it wasn't me who was run out. It was just another one of those silly bits of miscommunication. At the time, too many risky runs and singles weren't the best idea, but I didn't hear Eoin Morgan say yes, and he didn't hear me say no, and we ended up looking at each other, with him halfway down the wicket and me thinking: 'Oh my God, what has happened here? I've just run out our best player of the moment!' He had scored a century in the first innings, so it wasn't great timing.

I thought I'd best knuckle down. But by the time our ninth wicket fell, when Jimmy Anderson was caught behind off Shoaib Malik, I was still on only 63 not out. A century seemed a long way away. Steven Finn was our last man in, and I knew that he could block. I'd seen that the previous week when we'd met in a county championship match at Uxbridge. There, for Middlesex, he'd teamed up with Morgs, of all people, to bat for 12 overs to ensure that his side came away with a draw, eight wickets down. He faced 35 dot balls. That had been thoroughly annoying, but now I could use it to my advantage. As Finny came to the wicket I said something along the lines of: 'Same again today please, mate!'

And that's what he did. He did a fantastic job, facing 50 balls for his nine not out, so that I could reach my century. Those situations can be rather frustrating, as the fielding side often give the batsman an easy single from the first four balls of the over, and then try to pressurise him from the last two balls in the hope that he can be prevented from pinching a single. Then the tailender can be targeted the following over.

Finny was so confident that he could hold up an end that we started taking those singles from the early deliveries of an over. Obviously, I was trying to get twos or fours at the same time (or even sixes in the case of one over from leg-spinner Danish Kaneria when I hit two of them, one over long on and the other a sweep/slog over deep mid-wicket), but towards the end of my innings I wasn't quite hitting the gaps, and I didn't want to turn down the singles.

Those two sixes off Kaneria took me to 91, but from there to 99 I just dealt in singles. It got a bit frustrating, but eventually I cut Shoaib Malik's off spin down towards third man and I had made my third Test hundred. It was another special feeling. Andrew Strauss immediately declared, setting Pakistan 435 to win. They were all out for just 80, with Jimmy Anderson taking an incredible six for 17 off 15 overs.

We won the next Test at Birmingham by nine wickets, but we were not to have everything our own way in this series. Indeed, we had a serious blip in the third Test at The Oval, where we lost by four wickets after the debutant left-armer Wahab Riaz caused us huge problems on the first day, taking five wickets. We obviously hadn't seen him before and he took us by surprise, reducing us to 94 for seven, which is not the sort of score you ever expect when you've won the toss on what looked like a decent batting track. But as was often the case in that series, whenever the clouds rolled in, the ball swung around.

But Stuart Broad and I managed to put on 119 for the eighth wicket. I made 84 not out and Stu scored 48, which ended a pretty barren run for him with the bat and acted as the catalyst for his superb century at Lord's in the next Test. Even though he had made just 97 runs in 13 innings for England in all competitions that year up until then, Stu had been working very hard at his batting and he showed a huge amount of fight that day – as he always does. However, it was not enough, as we eventually lost the Test by four wickets as Pakistan chased down their target of 148.

I didn't play in the one-day series that followed the Tests, as Craig Kieswetter was preferred to me. Instead I went back to

Sussex and played a couple of games for them. One of them was a Clydesdale Bank40 match against Surrey at Hove and in the opposition was none other than Kevin Pietersen, who had been dropped from the England one-day squad and was playing four games on loan for Surrey.

This was quite a special match in many respects. In front of a healthy crowd of about 5,000, it ended up as a tie, after KP had made 116. But it was also an emotional ending for James Kirtley, who was playing his last game for Sussex after 16 years at the club. He'd had a fine career, taking 614 first-class wickets at 27.04, with 19 of those wickets coming for England when he played his four Tests in 2003. He also had to contend with doubts that were occasionally raised about his action, which would have broken a lesser man.

I also played another game at the end of that season, a county championship match against Northamptonshire at Hove, which we won by an innings, but there was a problem from my own view – I got a duck! No matter, Chris Nash got 169 and Yasir Arafat took nine wickets in the match.

Then, on 23 September, the day after the one-day team had beaten Pakistan by 121 runs at the Rose Bowl in Southampton to win the series 3-2, it was off to the Professional Cricketers' Association annual dinner, this time held at the Hurlingham Club. The whole England squad were there, but there was a twist for us. We had to be at Gatwick Airport the following morning for a 4.15am meeting at a hotel before a 6am flight. Guess what I did? Along with a few other lads, I decided that there was no point going to bed. I made sure that I enjoyed that PCA dinner to the full. But, looking back on it now, that turned out to be a really bad decision. What was I thinking?

We were told to bring our passports and little else, just a pair of hiking boots if anything. But it was all so vague. It was meant to be like that. There had been a lot of talk among the lads about this trip, with speculation rife about what it would entail. There were rumours that we were going to be dropped in the middle of the Amazon jungle or else that we would spending a week in Las Vegas doing some serious team-bonding! We looked at the flight times to try to work out where we might be going, and we'd come to the conclusion that we were not going too far, which ruled out Dubai, another option we had considered. In truth, we had no idea where we were going, and no idea either what we were going to be doing once we got there.

We soon discovered: we were flying to Munich. This was where the 2010-11 Ashes campaign began, with a five-day camp in the Bavarian forest. When we got to the car park at Munich airport, waiting for us were four big Mercedes mini-vans with their windows blacked out. That raised a few eyebrows for a start. Then, eight of the biggest blokes I have ever seen in my life got out of these vehicles. They were all dressed in full military gear.

The trip had been organised by our security adviser, Reg Dickason, the Australian with the walrus moustache who, along with his son Sam, has become such an important part of our back-up team. And we were later to discover that these huge, imposing men were members of the Australian police force.

At this stage, we were all still in high spirits. There was even talk that we might be going to the Munich Beerfest, which takes place around that time of year. Hadn't the Saracens rugby union team been there for some team bonding? But when we looked at these blokes, it seemed highly unlikely that they had a beer festival on their minds – they were sporting the sternest faces you could ever imagine. They just opened the doors and told us to get in. That was all they said. Then they drove us for about an hour and a half into the middle of the Bavarian forest near Nuremberg without saying a word. The guys sitting in the front of the vans tried to make some friendly conversation with them, but they got no response.

We eventually arrived and got out of the vans. Everyone was getting a little apprehensive by now. 'Did your driver say anything?' we asked each other – but the story was the same in all of the vans. Silence.

We were then told that we had ten minutes to get ourselves ready and that we should put everything we needed in a backpack that was given to us, along with the usual army kit such as utensils and a water carrier. They didn't give us any clue as to what we might require, or what we were going to do, mind. We were, however, told that we could not take phones, watches, cameras, money or even the sweets that some of the lads had brought with them.

There was still some banter flying around at this stage. But then one of the lads made a serious mistake. One of the instructors was talking to us, and he was interrupted. That was it. 'Get down and do fifty press-ups!' he screamed. So we all got down and started crunching out these press-ups.

We'd probably done about 20 each when he shouted at us to stop. He said: 'You've got a choice here. You can either carry on like that for a long, long time or you do fifty together all in unison.' So we started again, counting the press-ups as we did them. But then, when we'd got to about 30, one of the lads was really struggling and he swore loudly.

That was it again. 'Stop!' screamed the instructor. 'No swearing! Start again.'

Which is what we did. We were getting the message pretty quickly. This was not going to be fun. This was going to be hard-core military stuff. In that initial welcoming, I reckon we did 180 press-ups. And we hadn't even started! We now knew that we were in for five days of absolute hell. A group of pampered cricketers were about to be taken so far out of their comfort zones that they would not know what had hit them.

We were told that we could not call anyone by their nicknames. So I had to call my best mate Broady 'Mr Broad'. It wasn't too bad when I was concentrating on it, but the problem was that, when I was tired, that was the last thing I was thinking about. But the second any of the instructors heard a nickname, they would scream again: 'Get down and do press-ups!'

So, after all our press-ups, we began hiking. Now I've always thought of hiking as just walking. It's not hard, is it? Well, two hours later, we were still trudging through the forest, having already been up a few a nasty hills, and I was rapidly altering my opinion on that. When we got to the top of one hill, we were told to stop. We were told yet again to do more press-ups. I've never done so many of the damned things. Then we had to do burpees, then we had to hold our bags out in front of us for a minute or so, then we had to do sit-ups and then we had to do some squats. It was proper old-school fitness training, but it was really starting to hurt.

The silence was now intense. It wasn't just of the forest that was quiet, so was the group as well. All that early banter had dissipated very quickly. It was unbelievable. I would never have believed that people like Graeme Swann could be shut up like this. But he was. All you could hear was the heavy breathing of a group of blokes who were really hating life at this point. But we were just about to hate it a bit more. Up ahead of us we saw a huge hill, more of a mountain actually. 'We can't be going up there,' we all thought.

But, sure enough, we were. What an effort that was just to get to the top, with our bags on our backs and our arms and legs in bits from all the exercises we had been doing. Wondering what happened at the top? Yes, you guessed it. More press-ups, more burpees, more squats and more sit-ups. And more holding our bags out in front of us, where the minute we were supposed to do might become more like five minutes, because some of the guys couldn't do it and then we had to start all over again.

Once we'd finally completed all that, we were totally wasted. Then at last, relief was at hand as the instructors actually said to us: 'Good effort lads. Now you can go and get a drink.' This was exactly what we wanted to hear. We sat down and got our drinks. We needed that rest so badly. They'd taken us to the limit, and now that was going to be it for the day. It had to be. We had nothing left, and we began to relax.

Suddenly the shout rang out: 'Put your drinks down and get up. You've got two minutes. We've got something we need to do.'

What now? We all stood up and gathered ourselves together in silence. 'Unfortunately, we have left something at the bottom of the hill,' said one of the instructors. 'We need to go and get it.' Oh my God! We all wanted to shout and scream, but by now we knew that it was best not to. So we hiked back down to the bottom of the hill, wondering what on earth we had left behind, and rather fearing that whatever it was, we were bound to have to carry it back up the hill.

When we got there, we found another minibus waiting for us, doors open. We didn't know what to expect now, but knew better than to hope it would mean a lift to some more comfortable accommodation. It wasn't. 'Go into the van and go to the back and pick up two bricks each,' we were told.

Just when we thought things could get no worse, they did. It wasn't just that we were going to have to carry something up the hill, these bricks were going to be with us for the rest of the day. They were going to become part of us. We weren't allowed to carry them with our palms facing upwards, we had to do so with our palms facing downwards, which is much more difficult. We had to clasp them really hard just to keep them in our hands.

We then hiked for another two and a half hours with those things in our hands. Every so often we would stop to do more exercises, but this time with the bricks. So we would do shoulder presses with them, or more press-ups with them, or holding them out in front of us. I honestly cannot explain how bad it was. I have never had to dig deeper in my life. Any training session, any fitness session, anything I have ever done in a gym comes nowhere near how totally spent I felt after doing this. It was just incredibly painful.

I remember at the end of the day looking over at Andrew Strauss and Andy Flower when we were tucking into our army ration dinner (which was awful, but we were so hungry that we just smashed it up anyway – and we were doing ridiculous things like fighting over apples because we were so ravenous) and they were so broken. Flower looked at me and laughed. I said to him: 'You don't look happy, mate.' He was knackered.

But that was the good thing. All the management staff did all this physical stuff with us. I honestly think that if they had not done it with us – if, say, Flower and the other coaches had been riding alongside in minibuses – it would really have pushed buttons inside us. I think there might have been a mutiny. In that scenario, it would have done more damage than good. In fairness, all of them got stuck in. Phil Neale, our operations manager, who has always been keen on his fitness but was then in his late fifties, was trudging up those hills and doing really well.

We were in four different teams, with seven in each group. When we had finished our day, we had to build our own tents for the night. So we did that as quickly as we could because it was freezing cold. We got into our sleeping bags, and checked out the blisters that seemed to be everywhere on our bodies. We had just fallen asleep, or that's what it seemed like anyway, and then suddenly there was a commotion. 'You've got ten minutes! Get up!

Get up!' the instructors shouted. It was the middle of the night and it had started to rain. We were stranded in the middle of the Bavarian forest. It was so pitch-black, we could not see a thing. I didn't know where my boots were as I walked.

By this stage, we were petrified of these blokes. Whatever we were feeling about them, and it probably wasn't pleasant, there was no backchat whatsoever. We just did as we were told, and we set off hiking again. Then suddenly we stopped. We were told to put our arms out and after we'd done so, all we heard was this Aussie accent: 'It's nine am in Melbourne gents! I've heard that this team is going to win the Ashes,' he shouted. 'But I've seen **** all yet!' It seemed as though he was just abusing us for the sake of it. One instructor in particular seemed to relish shouting at us and making us work really hard. He would often wake us up in the middle of the night with his favourite phrase: 'Switch on, men!' That phrase would always scare us, because we knew then that something really tough was coming.

In matches since then, when things are getting tough in the field, you might hear one or more of the boys shouting out in a mock-Aussie twang: 'Switch on, men!' There will be knowing smiles all round and it would often galvanise the boys. A good example of that took place in the Trent Bridge Test against India in 2011. It's a game I have mentioned already in this book, for reasons which will become obvious in a moment.

We had been bowled out for 221, and on the second afternoon (on a Saturday because unusually this had been a Friday start) India were in a really strong position, with Rahul Dravid and Yuvraj Singh batting well and the score being about 260 for four. We were staring down the barrel at that point. Things just weren't going our way. India were looking at a huge first-innings lead that would have batted us out of the game. But out came the phrase: 'Switch on, men!' I can't remember who said it, but it certainly worked, because within moments Stuart Broad had got rid of Yuvraj and then taken an amazing hat-trick. With Tim Bresnan dismissing Dravid for a superb 117, India were suddenly 273 for nine and then 288 all out when Broady took the last wicket of Ishant Sharma.

The call had worked. Instead of our heads dropping and the game slipping out of our grasp, we had gone up a notch and turned the match on its head. Facing a much smaller deficit than anyone had ever imagined (especially India, no doubt) we then batted with real confidence, making 544 all out. Nearly everyone contributed, but the stand-out innings was that of Ian Bell, who made 159 (you may remember that this was the game in which he was given run out on the stroke of tea when he thought the ball had gone for four and was dead, but was then recalled by Mahendra Singh Dhoni after the break). Tim Bresnan made 90, I chipped in with 73, Eoin Morgan with 70 and Kevin Pietersen with 63. We ended up winning by 319 runs. We'd certainly switched on.

The fact that we all did it together really helped to draw together the squad. And the benefits of the trip did show on the field after that whenever we found ourselves in a tough situation. If it was a baking hot day and two opposition batsmen had put on 200 together without being parted, it was easy to think back to the trip and realise that what we were going through on the field was nothing really. It was certainly nothing compared with the hardship we endured in Germany, and we have often reminded each other of that.

In fact, it wasn't just hiking that we did in Germany, we also did some abseiling and even some boxing, too. But this was not a normal boxing match. It was actually what the military people call 'milling'. This does not involve the skills and ringcraft of boxing; you basically stand toe-to-toe for a minute and just keep throwing punches at each other. And of course there was a little bit extra, too. We were all stood in a big ring and everyone would have to get down and do ten press-ups. Then the two in the middle would have to jump up and start laying into each other. So we were doing ten press-ups for every bout. As I've said, I am a hard trainer and I always like to push myself, but during this trip I went to places I've never been before in my life. And I know that I wasn't alone in going to some pretty dark places.

At the end of it all, was the trip worth it? There are mixed views on this from the lads. Personally? If something like that is set up again, I will retire! I don't think I could do it again. It was that tough. What's more the trip did cause some controversy, because it emerged afterwards that James Anderson had cracked a rib while boxing with Chris Tremlett, and Trems also suffered bruised ribs. Mind you, it might have been worse. We heard that Joe Calzaghe, the former world champion boxer, had been due to come with us, but he pulled out at the last minute with food poisoning.

For a while, some newspapers reported that Jimmy might not be fit for the start of the Ashes, possibly even missing two Tests according to some of the reports. But fortunately, he had suffered only a small crack to his ribs and he was able to complete all the training in Germany, before realising when he got home that he was in such pain that an X-ray might be required.

We certainly had a really good team spirit before we went on that trip. It wasn't as if a great team spirit was discovered out there, but the key thing was that every single person completed every single challenge that was put in front of them. Whatever some said, we did come back from that trip as a really tight unit. People talk about shared hardship drawing you together, and this was an example of that. We definitely forged a bond because of what we had been through together. It just ticked boxes for me. It confirmed to me that, however tough the situation might get, we would stick together.

First-innings century-maker Eoin Morgan is run out against Pakistan in Nottingham in 2010 after some miscommunication between us. I knew I had to make amends. *(Phil Brown)*

Happily, I was able to walk off the ground at Trent Bridge after scoring an unbeaten century in what was a tough series for batsmen. *(Phil Brown)*

My first ball in
Ashes cricket in
Australia: not the
best of starts at the
Gabba, as Peter
Siddle set himself
up for a hat-trick.
(Getty Images)

The perfect Test?
Picking up an edge
from Simon Katich
off Graeme Swann
on the way to
England's stunning
innings victory at
the Adelaide Oval.
(Getty Images)

I wasn't happy with
Siddle's reaction
when he dismissed
me at Perth, and
we exchanged a few
words. Worst of all,
though, we lost the
Test. *(Getty Images)*

The final wicket. My catch to dismiss Ben Hilfenhaus ensured we retained the Ashes at Melbourne. Behind me, the Barmy Army get ready to go wild in celebration. *(Getty Images)*

On the way to my first Ashes century, at Sydney, as we won the Test by an innings. *(Phil Brown)*

The sign says it all: a 3-1 series victory in Australia, England's first win Down Under since 1986–87.

(Phil Brown)

The chance goes down. In someone else's kit, having just been called up to the England one-day side after the Ashes, I never felt quite right. *(Getty Images)*

Hitting out against Ireland in Bangalore in the World Cup of 2011. We lost that game, and were knocked out in the quarter-finals, as the team struggled to perform to its potential. *(Phil Brown)*

The 2,000th Test and the 100th against India, at Lord's – what better time to score a century? My mate Stuart Broad is on his way to congratulate me. *(Phil Brown)*

That number one feeling. The England squad celebrate on the balcony after we had beaten India in the third Test at Edgbaston, a result that meant we were officially ranked by the ICC as the best side in the world. *(Getty Images)*

Above: Tough at the top. Our next series – against Pakistan in the UAE – resulted in a 3-0 defeat, with our batsmen struggling to cope with their excellent spinners. *(Phil Brown)*

Left: I wasn't able to see much during the Edgbaston Test against West Indies in 2012, as I was suffering from conjunctivitis. *(Getty Images)*

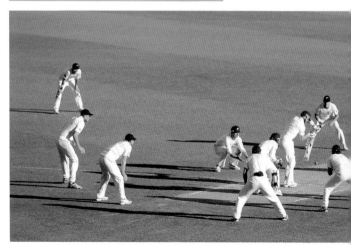

A year on from taking the number one spot, and we were battling South Africa to retain it. We soon found out just how hard the series would be, and they emerged worthy winners. *(Phil Brown)*

Our win in Mumbai, after losing the first Test, set us up for a famous series victory in India – the first for England since 1984–85. *(Phil Brown)*

I've rarely batted with a field like this around me, but my century to help save the Test and the series against New Zealand in March 2013 was a proud moment. *(Getty Images)*

With Emily in New York early in 2008. It was there that I learned I had been dropped from England – a huge blow. However, it did mean that we were able to get married sooner than expected.

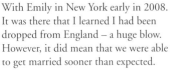

Proudly showing JJ my name on the honours board at the SCG, after we had secured our Ashes victory in 2010–11.

Recently, cycling has become a great passion of mine, and I love to ride through the Sussex countryside whenever possible.

(petewebb.com)

I took a huge amount from it individually. I didn't like it; it was disgusting. But, having done it, I found out that I could dig deeper than I'd ever believed I was capable of. I went back home and did the gym session that has been designed to really hurt me, and I absolutely cruised it. It wasn't because I was that much fitter, it was all down to my mentality – I knew that when I was hurting, I actually had another ten levels of pain to go to before I would have to stop and pull out. And, when we got back home after the Germany trip, we knew we had a month to spend at home before we left for Australia on 29 October. I felt that we were ready to take on the Ashes in the Australians' own turf.

8

Ashes Retained

We knew we had to be different. We knew that our mentality upon arrival in Australia for the 2010-11 Ashes had to be different from previous England teams. We had been talking about this before we set off; initially, we weren't discussing tactics or anything like that, we were considering what could happen to us in Australia on and off the field. For example, we even talked about what our attitude to Twitter should be, and how we should best deal with the media. That was the level of detail we were going into.

The most important thing we had to realise, however, was that there was nothing to be afraid of in Australia. Yes, the cricket was going to be tough, but we couldn't go there thinking things like: 'Oh my God, the taxi driver is going to sledge me, and the bloke in the lift is going to sledge me too.' If we did that, we were going to be defeated before we even started.

Something like that had happened when England teams had gone there in the past. They had been spooked by the hostility of the place. Certainly in 2006-07, it seemed to the England squad that the whole of Australia was determined to exact revenge for the 2005 Ashes defeat in England. Seven players in our touring party (Andrew Strauss, Alastair Cook, Kevin Pietersen, Paul Collingwood, Ian Bell, Monty Panesar and James Anderson) had been part of that 2006-07 tour, in which the Ashes had been lost 5-0. But fortunately they understood that that was just one bad experience. Many of them had been to Australia before and had absolutely loved the place. Of the others in the squad, Stuart Broad, Steve Davies, Chris Tremlett and I had been there as part of the Academy squad while that Ashes series was going on, and we had had a wonderful time.

We had other connections with the country: our bowling coach, David Saker, was Australian and he had played for Victoria. Andy Flower had played one season for South Australia. Straussy had lived in Australia as a child for a while and then returned to play grade cricket, while his wife is Australian. KP had once played grade cricket in Sydney. Belly and Cooky had both played in Perth, and Monty in South Australia. And Colly had done so well for the Richmond club in Victoria that he had won the famous Ryder Medal for the competition's player of the year.

So there were many more good experiences to be drawn upon than bad ones. When we thought about it, we realised what a phenomenal country Australia is. It has great restaurants, cold beer, brilliant golf courses and probably the best cricket pitches in the world for good cricket, given that there is always something in them for the bowlers, as well as loads of runs for the batsmen once they get in. And the whole country absolutely loves cricket. What more could you ask for? It is an unbelievable place to tour.

When we did eventually arrive in Perth to begin our preparations, we were pleasantly surprised by the reception we received. There was none of the abuse the 2006-07 players had talked about. Perhaps this was because Australia were struggling a bit. We had obviously beaten them in 2009 at home, then they had lost to India and now they were up against it in a one-day series against Sri Lanka. It meant that the locals were not so aggressive or as confident in their team's chances. Indeed, some even seemed to think that we were favourites to win the Ashes.

Not that we were lulled into any softness or complacency. We had some very definite and clear plans that we wanted to put in place, beginning with the three warm-up fixtures that we had before the first Test in Brisbane.

What had often happened in the past was that England sides would turn up for those games, have a hit, get used to the pitches and so on, but there wasn't much attention given to whether they won or lost. We had no interest in that. We decided that we wanted to play tough cricket in those games. They were all going to be proper 11-a-side matches, with none of this 14-a-side stuff to give everyone a go, and all the games were to have first-class status. There was no one-day match against the Prime Minister's XI to start the tour, as been the case in the past. It never made any sense in any case, playing a one-day match when you had your Test-match squad there.

We wanted to make an immediate statement. We could not go into the Test matches having lost any of those games, simply because they are just not games that you should lose. It is worth remembering that at the start of the tour, England had not won a match in whites in Australia since the last Test in 2003, which was only a consolation victory to make the series score 4-1. England hadn't won any warm-up games on that tour either, so you had to trawl all the way back to Cairns in 1998-99, when they just won by one wicket against Queensland, for the last warm-up victory in white clothing in Australia.

You could see why we wanted to win so desperately; we had to show our intent. We decided to make those games a series within the tour: it was a three-match series we had to win. It can be quite tricky to get results in three-day games on good pitches, but the first two matches (against Western Australia and South Australia) were three-day affairs, with the third match against Australia A being a four-day encounter. Despite this, we were still determined to do everything we could to ensure that we won those matches.

For the first match we picked what we thought would be the team for the first Test, as indeed turned out to be the case: Strauss, Cook, Trott, Pietersen, Collingwood, Bell, Prior, Broad, Swann, Anderson and Finn. Understandably there was some rustiness, especially when we made 223 for eight in our first-innings reply. It can be difficult to get out of net mode sometimes, and we were a little slow in doing that. We had talked a lot about adjusting to the different conditions, and how you have to be a little more patient in your stroke-play than in England, not driving at balls too early in your innings, for instance.

If our batsmen weren't quite right, the bowlers began really well, reducing Western Australia to 242 for eight before they declared at the end of the first day, with Broady looking as good as he had in the quick and bouncy nets at the WACA ground in Perth. Ah, those nets! There is nowhere like them in the world. The ball just flies through. And to make it worse, there are advertising hoardings situated on the netting right behind you as a batsman, so that when you leave the ball it thuds against them, making the sort of noise as if the ball has hit it at 120mph. You just feel so hemmed in. So, given all of that, it was no real surprise when Swanny got hit on the hand. Thankfully, nothing was broken because the rest of the series might have been very different had he not been playing.

When we returned there for the third Test later in the tour, the net session was even more intensive. Not only did we have all the fast-bowling members of the Test party roaring in, because Broady was by then injured and there was a place up for grabs, but also all the bowlers from the Performance Programme that winter. They were also all very keen to make an impression, and it was only afterwards that we discovered that their bowling coach, Richard Johnson, the former Middlesex, Somerset and England seamer, had told them all to tear in at us. He had said: 'Don't just come here and bowl half-volleys at these lads. Show them what you can do, and show the coach. Go hard at them.'

The likes of Liam Plunkett, Maurice Chambers, Chris Woakes and Jade Dernbach all bowled exceptionally fast. And at the end of the session one of the team management came up to me and said: 'I have no idea how we have not had casualties there.' I have never seen batsmen coming out of a net session and being so mentally tired. That is how you want training to be, but that was as frightening a net session as you are ever going to get.

Despite having scored our runs quickly, it looked like it was going to be hard to force a result when the home side began the final day on 109 for one. But Steven Finn made the breakthrough and Western Australia lost their last nine wickets for just 93, with Swanny picking up four of them. We needed 243 to win and Straussy set a great example by making an unbeaten 120 for us to win by six wickets, with only a few overs left. Apparently, it was the first time an England touring team had won their opening first-class match of the tour since 1965-66 when M.J.K.Smith's side also beat Western Australia.

We had enjoyed Perth. This was the first tour I had been on where we were allowed to take golf clubs with us. We had played at Royal Perth on our very first day on tour, and I partnered Jimmy Anderson against Straussy and Colly. Even that was competitive. It always is, and it always was throughout the tour.

We then moved on to Adelaide for the second match of the tour against South Australia. This match was important for Alastair

Cook, who made an unbeaten 111 in the second innings. Given what he has done in recent times, it is incredible to look back now and realise that he was actually under a little bit of pressure then (more from the media than within the team, of course). He had had a difficult time during the summer of 2010, when he had struggled against Pakistan before getting a hundred in the third Test at The Oval, which silenced a few critics who were suggesting that he might not even make the Ashes tour party. Then, in the first tour match, he had been out for single figures in both innings, so again this was a timely innings. And, of course, it was going to be the beginning of something really special.

Straussy also made a century to add to the one he had made in the first match, but we could not force a victory on what was a very flat pitch. In that respect, our bowlers did exceptionally well to bowl out South Australia for 221 in their first innings, with Swanny taking four wickets again and Jimmy Anderson chipping in with three. Me? I was happy to get a little 22 not out in this match, having made a fourth-ball duck in the first match. Just as importantly, I felt that I was keeping well. I grabbed a stumping in the first match off Swanny and was getting used to the conditions. The carry from the pitches suits me, as you can stand further back than in England and you don't have to contend with the wobble after the ball has passed the bat.

I was really looking forward to keeping in the Tests. In fact, I remember doing an interview in which I said as much, even if I was a little concerned about saying that – you always worry that this game of cricket can kick you up the backside, so I tend to be wary of making big comments. But I said: 'I'm a bit nervous saying this, but Australia for a keeper is quite a nice place to come. The challenges are getting used to the heat again and making sure you are fit enough to give the energy you want to give as a wicket-keeper and the engine room of the fielding side.'

Our last warm-up match was against Australia A in Hobart, but whereas we had fielded our full-strength side up until now – and that was particularly harsh on reserve batsman Eoin Morgan, who had finished the previous summer in the Test side but now found himself on the sidelines throughout these games – we now did something slightly different. It was decided that the first-choice bowling attack of Anderson, Broad, Finn and Swann should go to Brisbane to get ready for the first Test.

It was a good idea. The conditions in Brisbane, with its heat and humidity, are very different from those in Hobart and it gave us a good chance to demonstrate our strength in depth in the bowling, with also half an eye on the fact that we would not be using the same attack throughout the series. So in Hobart we went in with an attack of Chris Tremlett, Tim Bresnan, Ajmal Shahzad and Monty Panesar. It was still an excellent line-up, and they really showed that, and much more, in this match. The match was shown live on TV, in Australia and England, and we hammered Australia A by ten wickets. Ian Bell made a superb 192, and all the bowlers bowled excellently, with Trem looking especially danger-ous, taking seven wickets in the match, while Bres took six in the game, Ajmal grabbed three in the first innings and Monty three in the second. There was even a stunning catch from Monty, diving to catch Ed Cowan one-handed at mid-wicket off Bres.

The boys were on fire. It was time for some real Ashes and a visit to the 'Gabbatoir', as the Australians like to call the Gabba in Brisbane. And, to be honest, it was a fair enough name; England usually got slaughtered there. The statistics were there for everyone to see. No side had beaten Australia in 22 Tests there since the great West Indies team in 1988. England had not won there since 1986, when they last had won the Ashes in Australia, and had done so on just four occasions. It seemed as if England always went into the second Test of every series 1-0 down after a defeat at the Gabba. That's what had usually happened in recent times (although they did draw there in 1998-99). It was part and parcel of playing Test cricket for England in Australia.

We had to change that. We had done our preparation, and we had talked a lot about how we had to adapt to each pitch we came across during the tour. They were going to vary a lot, as they do in Australia, and we had to be aware of that and make sure we adapted accordingly.

The Gabba was going to be quick and bouncy, we thought, so we had to think about what shots we could play. As with all Australian pitches, we knew we had to get ourselves in first. Everyone is vulnerable early in their innings, but it is even more true in Australia. You really do have to work hard for those first ten runs. On the flip side, the bowlers had also talked a lot about the lengths they were going to bowl. And our analyst Nathan Leamon had done a presentation to us on the strengths and weaknesses of all the Australia batsmen.

Every base had been covered. We'd won that mini-series in the warm-ups 2-0, there had been lots of uncertainty about the Australia team (they had initially announced a squad of 17, which sounded like the sort of thing England used to do in the bad, old days when the side changed frequently), while we were certain about our line-up. We were ready. I was ready.

But on the very last day of practice, on the day before the first Test began at the Gabba on 25 November, I had a wobble. I'd been keeping so well on the tour up until then. I'd been catching the ball as well as I've ever done in my life. I was moving really well. My feet felt good, and so did my hands. My keeping preparation simply couldn't have gone better. Bruce French was delighted with the way I was looking. He thought we were good to go.

And then, on that day before the Test, I suddenly couldn't catch a cold. Nothing felt right. My gloves didn't feel as if they were mine, my legs felt heavy. 'Bruce, I've gone,' I said. 'What's happened? I've lost it.' What a time for it to happen. It was just incredible. But all it was really was a build-up of the pressure and anxiety around what was going to happen the following day. It was an indication of how much this match meant. Yes, I had a shocker at practice, but by the time I got back to my room afterwards I had calmed down. I looked in the mirror and gave myself a bit of a talking to.

I just likened the experience to that nightmare most cricketers have. It is the one where you are next in to bat and you just can't get ready in time. You might be naked in the dressing room when the wicket falls, or you might not be able to get your pads on in time, or you simply can't find your batting gloves. Most cricketers talk about these experiences, but you always wake up and everything is fine. That was what I was doing when I went back to my hotel room that evening in Brisbane. Everything was going to be fine. Of course, it was.

We arrived at the ground in good shape. What to do first, though, if we won the toss? Nasser Hussain had inserted Australia in 2002-03 and watched them rack up 492. The tone of the first day of an Ashes series can mean so much. For that, you only have to recall Steve Harmison's first ball of the series in 2006-07, which went straight to Andrew Flintoff at second slip.

This didn't look a straightforward decision, though. There was some green in the pitch. If the ball was going to do anything, it probably would do so on the first morning. But after quite a lot of consideration, Andrew Strauss decided that he was going to bat, if we did win the toss. And we did win that toss. I was happy with that. I could relax for a while.

Then what happens? Straussy cuts the third ball of the game, from Ben Hilfenhaus, straight to Mike Hussey in the gully. 'Oh, no. Here we go,' I thought. 'I'd better switch on.' I didn't have to put my pads on immediately, of course, as I was batting at seven, but it just gave me a sharp reminder of how competitive Ashes cricket can be and how there was going to be a such a tough time ahead.

That first day proved to be a real battle for our top-order bats-men, with the ball moving around just enough to make things difficult. Jonathan Trott made 29 and Kevin Pietersen 43, and all the while Alastair Cook was going along nicely. I sat there waiting to bat, feeling nervous. You have to be, and I always am, but I felt confident. I hadn't got a huge amount of runs in the warm-up matches, but I had felt in decent enough nick. Then suddenly Cook was gone, caught at slip off Peter Siddle for 67.

This was it, my first Ashes innings in Australia. I walked out, and immediately the noise struck me. It was so loud. But I blanked that out and went through my usual routine. I took middle-stump guard, and looked around the field. I told myself to watch the ball as Siddle came charging in.

I did watch the ball. It was full, and it was straight. It is always a decent combination for a bowler to give to a batsman facing his first ball. The next thing I knew my stumps were everywhere. Bowled first ball in the first Test of an Ashes series. What a start! What a horror story! Unsurprisingly the noise was even louder as I departed. I couldn't work out how I had missed it. To this day I don't really know how I missed it, but off I trudged for a first-ball duck. This was not good.

I don't think my mate Broady was even ready. He was probably living that nightmare I just mentioned. First-ballers tend to do that. But out he went eventually. And as I was coming to terms with my duck in the dressing room, I heard the deafening roar. It could mean only one thing. Siddle had got a hat-trick.

And he had. The first ball to Broady had been full and straight, too. It had hit him on the boot rather than bowled him, but umpire Aleem Dar had had no hesitation in raising his finger for LBW. Stu had reviewed the decision, but he'd had no luck. He was gone, and Siddle had been given a rather nice birthday present. Yes, it really was his birthday that day. It was a shattering blow for us, but you can look back and realise what a moment that was in Ashes history.

There was a funny ending to this story. As I have mentioned earlier, Broady and I always sit next to each other in the dressing room, and that was no different here for this match. On our bench it went Broady, myself and then Straussy. At the end of the day, after we had been bowled out for 260, we sat there looking at each other and it was Straussy who said it: 'Not a great day for this bench!' Yes, sitting there were three ducks in a row. And we all had a chuckle about it. 'When I was lying in my bed last night that was not what I saw happening today,' I said.

The fine margins in the game were no better illustrated than by Mike Hussey in this game. He had been under a lot of pressure for his place, and it was probably only because he made a century for Western Australia in their Sheffield Shield match against Victoria just before the Test that he was selected, firstly in the squad that was slimmed down to 13 players and then in the final team. It seemed quite a bold decision to pick him at that stage.

When he came in to bat in Australia's first innings with the score at 100 for three, he would have felt that pressure. His first ball was from Steven Finn and he edged it. Unfortunately, the ball fell just short of Graeme Swann at second slip – he was inches away from being out. I often wonder what might have happened had Swanny been standing just a tiny bit closer and had caught that ball. Would Hussey have been dropped (from the side, rather than by Swanny!)? How would the series have panned out then? Indeed, how would that game have turned out?

As it was, Hussey certainly made the most of his slice of fortune. He batted really positively, especially against Swanny, whom he knows well from their days at Northamptonshire together, going down the pitch to hit him over the top and then using the increasing slowness of the pitch to go back on his stumps and pull him. He made 195, which was actually his second successive Ashes century after he had scored 121 when we won at The Oval in 2009, and by the end of the series he topped Australia's averages with 570 runs at an average of 63.33.

In partnership with Brad Haddin, he put Australia in charge of the game here in Brisbane. Haddin made 136 as they put on a massive 307 partnership, which was then the highest for any wicket in a Test at the Gabba. Little did we know that record would last only a couple of days. As I mentioned earlier, when describing the spell of bowling by Jimmy Anderson and Stuart Broad on the third morning of this match as the second-best spell of bowling I have ever kept to, second only to Andrew Flintoff's at Lord's in the Ashes Test of 2009, Hussey and Haddin had some luck. But they rode it and it meant that Australia finished with 481, a lead of 221. But, crucially, we had finished their innings well, with Steven Finn mopping up the tail, with some hostile short-pitched stuff that helped him to figures of six for 125.

Furthermore, we had kept going. Our energy levels never dipped. At tea on the third day, Australia were 436 for five, with Hussey on 176 and Haddin on 134. During that break, one of the boys put on some ridiculous tune – it was called the 'Time (Dirty Bit)' by the Black Eyed Peas I think – but it was quite uplifting. So we pumped it on at full blast and as the bell went for us to return to the field, we were all bouncing around and laughing and joking. I can remember looking at Huss and Hadds as they waited to go out, and I could imagine them thinking: 'What are these blokes like? They should be knackered. They should be out of it.' But we weren't.

I honestly think it made a huge statement. We weren't going to sit down and die. And that has always been one of the most important attributes of this England cricket team. But still when we batted, starting our second innings so many runs behind and with so much time left to bat (we began our innings with 15 overs remaining on that third day), anyone who has played cricket knows that all you can do in that situation is just give it a good shot. You try to bat long and hope you can maybe get a 150 lead and see what happens from there. You just never know.

That spell on the third evening was obviously going to be challenging. And we very nearly lost our captain to the first ball of the innings. Straussy padded up to an inswinger from Ben Hilfenhaus, and there was a huge appeal. Umpire Aleem Dar said not out, but the Australians decided to review the decision, and thankfully the ball was shown to be going just over the stumps. It was a huge moment. To have lost him for a pair in the match would have been a massive blow.

But he survived that evening and so did Alastair Cook. The next day they did rather more than survive; they just batted and batted, as the pitch became flatter and flatter. They put on 188 before Straussy was out for 110. But there was more, because Cooky and Jonathan Trott then put on another 329 unbroken runs so that we ended our innings just before tea on the fifth day at 517 for one. Hussey and Haddin's record at the Gabba had gone and Cooky ended with a mammoth 235 not out, while Trotty weighed in with 135 not out.

It was just incredible. Afterwards, our batting coach Graham Gooch went up to the scoreboard and took a photograph of it and said: 'That's what every scoreboard should look like!' I replied: 'Yeah, as long as we aren't fielding!'

I've never experienced anything quite like it. It is such a long time to bat and save the game. Even when we got to 300 for one, it was still only a small lead. It was such a long way to safety. There was a group of us who just lay in the dressing room, not daring to move from our spots, because that would obviously mean that we lost a wicket. And we lay there for two days. When we lost a wicket, and it was only the one, when Straussy was out stumped off the off-spin of Marcus North during the afternoon session of the fourth day, we did think for a minute: 'Here we go. We'll have to be careful here.' But there was no need to worry – Trotty just went out and carried it on. To this day I still abuse Straussy for getting out. He should never have got out. He could have still been batting now.

Declaring and having a bowl at them for 26 overs at the end of the match was also another big statement. To be able to be safe enough to know that they couldn't get the 297 runs they required was a huge boost to us. To be able to walk out there, with hardly any Australian supporters left in the ground and with the Barmy Army singing their heads off, was a great feeling. We were actually putting pressure back on them as we tried to dent a few of their batsmen's confidence by dismissing them cheaply. And we did manage to get rid of Simon Katich for just four. That must have hurt them a lot.

We had escaped from the Gabbatoir with a draw. We were going into the second Test at Adelaide with the series still at 0-0. We were settled and going to pick the same side. It was Australia who were going to make the changes, dropping Mitchell Johnson and Ben Hilfenhaus and replacing them with Doug Bollinger and Ryan Harris.

It was a flat pitch. It usually is in Adelaide, and it usually turns late on, so it was obviously a toss you wanted to win. We were going to bat first, and that's what Ricky Ponting did when he won the toss. It would have been so easy to have been downhearted. It was a boiling hot day, too, with barely a cloud in the sky. And we all know that fast bowlers are temperamental by nature. Any toss you lose, they are not happy. They're often not happy if you win it and the pitch is a dirty green seamer on which they are bound to pick up wickets. But there was something different about this day. I remember finishing my warm-up and going into the dressing rooms. Broad and Anderson were remarkably upbeat.

Broady came up to me and said: 'If we can just get three wickets. If we can have them two hundred and fifty for three at the end of the day, maybe two hundred and eighty at tops, then we will have done well.' He was spot on. It wasn't about taking lots of wickets, or expecting to bowl them out quickly. It was about patience, about trying to control the day. That had to be our mindset.

Our attitude was really positive; we almost took energy from losing the toss. And that was backed up by our analyst Nathan Leamon, who had suggested to us that batting second at Adelaide wasn't that bad an option anyway. Usually both sides post a big first-innings total there, so, with time running out, it can often put pressure on the team batting third to force the pace and set up a game. That can often go horribly wrong.

So it's amazing what you can get when you are in such a positive frame of mind. And we got one of the most remarkable starts to a Test match you could ever imagine. The first thing to say was that the ball swung immediately for Jimmy Anderson, as he opened up to Shane Watson (so much for all the talk before the series that Jimmy couldn't use a Kookaburra ball). Then, from the fourth ball, came a bonus that we just hadn't expected. Simon Katich was run out by Jonathan Trott without facing.

There was a huge LBW appeal against Watson, and the ball ran away into the leg side. There was probably a single there if they had both gone straight away, but we knew that Watson and Katich were not a good running partnership. There was much confusion, so Trotty had plenty of time to set himself and hit the one stump he had to aim at from square leg.

I've never seen a bloke celebrate like Trotty did there. He ran for miles. I chased him for a little bit but gave up because I thought I'd better save my legs. It was a fantastic moment, which set the tone for the day. Trotty hasn't ever necessarily been one of our stand-out fielders, but he has always worked extremely hard and that direct hit just showed the value of that work.

It highlighted the work we put in on the training ground and in the gym. A lot has been said over the years about the size of our backroom staff, but if you want people to perform at a certain level, you need people to be thorough and precise. You need people in those roles who are looking specifically at low catches or hitting the stumps because those fine margins can be crucial. Take a bow Richard Halsall, our fielding coach.

But however hard you work, sometimes you still need that little bit of luck. Little things like that do change games, and when it's meant to be, they go your way. It was amazing that when we lost our number one world ranking in 2012, none of those little things seemed to go our way. You don't want to put everything down to luck or fate or whatever, because you have to be in control of a lot of things too, but it does play its part, of that there can be no doubt.

In came Ricky Ponting in his 150th Test. And, as Jimmy was about to run in to bowl, Andrew Strauss decided something was not quite right. He said to me and the rest of the slip cordon: 'Let's take it on a bit because it might not carry.' So we moved forward a yard. It was a vital yard. Ponting edged his first ball – a beauty it has to be said – low to Graeme Swann's left at second slip. It was a great catch as he dived in front of Straussy. Ponting was gone and Australia were nought for two, or two for nought as they say down there, in the first over.

Astonishingly, it then got even better for us. Michael Clarke had come to the wicket under some pressure in terms of his form. Given the match situation, he tried to begin his innings very positively. He had a big swish at Stuart Broad's first ball and then was in some trouble against a short ball from the same bowler. We sensed an opportunity here. With the first ball of his second over, Jimmy dismissed him, again caught at second slip by Swanny, as Clarke looked to drive a lovely outswinger. It was three for two or two for three. Whichever way round, it didn't look very good for Australia. For us it was heaven. We simply couldn't have dreamed of a better start to the Test.

In fact, it could have been even better, actually. There was a close LBW appeal on Watson that was reviewed, but was not overturned, and also Jimmy dropped a difficult caught-and-bowled chance off Mike Hussey when he'd made just three. Somehow they managed to get through to lunch at 40 for three, but the damage had been done. They were eventually bowled out just before the close of play for 245, with Jimmy taking four wickets. We had to face just one over, in which there were no alarms. We'd said 250 for three might be nice by the end of the day, but 245 all out? Wow.

In a situation like that, it would have been easy to relax and think the job was already done. Our batsmen were having none of that. They knew that there was still a lot of work to do, and that they had to bat long in order to score the runs needed for a substantial lead. Straussy may have gone early, but the rest just piled on the runs. By the end of day, we were 317 for two. Cooky merely carried on from where he had left off at Brisbane, making 148, and then there was an extraordinary innings of 227 from Kevin Pietersen. It was his second Test double-hundred, and his first Test century for 21 months. But he played as only KP can. By the end he was just taking the Australian attack apart.

We declared at 620 for five on the fourth morning. We had been a little unsure whether to continue batting that morning, especially because there was rain forecast for the last afternoon, but we decided to have a bit of a thrash so that there was no way, in the event of their batting really well, that Australia could get far enough ahead of us to put us under pressure. So we hit 69 runs in nine overs and then set about our work to bowl them out for a second time.

We didn't expect it to be easy, and it wasn't. By the end of day four, they were 238 for four with Mike Hussey, by now a serious thorn in our side, on 44 not out. And they were only four wickets down because KP sensationally took a wicket with what turned out to be the last ball of the day.

It was an interesting decision by Straussy to bring on KP. Swanny had been bowling excellently, but he did look a little tired. KP is a good off-spinner. He is tall and he gives the ball a rip. The ball he bowled to Michael Clarke was short of a length. Had Clarke not been playing for the close, he might well have gone right back in his crease and pulled it away for four. But because he was conscious of not doing anything too rash, and he wanted to be there on the last morning to help his side try to save the game (especially as he was on 80 at the time), he just looked to tickle the ball away on the leg side for a single. But it bounced and turned, and Clarke could only inside edge it onto his thigh pad and away to Cooky at short leg.

Clarke looked as if he was about to walk off. He actually took a few steps towards the dressing room, but then he appeared to realise that umpire Tony Hill was not going to give him out, so he stood his ground. You obviously start to worry then. Yes, there is the Decision Review System to fall back on, but will it show the edge? Well, there was only one way to find out. We reviewed the decision instantly. Surely it would show the edge. It was obvious, wasn't it? It was. It showed up immediately. It was a huge moment that gave us such a boost as we prepared for a tense final day, with Australia still requiring 137 runs to make us bat again.

There was a lot of talk about the weather on that final day. The forecast was still not good. Everyone seemed to be checking their iPads for weather radars, and there seemed a general consensus that there was a storm that was going to come in during the afternoon. When exactly in the afternoon it was going to come, no one was sure. We would have to crack on and finish the job as early as we could.

To make matters more difficult, we would have to do that without Broady. He had pulled up with an injury to his side during the fourth day. He had gone off and it became clear very quickly that it was a serious injury for a bowler – there was some hideous bruising around his rib cage. His tour was over (and so, too, in the opposition was Simon Katich's because of an Achilles' tendon injury).

I was absolutely gutted for Stu. As I've said before, he is my biggest mate in the side, and the way he had been bowling had been fantastic. He had hit the gloves hard, he had been bowling in difficult areas, and he had really been the bowler who had put the batsmen under a lot of pressure. That he had taken only two wickets in the two matches he played was hugely unfair. He would have bowled worse in the past and taken a lot more wickets. The shame is he was probably an innings away from taking a bundle. But bowlers work in partnerships and I do believe the performances he had put in allowed others to get wickets. He hit a great length throughout those two Tests and in the warm-up matches he played. The wickets suited him from the very first net session in Perth, when we knew that he was going to be a real handful.

We got a great start on that last morning in Adelaide, though, when Hussey pulled Steven Finn to mid on. It was an uncharac-teristically loose shot from Huss, but it was just the boost we needed. As I said, we had been having real problems getting him out. From there, it was the Swanny and Jimmy show. And I'm not talking about their video diaries (mainly featuring Swanny appar-ently, although I must admit that I did not actually watch any of them) which attracted so much attention during the trip.

Firstly Jimmy took two wickets in two balls, when Haddin edged a catch to me and then when Ryan Harris was LBW padding up for a king pair in the game (two first-ballers, in case you're wondering). Then Swanny took three wickets to wrap up the match and finish with figures of 41.1-12-91-5. We needed a review to get rid of Marcus North, but by now Straussy, Swanny and I were pretty good at judging what was out and what was not. Or rather, as I said, earlier, Straussy and I were getting good at telling Swanny what was out, because he thinks that absolutely everything is stone dead.

Xavier Doherty and Peter Siddle were both bowled and we could start celebrating. We had won by an innings and 71 runs. We were 1-0 up in the series, and we had just about avoided the rain. Our victory came at 11.27am and only a couple of hours later, the River Torrens that runs just behind the ground was bursting its banks, so hard did it rain in such a short period of time. Apparently, it was Adelaide's wettest December day ever. Lucky, lucky England. Not that we worried too much about the rain, as we celebrated long and hard in the dressing rooms until about 6pm.

A lot of people said that we had played the 'perfect Test' having lost the toss, and it is hard to disagree. Indeed, that *is* what Andy Flower said, and I never disagree with him! At the time, that last day was probably the proudest moment for me on a cricket pitch. And it wasn't necessarily because my own performances had stood out. I thought that I'd kept well – I dropped a chance from Hussey off Swanny on that last morning, but it was a tough one with the ball spitting at Hussey – and that I'd kept the team going well. But it was just the fact that it was such a fine team performance that made me so proud.

I remember thinking at the end of the match: 'I haven't even had a proper bat in this series yet.' And I hadn't. I'd got that first-ball duck in Brisbane, and then here in Adelaide I'd just gone in to slog a few at the death, making 27 not out from 21 balls. It felt quite strange but, don't get me wrong, I loved it. It just showed how well the boys were batting at the top, or how they were 'backing up the truck at the front' as I sometimes say.

There was now a respite from the Test series, as we travelled to Melbourne for a three-day match against Victoria. Not that the hype surrounding the Ashes was going to go away. After Australia's loss in Adelaide, all sorts of comments were made about the team and their performance, but the ones we found quite hilarious were the calls for Shane Warne to come out of retirement and save his country. I've recorded my total respect for Warne already in this book, but this did seem rather far-fetched, especially as Warne was very busy with TV commitments, whether commentating on the Tests or hosting his own show, where he interviewed a series of celebrities.

But that didn't stop the questions being asked when I did a press conference in between Tests. What could I say? 'Whoever comes into the Australian team, we'll have to look at it and see how we're going to play against them – whether it be Shane Warne, Merv Hughes or anyone else. We'd respect them like any other cricketer.' That's what I said. I could have mentioned Sir Don Bradman, but that might have been really taking the mick, I suppose.

Anyway, in the match against Victoria I did not keep wicket;

Steven Davies did. I just wanted to try to get some batting practice. I didn't get a bat in the first innings, but I did manage to get
an unbeaten hundred in the second innings, batting at four. I
must have impressed the Victorian management, because negoti-
ations began for me to play for their Twenty20 side, the Victoria
Bushrangers, in the Big Bash tournament after the Ashes had
finished.

Despite that, the truth is that the match was a bit of an incon-
venience for most of the guys, and it was not really much
preparation for the third Test in Perth because the drop-in pitch at
the MCG was horrendously low and slow. It is not like that in
Perth, and so the shoot-out for Broady's bowling place between
Chris Tremlett, Tim Bresnan and Ajmal Shahzad was a bit tricky
to judge on such a slow surface.

'This was not an easy wicket to get the batsman out,' I said to
the press afterwards. 'I don't think any bowler was going to charge
in and take a whole load. All three of them bowled beautifully,
held up ends, didn't let the batters score at a rate, and all did a very
good job on a wicket that wasn't helpful at all. They've all put their
hands up.

'Whoever comes into that eleven, we back one hundred per
cent, and I'm sure he'll do very well. They all bowl a heavy ball and
on their day can be very quick. Tremlett with his height and
bounce can be very awkward at times. Ajmal is always asking questions of the batsmen. He's very good with reverse swing and you
will struggle to find a bloke who works harder at his game.'

We actually got ourselves into a spot of bother on the last day.
Chasing 311 to win, we slumped to 55 for four just before lunch,
but we made sure that we didn't lose by finishing on 211 for six,
with our number eight (a chap called Strauss), who, believe it or
not, had taken a wicket earlier in the day with his filthy left-arm
spin, on 22 not out.

'Going in to lunch we were adamant we weren't losing this game,' I said afterwards. 'Winning is a habit and it's a habit that you want to protect. If we had lost today, I think we would have been very disappointed people. You can't take for granted being on a good run and you have to sometimes dig in and make sure you continue that run.

'It was just nice to get in the middle and have an opportunity to bat for a while, try to build an innings and get through a tricky patch as well. For me personally, it was perfect preparation for next week. I was delighted to get the hundred, but more important was the time in the middle and getting back into the rhythm of building an innings. If we carry on playing the brand of cricket we have been, there's certainly no reason why we can't go through the tour unbeaten. You go on any tour, you want to be unbeaten, whether it be an Ashes tour or anywhere else. If we could manage to do that, it would be a fantastic feat, but it's something we're certainly targeting.'

I was also aware that we had to avoid any complacency. This was danger time for us: we were one ahead in the Ashes series, thanks to a magnificent all-round performance where we had dominated the Adelaide Test from first to last. In those circumstances, it would have been very easy to do a lot of mutual back-patting. This was where England teams had sometimes stumbled in the past, and become a bit complacent. We had had a great innings win in Durban late the previous year against South Africa, but we had not carried that same form into the next match, where we had escaped with a draw at Cape Town only by the skin of our teeth. We had to guard against a repeat of that.

But there was no doubt that it was a very happy and united dressing room at the time. 'There are so many little things that come together,' I said to the press after that Victoria match. 'And the minute you start forgetting about the one per-centers, it becomes dangerous. It's very easy to look at the four hundreds, the big partnerships, the individuals taking five-fors, but it's putting your arm round a mate when he's struggling, celebrating someone else's success, genuinely enjoying Cook/KP double hundreds.

'You see the guys on the balcony and that excitement is not made up; it's not fake. It's very, very real, I can assure you. We've got a whole load of good mates in the dressing room. The minute you get to a place where the team's goal and the team's target is more than the individual's, that's a very powerful place to be, and that's what we have right now.'

We were determined that when we got to Perth, we had to hit that first session as we did in Adelaide, to make sure we got that first punch in. And we did. We won the toss on what looked like a green pitch, and we bowled Australia out for just 268. Chris Tremlett had got the vote to replace the injured Stuart Broad in our only change from the side that won in Adelaide. By contrast Australia made four changes. Phil Hughes replaced Simon Katich, Steve Smith came in for Marcus North, and both Mitchell Johnson and Ben Hilfenhaus were recalled for Xavier Doherty and Doug Bollinger.

Trem struck in his first over, bowling Hughes. He bowled superbly, using his height to great effect on a responsive pitch. He ended with three wickets, as did Jimmy Anderson, one of Jimmy's coming from a quite stunning catch from Paul Collingwood diving high to his right from Ricky Ponting's edge. At one stage Australia were 69 for five, so they might have thought that they had actually done very well to get to 268. But when Straussy and Cooky survived the final 12 overs of the day, ending on 29 for nought, we definitely thought that we had had the best of day one. We were buzzing. We were 1-0 up, and we were on top in this third Test.

And it continued that way into the second morning. Indeed,

just about half an hour before lunch we were 78 for nought. All was well in the world. Then Cooky rather poked at one from Mitchell Johnson which, surprisingly swung away from him, and was caught in the gully by Mike Hussey. 'Even the run machine is allowed to make a mistake now and again,' we thought. But the clue was there: Johnson was swinging the ball. He had swung it away from the left-handed Cooky, but it would be even more dangerous coming into the right-handers. A left-arm bowler swinging into the right-hander has a great chance of picking up LBWs, if he can get his line right.

Sure enough, in his next over Johnson pinned Jonathan Trott LBW. And then, in the same over, he did exactly the same to Kevin Pietersen third ball for a duck. With Straussy then nicking off to Ryan Harris after a good half-century and Collingwood also falling LBW to Johnson – after shouldering arms and an initial not out decision that was overturned upon review – we were suddenly in tatters at 98 for five.

Within an hour or so, the game had been turned on its head. We might have got the first punch in, but now we were on the ropes. And it was all because Johnson had unexpectedly starting swinging the ball. He had been so erratic at Brisbane that I think we had underestimated him, despite the fact he had recently been one of the top-ranked bowlers in the world. In the first Test, he had only really pushed the ball across the right-handers and he had been all over the place, if we're honest. But now, having also scored some runs in the first innings, he had rediscovered his rhythm and we just hadn't adapted quickly enough. It had taken us totally by surprise.

Along with Ian Bell, I tried to engineer some sort of salvage job. But after lunch on that second day, Peter Siddle decided that he was going to test me out with some bodyline tactics. He came around the wicket to me and posted a short leg and a leg gully, with two men back for the hook, too (one in front of square). We were under the pump and this was proper, competitive Ashes cricket. Usually I might have looked to attack my way out of his aggressive tactics, but, given the situation we were in, I didn't feel I could do that. If I got caught hooking or pulling, I would never have heard the last of it.

So I knew that I would just have to sit in there and take it. I resigned myself to the fact that I would probably get hit. This was a quick and bouncy pitch, and Siddle was fired up. He was racing in, just as he had when he'd bowled me first ball at the Gabba. And I did get hit, right on the shoulder as I ducked into one. That was annoying, but not half as annoying as the next ball, from which I was bowled for just 12. And it wasn't just the fact that I had been bowled. I'd been unlucky to be dismissed at all – the ball hit my gloves, then my chest and finally trickled onto the stumps. But Siddle then celebrated as if he had just bowled me with the ball of the century. He also followed that up with a few choice words for me as I left.

I lost it. It doesn't matter what he said, but the fact is that once you have dismissed somebody, you have done the job on them. There is no need to say anything else. There are not many boxing matches when a guy knocks someone out and then kicks him while he's on the floor. That isn't the way it works. I didn't enjoy him getting me out, but I don't think there was a need for him to say anything after that. Having said that, I didn't need to react in the way I did, either.

It turned into an incident that was really blown up afterwards. There was a photograph of me walking off, with my bat tucked under my arm and my gloves in my left hand. My right index finger was pointing at Siddle. Or rather it had been pointing at Siddle and then it was pointing somewhere off the ground. It was reported afterwards that I had offered to fight Siddle in the car park. I didn't say anything about the car park. I can't really remember what I said exactly, but it would have been something along the lines of: 'You are brave on the field, let's see you later.'

I was frustrated. But this was Ashes cricket. There are always going to be bust-ups. The way the Australians see it, that's what they expect to happen. That's how the game is played. There would be something wrong if there wasn't that competitive will to win for your country. If everyone was nice to each other all the time, it wouldn't be the same. It was said that the Aussies had really decided to up their sledging in this game. Had they? I don't think so. There was not, from our point of view, any more or any less than in any other Ashes Test and, if there was, it was all in the spirit of the game.

As I said at the time: 'It is being pumped up, but it's irrelevant. If I saw Peter Siddle right now, I would go over and talk about cricket and have a beer with him. I saw a couple of the Aussies the night after the match. There will be a lot said about it, but it's not the way I want to be remembered, and it's not the way Peter Siddle will want to be remembered. What is important is how we play.'

What I loved, though, was the fact that after all of this had been said and done, and after the Ashes had finished, I went off to play for Victoria. And you know who plays for Victoria? Yep. Peter Siddle. So there I am on the coach for my first game for Victoria, feeling nervous as hell, not really knowing anyone, when who should come onto the coach and sit next to me? Yep. Sids. And within minutes I was on nickname terms. He just said: 'How you going, mate?' and he proceeded to tell me everything about the team and how they worked. He couldn't have been more welcoming. What a top bloke. That's exactly how it should be: you can hate each other on the pitch, but then off it you must forget it and move on.

Not that long after I was out, we were dismissed for just 187, conceding a lead of 81 to Australia. Few would have thought that was possible after the first day. So our only way back into the game was to take early second-innings wickets. Finny did snare Phillip Hughes and Ricky Ponting, but eventually Mike Hussey (116) and Shane Watson (95) rallied and they just took the game away from us again. By the time we bowled Australia out on the third day, they had a lead of 390.

To say we were up against us was an understatement. By the end of that third day, we were out of it. We were 81 for five by then and in a real mess. There had even been a bit of a mix-up at the end, when Jimmy had gone in as nightwatchman and he and Paul Collingwood had not taken a single that was clearly there to be taken. Colly was then out to the last ball of the day. It was so unusual for us. The end was swift on the fourth morning, as we were bowled out for just 123 to lose by 267 runs. What a hammering.

It was just so unexpected. We had come from Adelaide holding all the cards and then we'd certainly handed a few back by being beaten so heavily. But in dissecting the third Test in all its aspects, we had to look at it logically and say that we were still in a good place on this tour. We were going to the MCG on Boxing Day at 1-1, and if somebody had offered us that at the beginning of the tour, we would probably have taken it. A couple of bad days – and they were bad days – didn't make us a poor team. A week before we had been talking about having played the perfect Test match and everything was rosy. But when you get ahead, you want to stay ahead and that was the most disappointing thing.

We simply had to dust ourselves down and stay away from the flak that was flying around. There was even talk in the media that we had lost in Perth because of the fact that most of our families had arrived then. Now that was rubbish. It would have been very easy to panic and start going: 'Right, this bloke out, this bloke in . . . he's ineffective, he's struggling.' We had to shut our minds to all that. It was a time when, as an individual, you really had to have belief in your own ability and in the team. We knew that if we won one more game we would retain the Ashes, but the target was still to win the series. We also had to remember that the opposition are allowed to play well sometimes. And they had. We just had to make sure they didn't do that again in Melbourne.

For me the Boxing Day Test at Melbourne was always my dream game. Yes, I've talked about how special Lord's is, and how it was such a thrill to score a hundred there on my Test debut, but there was always something about playing at the MCG that fascinated me. It was always a game that I dreamed I would be part of one day. And now I was going to get that chance. I insisted that my parents were there. I had never asked them to come to a game before, but I did it because that was how much it meant to me. And they were there. To play in this particular game was a real tick in the box.

When we had played Victoria in the three-day match between the second and third Tests, that had been my first visit to the MCG. It really is like a colosseum. I was staggered even by the scale of the TV screens. Each of them seemed to be as big as a house. Before the Test we actually spoke about the ground and its size. We don't often do that, but we felt it was necessary in this instance. There was already talk that there might be a record crowd there on Boxing Day, more than 90,000 it was said, although in the end 84,345 turned up, which wasn't as many as had passed through the gates in the 2006-07 Ashes and was some way short of the record, which, I'm reliably informed, is the 90,800 who attended the Boxing Day Test against West Indies in 1961. But still there was going to be a huge crowd, one that was going to be much bigger than those we were used to at home for instance, where we get superb crowds but the grounds can hold only about 20,000. We had to be ready to deal with this change.

We even spoke about minor details, such as making sure that we didn't lose our bearings out in the middle. For instance, batsmen have been known to be dismissed there and then walk off in the wrong direction. It must have been very embarrassing for them to have to walk around the boundary to get back to the dressing rooms!

The other thing was we just had to get Perth out of our system. Everyone was still hurting about that, but the truth was that, now we had let the Australians back in, they were favourites for this series. That's how dramatically things had been flipped on their head.

I thought at the time the first day might just be the moment when the Ashes were decided. That was why we had to be so right for it, so much so that we even practised properly on Christmas Day. We just did what we would normally do the day before the Test. Then we went back to the Langham Hotel, where we were staying with our families, and had a good Christmas lunch together.

I'm not sure that I have ever been as excited about a cricket match as I was when I turned up at the MCG on Boxing Day. This was it. This was huge. It was a vital toss to win, and bowl first. I know that there was quite a bit of discussion about that, because batting first at the MCG has more often than not been the way to go, but to me it always looked like a bowl-first pitch. Having said that, nobody could have ever envisaged quite how well we would do after winning that toss. If I tell you that we were batting by tea, then you can see that we did rather well.

In fact, we bowled Australia out for just 98 in 42.5 overs. It was truly remarkable. We did that despite having a nervous start, where we dropped a couple of early catches, but the Australia batsmen just kept coming in and playing shots. They played shot after shot so that, with the ball moving around, they were always likely to edge them, too. It played right into my hands, quite literally that is, because I took six catches, as all ten wickets were taken from catches behind the wicket. What a day! My prediction that this might be the most important day of the series had turned out well for us.

There were four wickets each for Jimmy Anderson and Chris Tremlett, and two for Tim Bresnan, who had been brought in to replace Steven Finn. That was harsh on Finny, but it was thought that he had been a little too expensive, even if he had been the leading wicket-taker in the series up until then, with 14. But Bres was picked because it was felt that he could keep it really tight, especially in the first innings, and that he could then reverse-swing the ball later in the game, because we expected the pitch to die somewhat as the game wore on.

We had said before the start of the series that it would require a massive squad effort to win the Ashes, and this was a good example of that. We needed those coming in to perform immediately, and that's what Trem had done in Perth and again here, and that's what Bres did, too. It was a great effort from both of them, because it can't be easy to come into the side and then fire straight away.

To make things even better, by the end of day one we were 157 without loss. We'd talked about silencing the home crowd, but we'd done more than that. We'd sent most of them home in disgust. It was estimated that just after tea 30,000 had left already.

It was an amazing day, and at the end of it, we were desperately trying not to think too far ahead, repeating all those clichés we use all the time about not looking too far ahead and about how things can turn around so quickly in cricket. But in this instance it was very hard to see how we could not win that Test. To be already 59 ahead with ten wickets in hand was cricketing heaven. We knew it would probably take much harder work to bowl Australia out a second time, but we were still delirious.

By the end of day two we were 444 for five, with Jonathan Trott 141 not out and Andrew Strauss, Alastair Cook and Kevin Pietersen all having made half-centuries. I was 75 not out, just 25 runs away from an Ashes century. I will freely admit that it was the only time I have never got a decent night's sleep before a day of Test cricket. It was terrible. I just could not sleep. Every time I tried to nod off, thoughts of how I might get those 25 extra runs ran through my head. I kept thinking: 'Not only would it be an Ashes hundred, but a hundred in the MCG Test.'

Maybe it affected me the next day, maybe it didn't, but what happened was that I chipped one to mid-on off Peter Siddle for 85. I was devastated to fall so near to a hundred, and stayed out there in the middle for an instant as I realised what I had done. All I could do was cross my fingers that I might get another chance in the series. Then again I had no reason to be too disappointed, because I had had a big piece of luck early on, when I had been caught behind on five, only for umpire Aleem Dar to call for a replay because he thought that that Mitchell Johnson had bowled a no-ball. And he had.

We were eventually all out for 513, with Trott still there on 168 and Siddle gutsily taking six wickets, but we had a lead of 415 and it was still only lunchtime on the third day. We knew that it was going to be harder the second time around; the pitch was getting lower and slower. It was time to unleash our plans for reverse swing. We had a very definite method for how to achieve that. We had to keep the ball dry, so that meant that sweaty palms had to be kept away from it. That meant only Cooky (who, of course, famously does not sweat), Jimmy and I were allowed to touch it.

And there were not to be any poor throws onto the green outfield. All throws had to come straight into my gloves, otherwise the fielder would be in serious trouble from me. That is the time when I am allowed to hand out bollockings.

Here we managed to get the ball reversing as early as the 11th over of Australia's second innings. And so Bres came into his element, ending the innings with four wickets, and in one spell taking the wickets of Shane Watson, Ricky Ponting and Mike Hussey (for a duck). That was just huge. So it was that just before noon on the fourth day, we retained the Ashes for the first time in 24 years. We had won by an innings and 157 runs. It took a while to get the final wickets – with Brad Haddin making an unbeaten fifty – but when we did eventually bowl Australia out for 258, it all really did kick off.

We all went absolutely mental, as did the Barmy Army. They had honestly been our 12th, 13th and 14th men during the series and it was wonderful to give them this superb victory to shout and sing about. By the end, there were barely any Australia fans left in the ground again. That was what we had set out to do: to end up with only England supporters watching the game. And that's what we had done.

Those huge screens confirmed the news: 'England retain the Ashes.' That felt good, but at that moment I so wanted them to say: 'England win the Ashes.' That was what we had come to Australia for, and there was still one Test left. There was no way we wanted to go home with the series score at 2-2.

I was fortunate enough to take the catch that ended the match, snaring an inside edge from Ben Hilfenhaus off Bres. It looked like a relatively straightforward catch, but the truth is that we were standing ludicrously close at the time. The wicket was becoming increasingly lifeless, and so we had decided to stand as close as we could to make sure it carried, giving someone an opportunity to take a special catch. If we weren't able to hold it first time, then there would still be a chance for a rebound.

Luckily, it was just a thin edge and it carried through, but we had trained for this moment. We knew that reverse swing was going to play a role in the series and that when it does, the ball doesn't carry as much, so we end up taking lower catches. Our slip practice that morning had been all about taking low catches and standing very close in preparation for this moment. If it still didn't carry, then so be it, as we could go only so close. Thankfully, this one came through and I hung on for dear life.

And I didn't let that ball go. Even when I got back into the dressing room after all the handshakes, I still had the ball nestled in my left glove. My right-hand glove was off, but the left stayed on and the ball stayed in that glove. I quite fancied keeping it. Maybe it would have made a very good auction item during the Benefit Year that Sussex so kindly granted me in 2012. I think there had been an argument between Alastair Cook and Graeme Swann over who kept the ball from the 2009 Ashes win at The Oval, so I knew there would plenty of debate over this. There were a few people who had a claim on it, not least Trotty, after his great innings, and Bres, who had bowled so well. In the end, I gave it to Bres. I can't even remember why, but that's what I was persuaded to do.

Immediately after our victory, Straussy called the team together for a huddle. It was a moment of pure emotion when everything else seemed to disappear – the noise from the Barmy Army and the rest of the crowd, everything. It sounds cheesy and corny, but we had been bonding not for weeks but for years as a group, and the release of emotion in those few seconds was incredible. We had been through tough situations that had brought us together and so to retain the Ashes felt very special.

As part of our celebrations, we performed the Sprinkler dance on the outfield in front of the Barmy Army. That had become the tour dance by then and was massively popular ever since Swanny had done it on one of his tour diaries.

It might be time to tell the truth about the Sprinkler. If I do so, Swanny might lose a lot of credit. It actually started after our second warm-up match of the tour, in Adelaide. After that game we knew that there was going to be small window in our training, so we decided to have a bit of a night out. And before we did so, Jimmy Anderson came and sat next to me and said: 'You know what? I think I am going to get on the table and do a sprinkler tonight.'

I replied: 'What on earth is that?'

'You know, the Sprinkler – the old dance move called the Sprinkler.'

I still didn't have a clue what he was talking about, so I said to him: 'Go on, then. Let's see it.'

So he showed me, and I loved it, as did everyone else. That night it came out more than a few times, and after that it simply had to become the tour dance. But when Swanny used it in his tour diary, it almost became Swanny's Sprinkler. I'm sure no one minds – he can have it. In any case, he and Jimmy are a brilliant and seriously funny double act.

But after the fun of the celebrations in Melbourne, which naturally went on some considerable time, first at the ground, then at a party organised by the ECB for us, and then God knows where, we had to focus our minds again on the final Test in Sydney. As I said, there was no way we wanted to go home having drawn the series 2-2. We'd already beaten Australia twice by an innings, so we thought that we more than deserved to win the series. There was no way that we were going to let up.

And Australia had a new captain for this game. Ricky Ponting had damaged a finger in the third Test at Perth, but had battled on in Melbourne. Now he was told that he had damaged it further, so he had to pull out. His place in the side was taken by debutant Usman Khawaja, while Michael Clarke stepped up to skipper Australia for the first time in a Test.

Immediately Clarke had a tricky decision to make at the toss. There was enough live green grass on the pitch for us to have decided to bowl first, if we had won it, but Clarke decided to be bold and bat first. That was mostly the way Ponting used to do it, although he famously went against that at Edgbaston in 2005, when he had just lost Glenn McGrath to injury and inserted England, only for Australia to lose the Test. But generally he thought that you batted first, and if it was going to do a bit, your batsmen had to 'suck it up', as they say, and be good enough to get through it.

In fairness, Phil Hughes and Shane Watson did do that here. They put on 55 and Australia were only one wicket down at lunch. When play was ended early at tea because of rain, they had gone on to 134 for four. We chipped away on day two and eventually Australia were all out for 280. We did slip to 225 for five in reply, but all along Alastair Cook had again been batting quite magnificently, ending with 189, and Ian Bell, who had come in at seven (demoting me to eight) because Jimmy Anderson had been used as a nightwatchman on the second evening, also made a century, his first in Ashes cricket.

Oh yes, and I made my first Ashes century, too. Wow! Talk about a special feeling. Before I'd missed out in Melbourne, I had been batting with Jonathan Trott when he reached his century and he had come up to me in the middle and said: 'It's the best feeling in cricket.' I desperately wanted to know what it felt like. Now, at last I discovered, and I'd have to agree. It is very, very special. And I will treasure the moment I got it for the rest of my life.

I came in when Cooky was out. His 189 meant that he finished the series with 766 runs at an average of 127.66. Only Wally Hammond, with 905 runs in the 1928-29 Ashes, has made more for England in a series (against anyone, not just Australia) and even then his average wasn't as good as Cooky's. So it was a formality that he went on to win the Compton-Miller Medal as player of the series. We were already calling him 'The Don', after the great Sir Don Bradman, in tribute to his efforts, but if there is a more down-to-earth sportsperson in the world, I have yet to meet him. Cooky would never let anything go to his head and we were all absolutely delighted for him.

When I came in we were 380 for six, already 100 ahead, so it was obvious what I had to do. It was time to take the initiative and attack, which, as you may have gathered, rather suits me and my game. The amazing thing is that, looking back now, at no stage during that series did I feel in the best of form. Even during that 85 at Melbourne, I still hadn't felt quite right. And when I walked out to bat here at Sydney I felt as if I wasn't moving too well again. But luckily it was the sort of situation where I could just say to myself that I could just give it a go. I did feel a little bit as if I was jumping on the back of all the runs that had come before, but that was my job. It was to be positive and hit boundaries. And that's what I did.

Sometimes you hit a few in the middle early on and then things click. So I just went with it and kept hitting. I put on 107 with Belly, before he went for 115, and then I put on 102 with Tim Bresnan. Before I knew it, I was in the nineties. Suddenly Brad Haddin piped up from behind the stumps. He hadn't said anything to me all series, but now he started saying: 'Don't get out now, mate. It's an Ashes hundred. They are so special. You don't want to miss out now.'

Normally I would simply brush off that sort of comment. He was trying to get into my head, and I would have ignored it, but in this instance I couldn't. I was actually thinking: 'Yeah, you are so right, mate. This might be my chance. I so don't want to muck this up.'

Then something happened that makes you think. I was on 97 and Michael Beer, the debutant left-arm spinner, was bowling. I'd just paddle-swept him for two, and I was thinking about the rule I'd agreed with Carl Hopkinson (to play that same shot whenever I reached 49 or 99) when Beer bowled me a juicy wide ball outside off stump. To left-arm spinners, I like to drive the ball very square when given any width (to be honest, I quite like to do that to any bowler, but with left-arm spinners it is often a more exaggerated movement when I really open up with my front leg and shoulders). So when Beer bowled me a ball right in the slot for that shot, I thought that was it. On 97 in an Ashes Test, this was the perfect opportunity. This was my Ashes hundred.

I absolutely crunched it; I couldn't have hit it any better, but Mike Hussey at cover stopped it. My heart sank. Was that my chance gone? Was it fate that I might not get another opportunity? It might sound irrational now, but that's how cricketers sometimes think in such situations. You worry that you might not get such an opportunity for quite a few balls afterwards, and that the pressure could build, and you end up doing something different from what you have been doing all innings. In fairness, though, I'd been 'seeing ball, hitting ball' throughout, so it should not really have been a problem.

Happily, I didn't have to wait long. The very next ball was in a similar spot. It may not have been quite as juicy as the ball before, but it was good enough for me. I threw everything at it. The ball went in the air, but this time it was in the gap. That was it. My first Ashes century! Just like my hundred on debut at Lord's, I wanted to be cool and calm, but I just couldn't. I charged off and jumped high in the sky. I ran towards the Barmy Army. I had got to know quite a few of them during that tour and their support was hugely important to me and the team. So many of them had been on previous tours to Australia, where England had got hammered, so now they were really enjoying this success. I genuinely felt that they were as happy as I was for scoring those runs. That's why I wanted to salute them. What a feeling!

I'd made my hundred in just 109 balls, which apparently was England's fastest Test century since Ian Botham's at Headingley in 1981. I was asked afterwards what had been the secret behind it: 'Luck, I reckon,' I said. 'I started off with not much luck and ended up with a whole lot of it. Sometimes it's just not your day, sometimes it is.'

This was certainly my day. I finished with 118 in 130 balls and was ninth man out as we finished with a remarkable total of 644. It was our third highest total against Australia, and our highest in Australia. There was only one regret for us: Paul Collingwood made just 13. He had decided that he was going to retire from Test cricket and it would have been so good had he finished on a high. He'd played 68 Tests, made ten Test hundreds and averaged over 40. But that was only a part of the story with Colly. What the fans don't see is the part away from the cricket ground. Everyone will know the stats and the important innings he played, the great catches he took and the wickets he picked up. But it's what a bloke like Colly brought to the dressing room that was so important. He was definitely one of the catalysts of why this team won the Ashes, and why the team spirit was as good as it was.

By the end of day four, the game was all but over. Obviously we would have liked to have finished it there and then, and we did take the extra half-hour in order to try to do that, but Australia held on to be 213 for seven, 151 runs behind. Again, reverse swing was a key factor, and all three of our seamers bowled magnificently. Jimmy Anderson in particular tormented Michael Clarke.

We knew what a huge wicket his was going to be, and Jimmy tied him up in knots with his swing. He just kept teasing him with in-swingers. In, in, in and in the ball kept going to him. I was wondering behind the stumps when the out-swinger would come. And doubtless Clarke was thinking something similar, but neither of us knew when it was going to happen.

When it did, Clarke still could do little about it. And he did something I don't think I've ever heard a batsman do before. He actually swore before he edged the ball. He knew that Jimmy had 'done' him. He knew he had poked at a ball that he shouldn't have, but there was no way of stopping himself. He did edge it and I caught it. Clarke was gone for 41 and his team were 124 for four. So much for all that talk about Jimmy's average in Australia being 82 before the tour. By the end of the series, he had lowered it to just under 36, having taken 24 wickets, the most in Australia since Frank Tyson's 28 in the 1954-55 series.

There was another moment during that day that I remember well, although Mitchell Johnson is probably still trying to forget it now. He'd bowled superbly in Perth, but in general it had been a very tough series for him. And he had really copped some stick from the Barmy Army, especially when they began chanting their favourite song: 'He bowls to the left, he bowls to the right, that Mitchell Johnson, his bowling is s****.'

So Johnson came out to bat with his side at 171 for six. The Barmy Army were in full cry by then. As he went to take guard, he was faced with the incredible sight of about 10,000 members of the Barmy Army swinging their arms from left to right and singing their song. Everybody on the pitch turned to look at them, including Johnson. I've never seen anything like it. Did it unsettle him? I reckon it might have unsettled most people. He was bowled first ball by Chris Tremlett. And the Barmy Army went even wilder. They were unforgettable scenes.

As I said, it would have been better if we could have won that day, but, as it was, when we did return for the final day, it did not make the celebrations any less riotous. As often happens in those situations, the three wickets did not come immediately. Australia battled hard, with Peter Siddle and Steve Smith getting some runs. But eventually, just before midday, Trem bowled Michael Beer so that Australia were all out for 281 and we had won by an innings and 83 runs, our third victory of the series by an innings. We had won the Ashes!

That's what we had come to do, and that's what we had now achieved. Little wonder that later on in the day I should write 'Job Done 2010-11' on my locker in the Sydney Cricket Ground dressing room, alongside other messages from down the years. That summed it up for me.

The SCG is an amazing cricket ground. It looks so modern from the outside, but the pavilion is so steeped in history that you can almost see Sir Don Bradman walking down the stairs to go out to bat sometimes. I love the place. That was why I thought 'I'm going to stamp my little mark on the SCG' when I wrote that message.

It is also why one of my favourite photos ever is of me holding my son JJ in that pavilion, as we look up at the honours board where my century was already remembered. It was great that all the families came into the dressing room after the game, and there were lots more photos to recall a momentous day.

Unsurprisingly it was all a bit of haze after we had won. The euphoria was remarkable. But there some things that still stick in the memory now. Firstly, there was walking back into the dressing room only a short time after we had won and seeing Jimmy Anderson fast asleep underneath a bench by his changing spot. It just showed what an unbelievable effort all the guys had put in. Yes, he was a little ill and for him the tour had been more arduous than for most. He had led the bowling attack superbly, but he had also popped home in between Tests to be at the birth of his second daughter, Ruby. Usually in that situation after winning, he would have been one of the first with a beer in his hand. But now he was so mentally and physically exhausted that he just had to rest. He was cooked, and he just had to go and shut down for a little while.

Meanwhile, the celebrations went on around him, though. And we went into the Australian dressing room to have a beer with them. I loved that, as I love doing so at the end of every series. We sang our team song (can't say what it is, sorry) and then we did something that I think is the most special moment of my whole career. We decided to grab an esky of beers and go and sit on the Sydney square. It was about five o'clock by now and the ground was empty. It was just the playing squad and the team management, and we went out there and sat in a circle to chat and reminisce.

It was fabulous. That is why you play international cricket for those moments. It was emotional, and it was out there that it began to hit home what we had achieved and what a marvellous experience we had just been through. Regardless of the result, it was undoubtedly the best tour I had ever been on. We had worked harder than on any other tour I'd been on, but we'd also enjoyed ourselves, too. We'd embraced Australia and we had reaped the rewards.

Personally, I thought I had done well. And by that I do not necessarily mean the runs I had scored. I'd averaged just over 50 for the series, so I was certainly happy with that. And I do not necessarily mean the standard of my glovework either, though I thought that was good, too. What I was most happy with was my energy. I thought that I had kept the side going throughout the series. As I have stated previously, that is my job.

So when one of the boys mentioned that Justin Langer,

Australia's batting coach and former opening batsman, had asked them: 'What is that Matt Prior on? He just keeps running and running all day long!' I took that as a huge compliment. As I write this, we are at the height of the Lance Armstrong drugs affair in cycling, so I am aware of the possible connotations some might place on that comment, but I do not think there was any malice in it. And I am certainly not on drugs. For me it was so pleasing that he had said that. My mostly unnoticed work had been seen, and not just by any old so-and-so, but by JL, a once-great player who had not exactly been complimentary about me when his so-called 'dossier' was leaked during the 2009 Ashes. I felt like I had really arrived in Ashes cricket.

Just as after the 2009 win at home, the only regret of this Ashes triumph was that we couldn't enjoy some sort of formal celebration. That would have been as nice for the people back home as it would have been for us, but it couldn't happen due to the simple fact that there were still two T20 internationals and seven one-day internationals to play on the tour. Not that I was involved, of course. I wasn't selected, so I went to play a few games for Victoria in the Big Bash before going home.

My first game for the Victoria Bushrangers didn't go well for the team, as we were thrashed by nine wickets by Tasmania in Hobart, but at least I scored 51, batting at four, with our wicketkeeper being Matthew Wade, who, as I write, is now the Australia keeper. Then it was off to Perth to play against Western Australia, where we again lost and I didn't even have the consolation of some personal runs.

But what I did get in Perth was a surprise phone call from Andy Flower, who told me that I had to go back to Hobart as they wanted me to play in the one-day international there three days later. I was in the World Cup squad and they were planning for me to open the batting.

What a turn up! I hadn't played a limited-overs international since March 2010, in Bangladesh, and I hadn't been expecting to add to my tally any day soon, even if I have always said that whenever England are playing in whatever format, I want to be the guy with the gloves on. It appeared harsh on Steven Davies, who had actually made 42 off 35 balls in the first match of the series. But, as I have said before, sentimentality doesn't come into these sorts of things. Davo and I had worked together all winter, as he had been the reserve keeper for the Ashes, but we always knew that we were pushing for the same place. That's the way international sport works. It can be cut-throat at times. There is always somebody ready to replace you.

That is why I have always said that security in international cricket is a strange thing, because you don't really have it. The day you feel secure is the day you are in trouble. I learned that early in my career and I've always been thankful for that lesson. My place in the England team holds a special place in my heart.

So here I was, having to say an abrupt farewell to my new Victoria team-mates, whom I hardly knew, and make my way back into the England tour party. As I said in an interview it felt like I was 'going home' in terms of going back to what felt like my second family. But this second family didn't have any clothes for me. There was no kit with the name of Prior on it. Steven Davies had been selected and so I had to wear his kit. Those who know me well will know how difficult that was for me. I am so particular about everything that I wear, that for me not to feel right when playing in an international match was just horrible.

There I was facing Brett Lee and I felt like I was playing for the Peckham third team, because I was playing in someone else's kit, rather than for England in a one-day international. Upon reflection it was little surprise that I got a duck in that first game in Hobart, but then I got another duck in the second match at the SCG.

I had missed the warm-up match against a Prime Minister's XI, two T20 internationals and the first 50-over game at the MCG, but this was not going well. All that winter, my focus had been on the Test matches. I knew that I had had to give every single ounce of energy to them and this was all rather unexpected. A series of seven ODIs (with those two Twenty20 games before them) seems too long anyway, especially having just played the Ashes. The schedule that winter was incredibly intensive, because after Australia, we had the briefest of stays at home – four days, three nights – before going off to the World Cup in India, Sri Lanka and Bangladesh.

We were away for five and a half months that winter and those three nights were all the time we had at home. In total, we went on more than 50 flights, and I know it was more than 50, because I remember us all pretending to raise our bats for our half-centuries as we boarded a flight somewhere. Where it was exactly, I can't remember. But it was that type of year, where I think out of the 365 days, we were away from home for something like 290 of them.

As a team we simply couldn't put in the same amount of effort and energy to the one-day series as we could for the Ashes. It was just impossible. So we lost 6-1. And by the end of that series I had been dropped down the order to number six. For the World Cup, that's where I stayed, or more often at seven, as Kevin Pietersen was given the role of opening and then Ian Bell took that over when KP went home with a groin injury.

It's fair to say that the World Cup did not go well. When you lose to both Ireland and Bangladesh, you know that things have not exactly gone to plan. But you know what? It might sound daft, but I was really proud at how we stuck at things during the tournament. As I said, we were tired and we were also carrying a lot of injuries. I honestly reckon that overall we were operating at about 70 per cent fitness. There were certain individuals who were really struggling, yet they carried on. Just imagine if the Chelsea football team put out a team at 70 per cent fitness on a Saturday. What chance would they have of winning?

The trouble is that a lot of people do not look at cricket in that way. They just expect players to be able to play through niggles. But if a bowler is having an injection into his ankle every two weeks because of the pain he is in, then it is going to have an effect. It is bound to catch up with him sooner or later. Added to all this, the tournament was played in conditions in which we have always struggled in one-day cricket. Those slow, spinning pitches have never really been to our liking.

And yet we played some outstanding cricket. There was that famous tied match with India in Bangalore in which Andrew Strauss scored a magnificent 158 in our pursuit of 338. There were also a couple of matches we won, when we had no right to do so, getting by through sheer grit and determination. Think of the victory over South Africa in Chennai where we managed to defend just 171, with Stuart Broad bowling phenomenally well to take four for 15 from 6.4 overs. And then at the same venue we beat West Indies (I was back opening for that match) when we defended 243, thanks to some brilliant spin bowling from Graeme Swann (three for 36) and James Tredwell (four for 48).

But then it all went horribly wrong in the quarter-final against Sri Lanka in Colombo, where we lost by ten wickets, as Tillekeratne Dilshan and Upul Tharanga both made hundreds to make a mockery of our total of 229. It had been a bridge too far, but it could not dilute what had happened before. We had gone to Australia and we had retained the Ashes. No number of one-day international defeats can take away what a thrill and achievement that was.

9

To the Summit and
Down Again

It all began in a room up at Loughborough where the England &
Wales Cricket Board's National Performance Centre is housed. It
was there, before our tour to South Africa in 2009, that we were
given a presentation by Nathan Leamon, our team analyst, the
Cambridge University maths graduate whom we call 'Numbers'.
He spelled out to us how we could get to the top of the Test
rankings. I had never been in a meeting like that before. Those
rankings were not something we as players really understood at
that stage, so Numbers had to explain them in great detail.

I have to admit that it was all a bit bewildering. There were all
sorts of permutations, most of which seemed to involve us winning nearly every Test and certainly every series. We could have
won every Test for the next 18 months and still not have been
number one. At that stage, it all seemed so far away and so difficult. We were ranked fifth in the world behind South Africa,
who were top, Sri Lanka, India and Australia. At that stage,

fourth-placed Australia were 11 points ahead of us, which was a big gap.

We thought it would take us at least two years to get to the top. So the meeting made us realise how hard we were going to have to work just to go upwards, and we certainly left with that knowledge much clearer in our minds. I do think we all believed that we were going to do it eventually, or, as a minimum, that we were going to go upwards. But we also recognised that this was not going to happen overnight; it would take a while.

By the end of the South Africa series that winter we were still fifth. Beating Bangladesh (home and away) and then Pakistan in the summer of 2010 meant that, by the time we began the 2010-11 Ashes in Australia, we were fourth, two points above Australia. But India had now moved to the top and they were still 18 points away. After we had won the Ashes, we had moved up to third, and narrowed the gap to India to just ten points. We knew that in the summer of 2011 we were playing India in four Tests at home, which was a great chance to catch up with them.

First, though, were three Tests against Sri Lanka. I have to admit that I was still completely burnt out going into that series. I didn't feel right physically or mentally, because I was very tired and still a bit sore from the winter's workload in the Ashes, then the one-day series in Australia and finally the World Cup. There was a lot of rain around and, no disrespect to Sri Lanka, but after the hype of the Ashes and World Cup it just felt like such a comedown.

We won the series 1-0 and that was only because of an unlikely victory in the first Test at Cardiff. It looked like the last day would be washed out and the Test abandoned as a draw, but somehow we managed to conjure a victory, bowling out the Sri Lankans for just 82 in 24.4 overs. And we didn't even have Jimmy Anderson, who was nursing a side strain, on the field. As it was, there were four wickets each for Chris Tremlett and Graeme Swann, and two for Stuart Broad.

We didn't really think we had a chance of winning when we went out onto the field. So much time had been lost, after all, and we even allowed Ian Bell, who had been on 98 not out overnight, to go out and complete his century first. But we had noticed the attitude of the Sri Lankans beforehand, and it looked as if they wanted it to rain all day. They didn't think we were going to play.

So there was a feeling that we might just take them by surprise, but really we were thinking more about setting down markers for later in the Test series than winning the match. You can always do that early in any series, whatever the situation. So here, for instance, we thought that if we could just get Mahela Jayawardena and Kumar Sangakkara for low scores then that might knock their confidence for the next Test match. We just wanted to inflict as much damage as we could.

We could never have imagined precisely what damage we would inflict. We just got on a roll and Sri Lanka capitulated. Our skill on that afternoon was exceptional. It was as good a bowling display as I have witnessed. It really was. There was only one soft dismissal that I can remember, and that was the left-arm spinner Rangana Herath having a bit of a hack, but that's the way he always plays. The rest went to superb deliveries. Quite a few of them were unplayable.

The next Test was at Lord's and I have already talked about that at length. I smashed a window and we drew. Nobody will remember it for much else, sadly. And so on to the third Test at Southampton where rain again ruined the match. But not before I was sent in to score quick runs again, just as I had been at Lord's. This time I wasn't run out, but instead cut my second ball from Tissara Perera straight to point for a duck. And I knew immediately what everyone was thinking: 'Mind the windows!'

So, as I walked into the dressing room, I glanced up at the television and could see that the cameras were panning through the big double windows at the front of the changing room. It was too good an opportunity to miss for some fun. With a huge grin on my face I picked up my bat and pretended to smash it through the window. It went down pretty well I hear, with commentator David Lloyd particularly impressed, apparently.

The serious stuff was about to begin, though. We were now only eight points behind India in the world rankings. If we could beat them by two clear Tests, then we would become the top-ranked side in the world. We really wanted to dominate them. We thought that they had come into the country with a slightly cocky attitude. They didn't seem too worried that they were under-prepared. They had just finished a Test series against West Indies, albeit with a weakened side, and five days later they were playing Somerset in their first warm-up game and not really appearing too interested.

In that Somerset side was none other than our captain Andrew Strauss, who was guesting in order to get some match practice. He hadn't got too many runs in the Sri Lanka series and had played just one county championship match for Middlesex in the lengthy break after the third Test, so this was ideal for him as he made 78 and 109 not out.

The first Test at Lord's was special, and not just because it was the 2,000th Test of all time and the 100th between England and India. In addition, there was a lot of talk about Sachin Tendulkar being on 99 centuries in international cricket, and whether he would reach that milestone at the home of cricket, a ground where he had never done well. It was to remain just talk during the series, as he didn't score a century against us.

However, the main reason it was special was that we won by 196 runs. And just for good measure I made 71 in the first innings and 103 not out in the second. But I wasn't man of the match, and neither should I have been. That honour went to Kevin Pietersen, and no one was arguing. His 202 not out, after we had been put in, was quite magnificent. Afterwards he said that he had never had to work harder at the start of an innings, and I could see why he said that. The ball moved around all over the place on that first morning. Our bowlers were superb throughout, too, with Stuart Broad taking seven wickets in the match, while Jimmy Anderson took five for 65 in the second innings.

Even with KP's innings, it was still one heck of a battle all through the game. There I was on the Sunday morning, expecting to have a quiet day, after we had begun the day 193 ahead with all ten wickets remaining. In fact so relaxed was I that I was even looking at the lunch menu and thinking how much I fancied the rack of lamb, when suddenly we had a bit of a collapse and were 62 for five in no time. My thoughts of lamb had to be shelved pretty quickly, as not only did I have my pads on, but I was even batting before lunch. Thankfully, although we lost Eoin Morgan soon afterwards, Broady and I managed to put on an unbroken 162, so that we could declare at 269 for six and set India 458 to win. They never really got close, and we were 1-0 up in the series.

We moved to Trent Bridge, where we could so easily have let India back into the series. It is a game I have mentioned already, but we were truly rescued by a partnership of 73 in the first innings between Broady and Graeme Swann. That got us up to 221 all out. Without that, goodness knows what might have happened, because we still needed Broady's hat-trick to keep us in the game.

Good teams on top form are never out of the match, and I think we proved that here. This was clearly an important game for me after what had happened four years previously against the same opponents on the same ground. That was Jelly Bean Central and we had a hammering on the field as well as off it. So when we were 124 for eight in the first innings, it felt like we could have potentially lost the game on the first day, and my thoughts went straight back to that match in 2007.

The toss had also been vital in that match and we were behind from early on. I remember thinking to myself this time around: 'OK, we are four years on, but we are in the same position. Have we improved since then? Have we moved forward?' Three days later we had provided the answers and I had a very different set of emotions. Winning the Test by 319 runs was a massively proud moment for the whole team. It was an epic effort built on hard work. We showed resilience and that resilience came from the amount of hard work we had put in as a team.

I was especially pleased for Broady. He had taken some real flak during the Sri Lanka series, and there had even been talk about him losing his place. It was all very harsh, and it came about because some commentators felt that he was bowling too short. In truth, he probably was bowling a little too short, but quite often he was doing so because he was performing a specific role for us. Wickets were not easy to take in that Sri Lanka series and, as quite a lot of their batsmen are not at their most comfortable when confronted with short-pitched bowling, that was a tactic that we tried to ruffle them with.

Broady was our best option when it came to executing that plan. But it can always be a bit tricky if you are that bowler and things don't go quite right, which was what happened to him here. He lost his rhythm and with it his natural length. Fortunately, between the Test series he was able to go away and play some games for Nottinghamshire, where there was not the same media scrutiny, and there he could sort himself out. He did that rather well. And he did bowl a tad fuller. Against India he was eventually man of the series, taking 25 wickets at 13.84, as well as averaging 60.66 with the bat. Not bad!

We needed to win at Edgbaston to become the top Test team in the world, and we were never going to fail in that mission. We just felt that at this stage we were playing such unbelievable cricket that India couldn't stop us. We were all over them. Our bowlers were causing their batsmen such problems that we honestly thought that some of them didn't want to be there. Rahul Dravid was an exception, of course. He was having a brilliant series.

We had had our little moment where we had momentarily let our ruthlessness slip at Trent Bridge, but from there on we were intent on doing what so many English teams of the past had failed to do: never let the opposition off the hook. We were going to grind them into the dust. And that's what we did at Edgbaston, or at least Alastair Cook did in particular. First, we'd won the toss and inserted India, bowling them out for just 224, with Broady taking four wickets and Tim Bresnan, who had replaced the injured Chris Tremlett at Trent Bridge, also taking four. He also ended up having a superb series, taking 16 wickets at 16.31 and averaging 77 with the bat. This was a team on fire.

In reply to India's 224, we made 710 for seven declared. Yes, 710, which apparently is England's third-highest team total ever and our highest since the war. Cooky made 294. I was gutted for him. He so deserved that triple hundred. He'd batted for 773 minutes and faced 545 balls. And the first time he tried to play an attacking shot – OK, that might be an exaggeration but you get my drift – he gets caught at deep point off Ishant Sharma. He came into the dressing room and we were all saying: 'What you doing, mate? You've bored us for two days and then you try a big square drive and get caught on the boundary!'

We were only joking, of course. We can do that with Cooky. He is a special player and a special bloke. What makes him such a good player is that however many runs he has scored before, he is still as keen to start from nought and go big again. That is a talent in itself. And he will always strip the game down to its extreme basics. That's why you might see him in practice being given drop-feeds by batting coach Graham Gooch. It's the sort of stuff you do at Under-12s, but they are the basics of the game and they will get you through those tricky situations when the ball is swinging and seaming.

Cooky is typical of this England team. There are no shortcuts; it is all about hard work and intense training. And that brought its due reward on Saturday 13 August 2011 when, just after 3pm, Tim Bresnan had Sreesanth caught in the gully by Kevin Pietersen. We had won the third Test by an innings and 242 runs, and we were now ranked number one in the world. We'd done it. We had reached the top.

We had played some unbelievable cricket, and there was still one more Test to go in the series. We were never going to let up there. We won again, this time by an innings and eight runs, after Ian Bell had made a remarkable 235 and KP had scored 175. Dravid stood firm in their first innings with 146 not out, but we enforced the follow-on and, though they battled hard, we won on the final afternoon.

India had arrived as the best team in the world and we'd beaten them 4-0. It had been the perfect series. We had performed as well as we possibly could in all facets of the game, and that included the catching department, where we had been outstanding, too.

Was it my proudest moment when we went to number one? It is so difficult to say because the Ashes are what I might call a 'different animal' when it comes to ranking any cricketing achievements, but it certainly seemed like it was my proudest moment at the time.

What to do next, though? We'd reached the summit, which had been such a huge goal for us, but now we had to decide how to deal with it. What was our next goal going to be? Saying that we were just going to stay at the top didn't seem enough of a challenge. There was supposed to have been a World Test Championship, involving the top four-ranked sides, in England in 2013. That would have been ideal as a long-term target for us, but it was postponed until at least 2017, so that the ICC Champions Trophy could remain in 2013.

However, if I am being truthful, I will say that we never quite got it right in terms of finding a goal or dealing with being number one. I think we put too much pressure on ourselves. We enjoyed doing the hunting, but, now we were being hunted, we were not so comfortable. We started worrying about things that we didn't need to worry about. Did the media want to see us knocked off our pedestal? I don't know if they did, but so what if they did. We should have just concentrated on the cricket. That was what we had done so well in getting to the top.

As a result, the three-Test tour we undertook to the United Arab Emirates to play Pakistan in early 2012 was just not enjoyable at all. And I am not just saying that because we lost 3-0. Something had changed. It is always difficult to put a finger on what exactly that is in such a situation, but there seemed to be more tension around the camp than normal. People seemed to be very worried about what might happen if we didn't win every single game as the best team in the world.

Did it help that it was five months after winning at The Oval before we played our next Test, in Dubai? All I will say is that we needed the break in terms of refreshing bodies and minds. As I said earlier, I was shattered going into the Sri Lanka series and it then took a huge effort to win against India. We needed some down time and to chill out for a while. But then, of course, the problem is that you need to get rid of the rustiness very quickly when you play again. And we probably didn't do that in the UAE.

We were then suddenly faced with the shock of our batsmen failing so spectacularly. We had been so used in 2011 to sitting back and watching them rack up the runs once we'd won the toss, that when we were bowled out for just 192 on the first day of the first Test in Dubai, we barely knew what to do. It set the tone for the series, unfortunately. We batted so poorly. All of our top order averaged under 30 for the series, with no hundreds, while Pakistan had five players who averaged over 30, with two hundreds. It was so unusual, and I still say to this day that, if a couple of our batsmen had had just half-decent series, we would have won it.

It was strange, because we had gone out there worrying about how we were going to take 20 wickets in each Test match. We really thought that the pitches would be incredibly flat. As it was, our bowlers were phenomenal. Time and time again they kept us in matches, but we just could not get the runs to back them up. As batsmen, we went in with one plan to attack, but the problem was that we attacked with the wrong shots. With the ball skidding on and keeping low often, it was not a place – in Dubai or Abu Dhabi – to be playing a lot of cross-batted shots. Instead of deciding that we would keep attacking, but play smarter shots in trying to do so, we then decided to sit in and be patient. We had gone from one extreme to the other. And that didn't work either. One of us would bat 40 overs for 20-odd, then get out, and, as happened throughout the series, a cluster of wickets would fall.

One thing to bear in mind is how brilliantly the two Pakistan spinners, the mystery off-spinner Saeed Ajmal and the slow left-armer Abdur Rehman, bowled. Ajmal took 24 wickets at 14.70 and Rehman 19 wickets at 16.73. I am not sure they will ever bowl as well as a pairing again. Rehman was the real surprise. The conditions really suited him because he would get one ball to turn sharply and then the next would slide on and have a good chance of an LBW. There did not appear to be anything in his action that suggested a difference in those deliveries. Maybe he was just getting a little lucky. Graeme Swann will admit that that sometimes happens to him. He will try really hard to spin a ball, but it will sometimes land on the shiny side and skid straight on.

With the Decision Review System in place, too, it often meant that you were trying to cover an area of about two feet when facing Rehman. You'd be worried about the one that skidded on for that LBW and you'd also worry in the back of your mind about the odd ball that ragged square. It was a nightmare. I genuinely believe that they were the most challenging conditions I've ever encountered when facing spin, and that includes coming up against Muttiah Muralitharan in Sri Lanka in 2007. It was that difficult.

So it was a bit of a relief when we ended that debacle and moved to Sri Lanka for a two-Test series in late March and early April. We were still ranked number one, after all. But we went to Galle and were ambushed by spin again. 'Oh no, here we go again,' I thought, as Rangana Herath took 12 wickets in the match. Our critics were saying that this England team could not play spin, and I was beginning to worry that we were all starting to believe it. We needed to stop the chat there and then. And, in fairness, we did that in Colombo, thanks to a remarkable innings of 151 from Kevin Pietersen and ten wickets in the match for Graeme Swann.

In this match, we had to chase 94 to win. Some minds went back to the second Test in Abu Dhabi, when we had been chasing 145 and had been bowled out for just 72. Then we had got off to a slow start, with the first wicket going down at 21 and after 15 overs. This time I looked across at Andrew Strauss and Alastair Cook as they prepared to go out to bat and they both gave smiles which said something like: 'We ain't blocking it this time!'

That is always the best way to go about small run chases, and they had learned from their mistake in the UAE. In fact, we all had. As it was, Straussy was out in the first over – bowled by off-spinner Tillekeratne Dilshan – but Cooky (49 not out) and KP (42 not out) blasted it and we won by eight wickets.

Straussy had made 61 in the first innings, and that had at least relieved some of the pressure that was beginning to surround him. He hadn't been scoring many runs in previous Tests and there was chat in the media that he might have to stand down as captain. Would anyone in the dressing room have known that he was under pressure? Not a chance. It never affected him one bit as a captain or as a bloke. He was flawless in that regard. You just wouldn't have known.

For the rest of us, we just realised that that was how these things work: there is always someone who is under pressure. But we are always thrilled when that person comes out of a lean spell and silences the critics, for example when Broady came through against India in 2011 or Cooky did the same against Pakistan in 2010. We all know what it is like because we have been through it ourselves. We know how horrible it is, so we can feel the shared joy when a team-mate survives it. And that's what Straussy did with that half-century. He then followed it up with centuries in the first innings of the next two Tests, against West Indies at Lord's and then at Trent Bridge, matches we won by five wickets and nine wickets respectively.

One thing I love seeing in the dressing room is how we wish a player to a hundred and then the genuine elation we feel when he gets there. When a player has got a hundred or taken five wickets, we have a custom that at the close of play that day someone has to propose a toast to that man. And in the second Test at Trent Bridge I was the one randomly chosen to have the great honour of toasting Strauss's hundred. I can't remember what I said exactly, but I think that it was something along the lines that he had been through a tough few months before getting his hundred at Lord's, and to back it up with another hundred was truly the sign of a class player. I was really, really delighted for him, as was everyone else. Little did I, or anyone else, know that it was going to be his last Test century.

That West Indies series sticks in my mind for only a couple of other things. Firstly, there was the cold during the Test at Lord's. I've only ever been colder once on a cricket field, and that was against West Indies again, this time at Durham in 2007. Secondly, I found out that it is not a good idea to try to play Test cricket with conjunctivitis, which is what I tried to do in the third Test at Edgbaston. I think I had picked up the infection from one of my children, and it was touch and go whether I played in the Test at all. Steven Davies had been called up as cover, but I was desperate not to pull out, even when a specialist told me just before the game that it might get worse before it got better.

Thank goodness it rained, and we did not get any play at all on the first two days, because when we did eventually start on the third day, and we won the toss and bowled, I did not see the first ball of the match bowled by Graham Onions. As a wicketkeeper that is a bit of a problem. 'I should not be out here,' I thought, and I really shouldn't have been. For most of that innings I was guessing a lot of the time. At least I managed to just about get away with it, and the match only fizzled out into a draw. But I had learned a valuable lesson.

The condition did worsen, and there was a stage where I was quite concerned about my eyesight, but that was all put into perspective a month later when South Africa's Mark Boucher suffered his terrible eye injury while keeping in a warm-up match at Taunton, ending his career.

Thus far, I am fortunate that the worst accident I have had while keeping came when I was standing up to the stumps for Sussex against Middlesex. Andrew Strauss was batting, funnily enough, and a ball from Robin Martin-Jenkins bowled him through the gate, then bounced up off the stumps and hit my bottom teeth through my lip. Ouch.

When I heard the news about Bouch, I tweeted: 'Absolutely gutted for Mark. Three games away from 150 and 999 dismissals is a phenomenal feat, deserved 1,000! Get well soon, mate.'

He had played 147 Tests and had 999 dismissals across all forms of the game, and he was the world record-holder with 555 Test dismissals at the time of his horrible accident. He will probably remain the record-holder for many years to come, because wicket-keeping in Test cricket is so physically and mentally demanding. It is not just the knocks on your fingers and the strain on your knees and Achilles' that makes it so hard, let alone the time on the road and being away from your family. It's also the sheer physical effort involved: a keeper, it has been worked out, does about 2,500 squats in the course of a Test. Multiply that by 147 Tests in Bouch's case and that is an awful lot of squats. The ground he covered when standing back was exceptional, but all the great keepers do that. He had excellent footwork and reflexes, too. But the ultimate compliment that I can pay to Bouch is to say that he was consistent. That's what keepers crave. He was a very, very solid performer.

Bouch was a fierce competitor on the pitch, but he was always ready to share his thoughts off it. When we first played against each other, I remember that he gave me a few pointers about keeping in the sub-continent, about getting closer to the stumps and staying lower for longer. So it was a huge disappointment that he was not going to be in the South Africa team that we faced for three Tests at the end of the 2012 summer, in a series that gave our opponents the chance to overhaul us as the best side in the world.

The loss of Bouch did not mean that they were going to be any easier opponents, as we discovered very quickly. Well, in fact, we actually had a very good start to the series at The Oval. The first day probably went as well as we could have expected. Having won the toss, we finished the first day on 267 for three, with Alastair Cook on 114 not out. It was all set up. This was how we'd always played our best cricket when getting to the top. We would make a huge total and then set about their batting line-up.

That's what we were thinking anyway. And maybe we were a little bit too complacent. Maybe we did just turn up on that second day and expect Cooky to score a double hundred. But on that second morning the ball began to move around a lot, and we were bowled out for 385. I did think at the end of our innings: 'If it keeps moving around, that could actually be a decent score.'

But I hadn't banked on the brilliance of the South Africa batsmen. Opener Graeme Smith's 131 paled into insignificance alongside Jacques Kallis's 172 not out and Hashim Amla's monumental 311 not out, as South Africa made 637 for two. What to say about Amla? He has come on so much that it is almost incredible. He is now one seriously good player. As for Kallis, for me he is the greatest all-round cricketer to have played the game.

I know the old boys won't be happy with that statement and will be shouting out the name of Sir Garfield Sobers, but just look at Kallis's statistics. They are amazing. As I write, he has played 161 Tests, making 13,105 runs at an average of 56.48 with 44 centuries, and he has taken 288 wickets at 32.22, while also pouching 194 catches.

Sobers played many fewer Tests and has a slightly higher batting average but also a higher bowling average, and nowhere near as many catches. It's Kallis for me, because I just don't think he ever gets the credit he deserves. At The Oval, he and Amla slaughtered us. We didn't know how to get them out. And by the time we batted, we were shell-shocked. Dale Steyn ran through us with five wickets, and South Africa were 1-0 up.

I had found preparation for that match quite tricky. I had one championship game against Warwickshire after a month and five games of Twenty20 cricket for Sussex. But two of the days of that championship match were rained off, so I didn't have much opportunity to bat in the middle (I faced five balls and was out for one) and change my mentality and technique from 20-over white-ball cricket.

When I got to The Oval for net practice, I found a red ball swinging around. So it was little surprise that my first net was a shocker, an absolute nightmare. I was thinking: 'What's going on here? I'm in trouble here.' I got bowled three or four times. I didn't know where my off stump was and I wasn't picking the ball up or hitting it cleanly.

So the biggest challenge was to find my off stump again and to start to leave balls in the channel outside. It is a very different technique and mentality, and it was a sharp reminder of what county cricketers face all the time. They don't have that opportunity to switch modes, because of the hectic scheduling. They play a 20-over game, then a four-day game, followed by a 40-over game – it is quite tough to expect guys to perform at the top level when chopping and changing without any preparation.

You can argue that the basics of cricket are the same for every form of the game, that you still want to hit from a solid base and play cricket shots. But it is more the mental side that you have to change, like how and when are you going to attack a particular bowler? And making that switch takes a couple of days. My way to do that is to break things down and keep them very, very simple. I spend a lot of time with Graham Gooch, who thinks the same way, and that's why I believe he has been such a fantastic batting coach and has had such a great effect on me and the rest of our batting line-up.

Despite the results, for me personally, the South Africa series went really well. I took a huge amount from it. I added quite a bit to my game and gained in confidence from this series. I often found myself batting against Steyn and Morne Morkel in high-pressure situations and I managed to score a few runs and come out of it pretty well, well enough in fact to be named England's man of the series.

I was also named for the first time in the International Cricket Council's Test team of the year alongside Cooky and Broady. That was a huge honour, and real recognition for my efforts over the year. The team was: Alastair Cook (England), Hashim Amla (South Africa), Kumar Sangakkara (Sri Lanka), Jacques Kallis (South Africa), Michael Clarke (Australia, capt), Shivnarine Chanderpaul (West Indies), Matt Prior (England, wicketkeeper), Stuart Broad (England), Saeed Ajmal (Pakistan), Vernon Philander (South Africa), Dale Steyn (South Africa); 12th man was A.B.de Villiers (South Africa).

However, there was no doubt I would have swapped any of that for a series win, and therefore the retention of our number one spot. Instead, we ended up losing the series 2-0, and so were overhauled by South Africa. After losing that first Test by an innings and 12 runs, the second Test at Headingley was drawn. Kevin Pietersen had made an astonishing 149 and then Graeme Smith surprised everyone by setting us a target of 253 from 39 overs at the end. I was even promoted up the order to five for that chase, above Ian Bell and debutant James Taylor, but it proved a vain chase as we ended on 130 for four. Sadly, all that Test will be remembered for is KP's comments afterwards and his subsequent dropping for the final Test at Lord's.

Did KP's unhappiness throughout the summer – remember that he had retired from one-day internationals, and therefore Twnety20s, earlier in the season – have an effect? I think it would be naïve to suggest otherwise. It's amazing how a small thing can change the dynamics of a team. Looking back now, it did have an effect. But it was not the only problem, of course. We just didn't play well enough, and we hadn't done so since we had been crowned as the number one team.

We had our moments in that last Test at Lord's. South Africa had won the toss, but we were very happy, thanks mainly to Steven Finn's four wickets, to have bowled them out for 309 and then to have secured a six-run advantage in the first innings, with Jonny Bairstow making an eye-catching 95. In the second innings our nemesis, Hashim Amla, returned to make 121 and ensure that we had to chase a very difficult 346 to win. There was a time during the last afternoon when we thought we had a chance. I was batting then (I ended up with 73) and we really did believe it was possible. But it was weird because we had been so outplayed throughout the series, yet suddenly we thought that we could pinch the match, save the series and, in doing so, also preserve our status at the top of the rankings.

But it didn't happen. We were bowled out for 294 to lose by 51 runs, and South Africa were given the mace that we had received a year earlier for being the number one Test side in the world. This is going to sound a little daft, and I hope that it is taken in the right way, but it was almost a relief. We had dealt so badly with being number one that it was as if a huge burden was now being lifted from our shoulders. We could go back to hunting again.

And we quickly discovered that we would have to do that with a new captain, because after the Lord's Test, Andrew Strauss announced that he was stepping down as captain and retiring from all cricket. I'd love to be able to sit here and tell you that I knew it was coming, but the truth is that I didn't. I didn't have a clue. Once I knew, a few things that had happened and a few things that had been said made more sense, but that is not to say that it wasn't a huge surprise when I discovered his intentions.

I discovered by letter, as did the rest of the team. What a classy gesture that was. Straussy had taken the time to sit down and hand-write a letter to all of us. They were all different in their content. It wasn't just some standard letter to us all. Mine was addressed to 'The Cheese'. Straussy was one of the people who always called me by that name. In the letter, he thanked me for all my support and for the effort I had put into the team ethic, as well as explaining his reasons for stepping down. He said that he genuinely thought that it was the right decision, and that it was nothing to do with KP or anything like that. He just felt that it was the right time for the team to move on with a new captain.

I'll admit that I got quite emotional reading it. As a team, you go through an awful lot in international sport. There are some huge highs and lows, and you spend so much time together that a bond is created that makes you just like a family. So when one member of that family decides that it is time to fly the nest it is bound to be emotional. I miss Straussy. He used to make me laugh. He was always a bit clumsy: every day, it seemed, he would spill lunch down his front. He would, honestly. When he finished playing he was 35 years old, he was captain of England and yet he still couldn't feed himself! The number of times we walked out on the field and he had spaghetti bolognese down his white shirt was ridiculous.

Cooky was always the right man to take over. And he certainly hasn't changed since he became captain. He has always been far too sensible anyway. It was difficult to dwell on things too long after Straussy's retirement. As a professional sportsperson, you can't really do that. You just have to steel yourself for the next challenge and get on with it. And that's what we had to do. We had to go to India for four Tests as the second-ranked side in the world. We were on a new quest with a new captain.

We won that series in India and I spoke to Straussy about it afterwards. He was naturally delighted for the team, but I could sense that there were no regrets on his part. It showed to me that he had left at the right time and that he had made his decision with the team's best interests at heart.

Going to India was a huge challenge. We'd been to Australia, where we had not won for 24 years, now we were going to India where we hadn't won for 28 years. It was going to take a monumental effort to win. For any cricketer in the world, winning in India is as big as it gets. With the Ashes you have the motivation of the enormous amount of hype. But a tour of India is different. You have to find a different motivation. You can't just use the hype and the crowd. Going out to Australia, we knew that if we played our best cricket, we would win the series. Going to India, you can play your best cricket and still get beaten, and that's the difference.

But as we embarked upon this task, I reflected upon something I have talked about before in this book – our team's love of trying to break records, our desire, as Peter Moores first pointed out to me all those years ago at Sussex, to create a legacy. Making records has always been a massive turn-on for this team. Our goal has always been to create history. And this challenge in India may even have been bigger than retaining the Ashes in Australia. I described it at the time as the 'final frontier' and I meant it. It was something we hadn't done and something we desperately wanted to do.

Not that it began well, of course. We lost the first Test in Ahmedabad by nine wickets. Two days before the match, I'd told the press that the talk was over and it was time to go out and do the business. But I was still genuinely nervous; I think we all were. That cloud about us not being able to play spin was still hanging over us.

I think we got a bit panicky about dispelling it. India had made a huge total of 521 for eight declared, with Cheteshwar Pujara making a double hundred. And then we were rolled for just 191. All that talk and now we had failed to do the business – it was as simple as that. We had all been very keen to get to this Test match, especially the batsmen, who wanted to prove a point. We knew the pitch was going to turn, but I just think that we got too ahead of ourselves.

Just like Galle earlier in the year, we had failed to deliver when we thought we had learned our lesson from previous mistakes. There were players all around the dressing room scrambling to get pads on and there was almost an air of panic. The crowd was extremely loud and enthusiastic, believing they were getting some measure of revenge for their team's poor showing in England in 2011.

We were asked to follow on. As it was only tea-time on the third day, the chances of us saving the match were remote, but we had a real opportunity to make a statement. We had to show that we could play spin. We had to show it there and then.

And we did. Cooky and Nick Compton on debut made sure that we were 111 without loss at the end of that third day. There was a calmness about their batting that had not been evident in our first innings. By the end of day four we were still batting. Cooky was 168 not out and I was 84 not out. He was out for 176 early on the final day, and we eventually lost, bowled out for 406, but we took so much from that batting effort. Remember that we had failed to make more than 327 in any innings against Pakistan in the UAE. It was undoubtedly the turning point of the series.

Cooky's innings was a proper captain's knock, just like many we had seen from Straussy over the years. They are very similar captains in that they both lead from the front. But they do it in slightly different ways. Straussy was a very good speaker, very articulate in the dressing room, whereas Cooky is hell bent on leading on the pitch through his own actions. He said he wanted his batsmen to bat long in India and then he went and did it himself, starting in Ahmedabad. I just know that while he was out there, he would have been thinking: 'I said I wanted my batsmen to bat long, so I'd best go and do it first.'

Both are very calm characters. They don't get flustered very easily. I have already mentioned how impressive Straussy was in the post-match press conference when we lost badly against Australia at Headingley in 2009. Well, Cooky was similar here in Ahmedabad. Just like Straussy was back then, he was so calm and logical in what he said that it gave the team a huge amount of confidence.

I tried my best to help him in our long partnership of 157. I made 91 before I was caught and bowled by the left-arm spinner Pragyan Ojha. To say I was gutted would be a huge understatement. I so wanted to get a Test hundred in India. It is such a challenging place to bat. I may not get another chance to play in a Test series out there, as England are not scheduled for another Test tour there until 2016. I'd love to be on that, of course, but you just never know. It seems a long way off at the moment.

It was such a soft dismissal, too. Ojha bowled me a short ball – it might even be described as a long hop – which I went to punch off the back foot, but the ball just stopped in the pitch and I ended up just dollying it back to him. It was so annoying because, in normal circumstances, I'm pretty sure that I would have gone back in my crease and smashed that ball over mid-wicket. But because I was in defensive mode, which I had to be in the situation, I just lobbed it back.

If we had made a statement with our second-innings batting, then it didn't really register with the Indians. Judging by the pitch prepared for the second Test in Mumbai, they still didn't think we could play spin. It was an absolute Bunsen (burner in rhyming slang, for the uninitiated). We saw immediately that it was going to rag and bounce, and knew we'd better get used to it quickly. We might have preferred to win the toss, but we were reasonably pleased to have dismissed India for 327, with Pujara again batting very well in making a century.

But then we were treated to a batting masterclass by KP. Cooky made a superb 122, but it was KP's 186 that took the game away from India and made sure we had a vital lead of 86 on the first innings. It was like the knocks KP had played earlier in the year in Colombo and at Headingley. They were knocks that no one else in the world could have played. They were that good. But then I'm never surprised by what he does. Good players of spin use their feet well and that's what Kev did so brilliantly here. The moment that their spinners dropped short, he was well back and hitting the ball through the covers. Any bowler who gets it slightly wrong knows that he'll disappear. That's what makes Kev so hard to bowl at.

This was why we had to have him back in the side. With Kev in it, the England cricket team will always be stronger, as long as he is pulling in the same direction as everyone else. And that goes the same for any player; any player pulling in a different direction is going to cause harm to that team. Kev had said the things he needed to say to a few people and they had said the things that they needed to say to him. Ultimately everyone had to agree to get on with it in an adult fashion.

And that's what had happened. The way he came in – and this isn't rubbish I assure you – and the way he behaved and pulled with the team in India was phenomenal. It was everything you want from any team-mate. If we hadn't had the team spirit right in India, we could easily have lost the series 4-0 after Ahmedabad (as our former skipper Michael Vaughan suggested we would do on Twitter – we did notice that!). When you genuinely have that team spirit, it is something to cherish and preserve, which was one of the main reasons why I had made that phone call to KP that I mentioned earlier on.

Of course, we also needed the bowlers to do their jobs in Mumbai, and Monty Panesar and Graeme Swann duly obliged, sharing 19 wickets in the match – 11 for Monty and eight for Swanny. Monty hadn't played in Ahmedabad, but he had watched Ojha (who took nine wickets in the match) closely and tried to learn from him. I had a net with him during that game and he was constantly asking me: 'What pace does Ojha bowl? How does he vary it?'

I can always tell when Monty is in a good rhythm. It all looks so easy. You can see the revs on the ball. The flight of the ball usually has more shape on it, more turn and bounce. Monty's variations now are quite subtle. He doesn't have a 'carrom' ball or anything mysterious like that, but he does land the ball in the right area with good pace and plenty of revs, and if you do that you are going to ask questions of the batsman. He is also lucky that his stock delivery is quite quick. People have sometimes criticised him for it, but it is definitely his strength.

As for Swanny, he is very good at adapting. He assesses the pitch and the batsman well. He's always trying to spin the ball hard, and that's what gets him that fantastic drift and dip. Cricket in India is a very different game from the one that we play in England. You need to embrace the conditions and in these two bowlers we had players who can do that. They both bowled superbly, but I do reckon that, if you asked them to nominate one pitch in the world that they could roll up and carry around with them, they would say this one. That's why I think it was the way Cooky and KP batted that won us the game, and why KP was quite rightly named man of the match.

How big a win was it? A few of the lads compared it with the Ashes win in Adelaide in 2010-11, where we lost a big toss and managed to turn the game around. But here we lost the toss and the conditions were so completely in India's favour. No one gave us a prayer, but our batsmen and spinners outperformed theirs in their back yard. For me it was a huge win, the biggest I've been involved in, and one of the proudest.

Touring India is a unique experience, but I have to say that it is not easy to get out and about. You simply get too much attention. The people are so cricket-mad that you just can't go anywhere without being mobbed. I prefer the tours where you can get out a bit more, even if it is only to play a round of golf, but in India it meant that long hours were spent in hotel rooms.

Quite often you are only as good as your DVD collection on trips out there. I remember when we went there in 2008-09, Stuart Broad and I watched about 60 DVDs in three weeks. *The Office* has always been a favourite. And we have been into *Entourage*, the American comedy-drama series. But on this trip

Broady and I really got into *Homeland*, the American psychological thriller television series. I think that we stayed in Ahmedabad for 12 nights, and series one of *Homeland* consists of 12 episodes. So we allowed ourselves one episode a night. But anyone who has watched the show will know that an episode often finishes with you screaming: 'I need to watch the next episode!' Often we had to physically stop ourselves from jumping the gun. One episode a night, that was the deal. Meanwhile, every night Swanny, Cooky and Jimmy Anderson were watching *The Killing*, the American version of the Danish crime drama series.

Before the third Test in Kolkata we did get out and about, though, and it was a pleasure to visit the Future Hope School and meet some 200-odd underprivileged children. It was a truly humbling experience, as the kids were amazing. We played cricket, hockey and chess with them, as well as singing some hymns. It really was uplifting and I hope we made their day, as it was certainly something I won't forget.

While we were relaxing, the Indians seemed to be getting themselves into a bit of a state about the pitch for Kolkata. The team management wanted one thing, and the groundsman, an 83-year-old who quickly became a bit of a celebrity, wanted another. To be honest, it was music to our ears. I thought that the Indians had become a bit complacent after Ahmedabad. They thought they could just slaughter us on spinning pitches. Now they had seen what Monty and Swanny could do to them, and they did not know what to do and what pitch to prepare.

We still lost the toss again, though. But once more India did not get the sort of score they would have been hoping to get. They made just 316, with Monty taking four wickets. It gave us the opportunity to post a big first-innings total, and that's what we did. Cooky again led the way, making 190, and virtually everyone else backed him up so that we scored 523. It was Cooky's fifth hundred in five Test matches as captain, which was an amazing record.

He had a new vice-captain for this match, too. Me! It was a huge thing for me to be asked to do that when Broady did not play. When Cooky was first made captain, I did think that maybe I had a chance of being given that role, and it is certainly something I would love to do for as long as I can. I really like the responsibility. It is never going to change my role in the team, as I don't think I will say any more or any less doing it, but I do consider it a great honour.

I've occasionally heard Nick Compton calling me 'the lieutenant' out on the field, and I think that is fair enough. I have always been a reasonably hard task master, whether it is making sure that we look after the ball, that we maintain our energy levels, that fields are in exactly the right position rather than simply in the general vicinity of where they should be, or just that the throws into me are precise.

Once we had that first-innings lead of 207 in Kolkata, we were always in control. And India simply could not fight their way out of the trouble, being bowled out for 247, with the seamers taking centre stage this time, Steven Finn and Jimmy Anderson taking three wickets each. It left us requiring 41 to win, but before we knew it, we were eight for three and I had my pads on. Thankfully, Ian Bell went out and scored one of the best twenties I have ever seen in my life. I'm not joking. It was superb, it really was. He made 28 not out off just 28 balls, and we won by seven wickets. We were 2-1 up, with one to play. It all looked set up for us to win the series.

And we did. The last Test, on a surprisingly flat pitch at Nagpur, was drawn, with Joe Root making a sensational debut. It was a pleasure to bat with him in a decent partnership in our first innings, but there was some even better batting in our second innings as Jonathan Trott made 143 and Ian Bell also hit a hundred. By then the Indians were thoroughly frustrated. We just hadn't succumbed as they thought we would. They try to take you out of your comfort zone in India. The crowds and the players can all wind you up, and suddenly you can find yourself involved in a sledging battle rather than playing cricket. But we just didn't take the bait.

There was no better example of this than in Trotty's innings. The Indians were unhappy because they felt a catch behind had not been given (use the Decision Review System, then!) and they really tucked into Trotty. But, as I have said before, he bats in a bubble. They were wasting their time and energy on him. He knew exactly what he needed to, and that was to take us to safety in that match. He did that, and history was made: we had beaten India in India.

It was a little strange, though. As I said earlier, purely from a cricketing point of view, it was a bigger challenge than the Ashes, but that is not how the public sees it. For them, the Ashes is everything. So when we were celebrating, it was almost as if we were just celebrating among ourselves, without many others really recognising the importance and toughness of the achievement. However, what it really meant was brought home to us by Graham Gooch, who made an emotional speech at the end of the game. He emphasised what a big deal it was, telling us how he had struggled during his Tests in India (he had played in only one victory in nine Tests there). I am absolutely certain that every player in that dressing room in Nagpur will remember that moment for a very long time.

I certainly will, and on a personal note there were some further special memories for me during the three-Test tour to New Zealand in March 2013. Ultimately, the result of that series – drawn 0-0 – was not what we wanted, but we also thought it unfair that some in the media expected us just to turn up and win 3-0. That was hugely disrespectful to New Zealand for a start, and Test cricket just does not work like that. There is a lot of hard work that goes into beating any team in that form of the game.

What was more, New Zealand played really well. The pitches for the three Tests at Dunedin, Wellington and Auckland were flat, but I thought their bowlers were very good. Sometimes the opposition are allowed to play well, and that's what New Zealand did. Yes, we weren't at our best, but a lot of credit must go to the Kiwis.

It was my first tour of New Zealand, and what an unbelievable place it is. I thoroughly enjoyed the whole trip off the field; doing some serious cycling in Queenstown was one of the highlights. On it, I was made vice-captain again, which, as mentioned, is such a huge honour. And, with the bat and gloves, I think I had my best tour. I say that because I was consistent in both departments. It is rare for that to happen. There is usually a slight drop-off in one facet of the game or the other.

In New Zealand I felt that I was at my best with both. With the gloves, I was in a really good rhythm. And with the bat I got a couple of twenties in the first Test, 82 in the second Test, but I suppose it is the final Test for which my batting will be remembered. And I don't necessarily mean my 73 in the first innings.

I got 110 not out in the second innings, but it didn't really matter how many I scored. It was the fact that I was still there at the very end of the game and we were only nine wickets down, so that we had added another heart-stopping draw to those at Cardiff, Centurion and Cape Town in recent times. That was all that mattered. I was very proud that I managed to do it, but I do have to say that I found it all a rather strange scenario. I don't like the concept of blocking out for a draw at all. It does go against the way I normally play.

But the way the team tried to look at it at the start of the final day was that, if we did escape with a draw, then one, two or three of us would be considered England heroes. I know that I got a lot of attention for my effort, but people should not overlook Ian Bell's innings. Belly played an amazing knock, making 75 but using up 271 balls. We would never have saved that match without him. And what about Stuart Broad, too? He made just six, but it occupied 77 balls – he didn't get off the mark until he had faced 62 balls.

I came in just after lunch on the last day with the score at 159 for six (we had used Steven Finn as a nightwatchman) and the new ball not long having been taken. Belly was going well on 42 and we knew that if we could see off the new ball, then New Zealand might get twitchy later on. We managed to do that, but then Belly went and my whole mindset had to change. I was in charge now. Batting with the tail (I know Broady won't like me using that term!) is a skill in itself, but it is something I really enjoy. It's almost as if you are batting for the two of you, and the key thing is to communicate a lot and to do so very clearly. It is a case of walking down the pitch and saying to the other batsman, whoever he is: 'This is the plan. This is what this bowler is looking to do and this is what I think you should do.'

When we do save a Test in such tense circumstances, it is always a reward for all the hard work put in at the nets by bowlers such as Finny (witness his monumental 56 as nightwatchman in the first Test), Broady, Jimmy Anderson and Monty Panesar.

I had some luck in my innings, of course. Sometimes the fates smile on you. When I had made only 28, a ball from Neil Wagner hit the stumps (twice, I think), but somehow did not dislodge the bails. I'm not sure that has ever happened to me before, certainly not when the ball has hit the stumps that hard, but it was my day. I just had to laugh. Suffice to say, the Kiwi bowlers were not best pleased.

Reaching my hundred was strange in these circumstances. Normally, it's a great moment, but this time I berated myself first for hitting the ball in the air and then celebrated, but not wildly. The milestone was almost irrelevant, it was all about getting to the end. We were so close, and that was a reminder of how close we were. The intensity was really building, with every ball feeling like it was taking an hour, and getting the hundred was almost a way of letting off a bit of steam momentarily.

But then it was back to the graft. And it came down to the fact that Monty and I had to survive 19 balls. It's always Monty, isn't it? Well, it was in Cardiff, too. And it's always fun. I was obviously trying to take as much of the strike as possible, but unfortunately for the start of the penultimate over, to be bowled by spinner Kane Williamson, I couldn't manage that.

Monty was facing and I took a bit of a punt. I said to him: 'If the ball is there to be hit, hit it and we can get a one.' Even as I was saying this, I was thinking to myself: 'My God, what are you saying?' So I then reinforced the key message several times: 'Nothing crazy, mind, Mont. If he bowls you a long hop, just push it into the gap.'

Luckily, with the first ball of that over he was able to take a comfortable single. I got in easily and was congratulating Monty in my mind when I suddenly heard a commotion behind me. I turned around to see Monty leopard-crawling down the pitch, possibly in search of a second run. 'What are you doing, mate?' I thought. It could only happen to Monty.

But he survived, and I survived. And we drew the Test. It's another memory I won't forget, even though we all much prefer the winning ones. And I sincerely hope that there are still a few more of those moments in store for me in my cricketing career.

Matt Prior's Career Record

Statistics compiled by Ian Marshall

(to 1 April 2014)

FACTFILE

Matthew James Prior, born Johannesburg, South Africa, 26 February 1982

Education: Brighton College

Height: 5'11"

County: Sussex; county cap 2003; benefit 2012

Wisden Cricketer of the Year 2010

Other teams: England A/Lions; MCC; Sussex Cricket Board; Sydney Thunder

Test debut: England v West Indies, 17-21 May 2007, at Lord's, scoring 126* and 21

One-day international debut: England v Zimbabwe, 5 December 2004, at Bulawayo, scoring 35

Twenty20 international debut: England v West Indies, 28 June 2007, at The Oval, scoring 25

First-class debut: Sussex v Worcestershire, 25-8 April 2001, at Worcester, scoring 25*

Limited-overs debut: Sussex Cricket Board v Berkshire, 16 May 2000, at Hastings, scoring 3

Twenty20 debut: Sussex v Hampshire, 13 June 2003, at Southampton, scoring 4

MATT PRIOR'S MATCH-BY-MATCH TEST RECORD

Test	Opponent	Venue	Date Started	1st Inns Score	1st Inns Dis	2nd Inns Score	2nd Inns Dis	Result
1	West Indies	Lord's	17-May-07	126*	0	21	0	Drawn
2	West Indies	Leeds	25-May-07	75	2	–	2	Won I/283
3	West Indies	Manchester	07-Jun-07	40	1	0	0	Won 60
4	West Indies	Chester-le-Street	15-Jun-07	62	1	–	2	Won 7w
5	India	Lord's	19-Jul-07	1	2	42	1	Drawn
6	India	Nottingham	27-Jul-07	11	5	7	1	Lost 7w
7	India	The Oval	09-Aug-07	0	2	12*	1	Drawn
8	Sri Lanka	Kandy	01-Dec-07	0	3	63	1	Lost 88
9	Sri Lanka	Colombo	09-Dec-07	79	2	–		Drawn
10	Sri Lanka	Galle	18-Dec-07	4	1	19*		Drawn
11	India	Chennai	11-Dec-08	53*	0	33	1	Lost 6w
12	India	Mohali	19-Dec-08	2	2	–	0	Drawn
13	West Indies	Kingston	04-Feb-09	64	2	0		Lost I/23
14	West Indies	North Sound	13-Feb-09	–		–		Drawn
15	West Indies	St John's	15-Feb-09	39	2	15*	1	Drawn
16	West Indies	Port of Spain	06-Mar-09	131*	1+1	61	0	Drawn
17	West Indies	Lord's	06-May-09	42	2	–	0	Won 10w
18	West Indies	Chester-le-Street	14-May-09	63	1	–	0	Won I/83
19	Australia	Cardiff	08-Jul-09	56	3	14		Drawn
20	Australia	Lord's	16-Jul-09	8	1	61	0	Won 115
21	Australia	Birmingham	30-Jul-09	41	3	–	3	Drawn
22	Australia	Leeds	07-Aug-09	37*	0	22		Lost I/80
23	Australia	The Oval	20-Aug-09	18	1	4	0+1	Won 197
24	South Africa	Centurion	16-Dec-09	4	2	0	0	Drawn
25	South Africa	Durban	26-Dec-09	60	2	–	1	Won I/98
26	South Africa	Cape Town	03-Jan-10	76	4	4	2	Drawn
27	South Africa	Johannesburg	14-Jan-10	14	1	0		Lost I/74
28	Bangladesh	Chittagong	12-Mar-10	0*	1	7	3	Won 181
29	Bangladesh	Mirpur	20-Mar-10	62	4	–	1+1	Won 9w
30	Bangladesh	Lord's	27-May-10	16	2	–	3	Won 8w
31	Bangladesh	Manchester	04-Jun-10	93	2	–	3	Won I/80
32	Pakistan	Nottingham	29-Jul-10	6	2	102*	0	Won 354
33	Pakistan	Birmingham	06-Aug-10	15	3	–	1+1	Won 9w
34	Pakistan	The Oval	18-Aug-10	84*	3	5	0	Lost 4w
35	Pakistan	Lord's	26-Aug-10	22	2	–	1	Won I/225
36	Australia	Brisbane	25-Nov-10	0	2	–	0	Drawn
37	Australia	Adelaide	03-Dec-10	27*	1	–	2	Won I/71
38	Australia	Perth	16-Dec-10	12	2	10	2	Lost 267
39	Australia	Melbourne	26-Dec-10	85	6	–	1	Won I/157
40	Australia	Sydney	03-Jan-11	118	2	–	5	Won I/83
41	Sri Lanka	Cardiff	26-May-11	–	2	–	2	Won I/14

MATT PRIOR'S MATCH-BY-MATCH RECORD (continued)

Test	Opponent	Venue	Date Started	1st Inns Score	1st Inns Dis	2nd Inns Score	2nd Inns Dis	Result
42	Sri Lanka	Lord's	03-Jun-11	126	2+1	4	0	Drawn
43	Sri Lanka	Southampton	16-Jun-11	0	4	–	1	Drawn
44	India	Lord's	21-Jul-11	71	2	103*	3	Won 196
45	India	Nottingham	29-Jul-11	1	2	73	1	Won 319
46	India	Birmingham	10-Aug-11	5	3	–	2	Won I/242
47	India	The Oval	18-Aug-11	18*	2+1	–	1	Won I/8
48	Pakistan	Dubai	17-Jan-12	70*	2+1	4	0	Lost 10w
49	Pakistan	Abu Dhabi	25-Jan-12	3	0	18	1	Lost 72
50	Pakistan	Dubai	03-Feb-12	6	2	49*	0	Lost 71
51	Sri Lanka	Galle	26-Mar-12	7	2	41	0+1	Lost 75
52	Sri Lanka	Colombo	03-Apr-12	11	3	–	1	Won 8w
53	West Indies	Lord's	17-May-12	19	1	–	2	Won 5w
54	West Indies	Nottingham	25-May-12	16	0+1	–	0	Won 9w
55	West Indies	Birmingham	07-Jun-12	–	1	–		Drawn
56	South Africa	The Oval	19-Jul-12	60	0	40		Lost I/12
57	South Africa	Leeds	02-Aug-12	68	1+1	7	1	Drawn
58	South Africa	Lord's	16-Aug-12	27	5+1	73	1+1	Lost 51
59	India	Ahmedabad	15-Nov-12	48	1	91	0	Lost 9w
60	India	Mumbai	23-Nov-12	21	0+1	–	1	Won 10w
61	India	Kolkata	05-Dec-12	41	1	–	2	Won 7w
62	India	Nagpur	13-Dec-12	57	1	–		Drawn
63	New Zealand	Dunedin	06-Mar-13	23	2	23*		Drawn
64	New Zealand	Wellington	14-Mar-13	82	3	–	0	Drawn
65	New Zealand	Auckland	22-Mar-13	73	5	110*	0	Drawn
66	New Zealand	Lord's	16-May-13	0	3	0	1	Won 170
67	New Zealand	Leeds	24-May-13	39	1	4*	1	Won 247
68	Australia	Nottingham	10-Jul-13	1	3	31	2	Won 14
69	Australia	Lord's	18-Jul-13	6	1	1*	2	Won 347
70	Australia	Manchester	01-Aug-13	30	1	–	1	Drawn
71	Australia	Chester-le-Street	09-Aug-13	17	4	0	1	Won 74
72	Australia	The Oval	21-Aug-13	47	1	0*	2	Drawn
73	Australia	Brisbane	21-Nov-13	0	1	4	2	Lost 381
74	Australia	Adelaide	05-Dec-13	0	3	69	1	Lost 218
75	Australia	Perth	13-Dec-13	8	3	26	0	Lost 150

MATT PRIOR'S TEST MATCH AVERAGE BATTING AND FIELDING

	M	I	NO	HS	Runs	Avge	100	50	Ct/St
v Australia	18	30	4	118	753	28.96	1	4	62/1
v Bangladesh	4	5	1	93	178	44.50	-	2	19/1
v India	13	20	4	103*	690	43.12	1	5	37/2
v New Zealand	5	9	4	110*	354	59.00	1	2	16
v Pakistan	7	12	4	102*	384	48.00	1	2	17/2
v South Africa	7	13	-	76	433	33.30	-	5	20/3
v Sri Lanka	8	11	1	126	354	35.40	1	2	25/2
v West Indies	13	16	3	131*	774	59.53	2	5	21/2
Overall	75	116	20	131*	3920	40.83	7	27	217/13

MATT PRIOR'S TEST CENTURIES

Score	Balls/Fours/Sixes	Opposition	Venue	Season
131*	198/12/0	West Indies	Port of Spain	2008-09
126*	128/19/0	West Indies	Lord's	2007
126	131/19/0	Sri Lanka	Lord's	2011
118	130/11/1	Australia	Sydney	2010-11
110*	182/20/0	New Zealand	Auckland	2012-13
103*	120/5/1	India	Lord's	2011
102*	136/7/2	Pakistan	Nottingham	2010

Matt Prior's longest innings, in terms of balls faced, was 91 (225/11/0) v India (Ahmedabad, 2012-13).

100 WICKETKEEPING DISMISSALS IN TESTS FOR ENGLAND†

Total		Career	Tests	Ct	St
269	A.P.E.Knott	1967-1981	95	250	19
241†	A.J.Stewart	1990-2003	82	227	14
230	M.J.Prior	2007-	75	217	13
219	T.G.Evans	1946-1959	91	173	46
174	R.W.Taylor	1971-1984	57	167	7
165	R.C.Russell	1988-1998	54	153	12
133	G.O.Jones	2004-2006	34	128	5
112†	J.M.Parks	1954-1968	43	101	11

† *Excluding catches taken in the field.*

2000 RUNS IN TESTS BY AN ENGLAND WICKETKEEPER

	M	I	NO	HS	Runs	Avge	100	50	Ct/St
A.J.Stewart	82	145	15	173	4540	34.92	6	23	227/14
A.P.E.Knott	95	149	15	135	4389	32.75	5	30	250/19
M.J.Prior	75	116	20	131*	3920	40.83	7	27	217/13
T.G.Evans	91	133	14	104	2439	20.49	2	8	173/46
L.E.G.Ames	44	67	12	149	2387	43.40	8	7	72/23

Matt Prior's Career Record

FIVE OR MORE DISMISSALS IN AN INNINGS MOST TIMES FOR ENGLAND

Total		Career	Best
5	R.C.Russell	1988-1998	6
5	G.O.Jones	2004-2006	6
5	M.J.Prior	2007-	6
4	A.J.Stewart	1990-2003	6
4	C.M.W.Read	1999-2007	6

MATT PRIOR'S ONE-DAY INTERNATIONAL AVERAGE BATTING AND FIELDING

	M	I	NO	HS	Runs	Avge	100	50	Ct/St
v Australia	13	13	-	67	250	19.23	-	1	9/1
v Bangladesh	4	3	1	42	87	43.50	-	-	4
v India	19	18	1	46	304	17.88	-	-	20/2
v Ireland	2	2	-	29	35	17.50	-	-	–/2
v Netherlands	1	-	-	-	-	-	-	-	1/1
v Pakistan	5	5	-	45	94	18.80	-	-	–
v Scotland	1	1	1	1*	1	-	-	-	1
v South Africa	9	6	1	45*	146	29.20	-	-	22/1
v Sri Lanka	2	2	2	28*	50	-	-	-	2
v West Indies	11	11	3	87	280	35.00	-	2	11/1
v Zimbabwe	1	1	-	35	35	35.00	-	-	1
Overall	68	62	9	87	1282	24.18	-	3	71/8

MATT PRIOR'S ONE-DAY INTERNATIONAL FIFTIES

Score	Balls/Fours/Sixes	Opposition	Venue	Season
87	86/5/0	West Indies	Birmingham	2009
67	58/8/1	Australia	Adelaide	2010-11
52	73/3/1	West Indies	Birmingham	2007

50 WICKETKEEPING DISMISSALS IN ONE-DAY INTERNATIONALS FOR ENGLAND†

Total		Career	ODIs	Ct	St
163†	A.J.Stewart	1989-2003	138	148	15
75†	M.J.Prior	2006-	56	68	7
72	G.O.Jones	2004-2006	49	68	4
64	C.Kieswetter	2010-	43	52	12

† *Excluding catches taken in the field.*

MATT PRIOR'S FIRST-CLASS AVERAGE BATTING AND FIELDING

	M	I	NO	HS	Runs	Avge	100	50	Ct/St
2001	16	24	2	66	433	19.68	-	1	39/2
2002	16	27	3	102*	741	30.87	1	5	39/2
2003	16	24	3	153*	1006	47.90	4	3	28
2003-04	3	6	1	82*	310	62.00	-	3	4/1
2004	18	26	1	201*	1158	46.32	3	6	25/2
2004-05	2	4	2	104	220	110.00	1	1	10
2005	17	27	1	109	874	33.61	2	6	45/1
2006	14	22	2	124	934	46.70	3	4	34/11
2006-07	2	3	-	50	90	30.00	-	1	7
2007	11	19	2	126*	555	32.64	1	2	31/1
2007-08	4	7	2	79	202	40.40	-	2	13
2008	15	23	1	133*	1040	47.27	3	7	37/1
2008-09	7	10	3	131*	434	62.00	1	3	12/1
2009	13	21	2	140	788	41.47	1	6	30/1
2009-10	6	10	1	76	227	25.22	-	3	21/1
2010	13	19	3	123*	639	39.93	2	2	41/1
2010-11	9	10	3	118	403	57.57	2	1	36/2
2011	12	17	3	126	685	48.92	2	4	43/4
2011-12	8	12	2	84	339	33.90	-	2	21/3
2012	11	13	-	86	424	32.61	-	4	20/4
2012–13	10	15	2	110*	772	59.38	1	6	23/2
2013	14	22	3	62	421	22.15	-	1	39
2013-14	5	8	-	69	137	17.12	-	1	13
Overall	242	369	42	201*	12832	39.24	27	74	611/41

Index

Index

Index

Index